Labour Unions, Public Policy and Economic Growth

Collective bargaining is still the main vehicle for labour worldwide to negotiate wages, benefits, retirement policies, training and other terms of working with management in both the public and private sectors. Labour economists have long been active in modelling the relations among collective bargaining agreements, labour markets and social welfare conditions. This book presents a new theoretical framework for unions which offers a unified treatment of the centralization of bargaining, the credibility of labour contracts, the unionization of labour markets and the relative bargaining power of the union. It assesses the microfoundations of bargaining and examines collective bargaining interacting with public policy, investment and growth, and international trade and specialization. In conclusion Professor Palokangas challenges the commonly held view that collective bargaining has a negative impact on economic welfare, and argues that, with the existence of market failure, collective bargaining can be welfare-enhancing.

TAPIO PALOKANGAS is Professor of Economics at the University of Helsinki, Finland.

Labour Unions, Public Policy and Economic Growth

TAPIO PALOKANGAS

CAMBRIDGE
UNIVERSITY PRESS

PUBLISHED BY THE PRESS SYNDICATE OF THE UNIVERSITY OF CAMBRIDGE
The Pitt Building, Trumpington Street, Cambridge CB2 1RP, United Kingdom

CAMBRIDGE UNIVERSITY PRESS
The Edinburgh Building, Cambridge, CB2 2RU, UK http://www.cup.cam.ac.uk
40 West 20th Street, New York, NY 10011-4211, USA http://www.cup.org
10 Stamford Road, Oakleigh, Melbourne 3166, Australia

First published 2000

Printed in the United Kingdom at the University Press, Cambridge

Typeset in 10/12pt Monotype Times [KW]

A catalogue record for this book is available from the British Library

ISBN 0 521 66323 7   hardback

To my daughters Silja and Tarja

Contents

Figures

Preface

This book examines collective bargaining in interaction with (i) the exercise of public policy, (ii) investment and growth, and (iii) international trade and specialization. So far, the common assertion has been that non-competitive wage-setting in collective bargaining is either insignificant or welfare-decreasing. This assertion, however, arises from some of the following assumptions being used in the analysis:
  (i) Wages are exogenously determined.
 (ii) Whenever wages are taken as endogenously determined, the analysis is carried out in a partial equilibrium framework that ignores macroeconomic aspects.
(iii) Whenever the general equilibrium framework is used, the first-best equilibrium of the economy (i.e. an economy without distortions) is taken as a starting point. However, if the non-competitive determination of wages is assumed to be the only distortion in the economy, the welfare-decreasing nature of it is a trivial matter.
(iv) Labour is fully homogeneous, even at the macrolevel. The homogeneity of labour eliminates the effect of relative wages on the allocation of labour over the sectors of the economy.
In contrast, the approach of this book (i) starts with sound microfoundations of bargaining, (ii) uses a general equilibrium framework, and (iii) introduces market failure or some other sort of externality into the economy. Furthermore, although the assumption of homogeneity (iv) is in some cases a plausible simplification, we require that any robust theory should not be sensitive to it.

This book integrates many issues of labour economics – such as the unionization of the economy, the credibility of labour contracts, the level of the centralization of bargaining, as well as the relative bargaining power of the union – into a single framework. If something general can be concluded from the various models of the study, then it might be the following:

- If union power is distorting, then it is better to use corrective taxes, for the outcome of a direct attempt to undermine union power can be harmful or highly unpredictable.
- If there is some other distortion in the economy already, then, in some circumstances, union power can be welfare-enhancing.

The proofs employ some basic results of mathematical economics (duality etc.) as well as some basic concepts of calculus, differential equations, game theory and control theory. Therefore, one or more courses on these topics might be regarded as a prerequisite. With technical details being placed in the Appendices, the exposition is such that the book is intended to be readable for most graduate students in economics. Although some of my early thoughts on the ideas of some chapters are found in previous publications (Palokangas 1987, 1989, 1991a, 1991b, 1992, 1996, 1997), chapters 2–9 all contain new material that has not been published before.

I am greatly indebted to the Finnish Academy for research grants (nos. 48013 and 51606) as well as to the University of Helsinki for the exchange fellowship to Cambridge. Their support made it possible for me to spend my sabbatical year 1996–7 at Clare Hall, Cambridge. It was during this time that the bulk of this book was written. Finally, I would like to thank the editors and referees of Cambridge University Press for their co-operation during this project.

Overview

Chapter 1 gives a game-theoretic basis for models of collective bargaining. It starts by introducing general concepts of two-person strategic, extensive and repeated games. It is assumed, for simplicity, that the two parties in bargaining have a constant discount rate and that they make an arbitrarily large number of alternating offers. It is shown that in such a case, the equilibrium of the game is obtained through the maximization of some weighted geometric average of the objectives of the parties. As either of the parties becomes more patient (or quicker when responding to the opponent's offers) relative to the other, the geometric weight of its objective approaches unity, and as it becomes more impatient (or slower when responding to the opponent's offers), the geometric weight of its objective approaches zero. Finally, it is shown that in the absence of uncertainty, the outcome of the game takes the simple form that either of the parties proposes the equilibrium offer and then the other immediately accepts this.

Chapter 2 gives microfoundations for models of collective bargaining when there is no investment. The same analysis also holds when there is no adjustment cost for investment, since in this case the firm will always hold its capital input at the optimal level. We start by introducing the monopoly-union model and extend this model for the case of profit-sharing. In the ordinary-wage system, only the basic wages are used as instruments of bargaining and the workers do not receive any share of profits, while in the profit-sharing system, the basic wages and the workers' profit share are determined simultaneously in bargaining. It is shown that if there is no investment or no adjustment cost for investment, then the behaviour of the monopoly union does not qualitatively differ in the two systems; also, in the case of profit-sharing, the monopoly union chooses its optimal wage–employment combination on the labour demand curve.

Finally, it is theoretically proven that either highly centralized systems with bargaining at the level of the whole economy, or highly decentralized systems with bargaining at the level of small industries or firms, seem to perform well in terms of employment, while lower levels of employment are found in systems where bargaining is carried out at some intermediate level of centralization. The starting point is that since firms produce different commodities and purchase intermediate inputs from each other, the degree of centralization has opposing impacts on wages: one of these operates through the macroeconomic effects of a single union's wage policy, while the other operates through the elasticity of the labour demand that the single union faces. It follows that a union facing the whole productive sector of the economy and a union facing a very small part of that sector both set low wages, but for different reasons: the former because it can internalize the macroeconomic effects of its wage policy, and the latter because it observes a high elasticity of labour demand.

Chapter 3 examines the prospects for public policy when the response of the government is internalized in wage-setting. We assume that the government uses some taxes or subsidies to correct the distortions of the economy, but that it must balance its budget by other 'revenue-raising' taxes. In such a case, the tax incidence on the workers has an impact on wages. Standard results based on the assumption of exogenous wages suggest that if wages are fixed arbitrarily high in some part of the economy, it is desirable to provide a subsidy to counteract the distortion. We show that when collective bargaining is properly incorporated into the model, this result holds only for very decentralized bargaining but otherwise, it is reversed; then the effect through the government budget on the workers' tax burden will outweigh the direct effect of the subsidies, so that a tax is preferable for this purpose.

While chapter 3 focuses on public policy from the viewpoint of setting small distortion-correcting taxes and subsidies, chapter 4 examines optimal taxation and public production when the government can set its instruments at any level. It is shown that optimal taxation and public production must change the unions' choice-sets so that (with a utilitarian social welfare function) the union wages will be uniform. Since the subsidies create a gap between consumer and producer wages, production and consumption decisions are independent and aggregate production efficiency is desirable. An interesting result is that although it is possible to maintain full employment by public policy, this is not necessarily socially optimal. When jobs cannot be divided and wage-fixing is non-competitive, an equilibrium with unemployment is possible. Then, with decreasing returns to scale in aggregate production, it can be optimal to employ only some of the workers and to pay benefits to the rest of them rather than to attempt to employ them all.

In chapter 5, the static model of bargaining is extended so that there exist sunk costs in investment. It is shown that if the union is strong, then there exists a reputational equilibrium. In the presence of *credible* contracts, the firm can, when making its plans, take the union's pay parameters as given, but in the absence of credible contracts, the employer and the union bargain after the former announces its investment plan. In the absence of credible contracts, the union has an incentive to renege and reap the benefits of investment, so that the firm has less incentive to invest than in the presence of credible contracts. If the union is powerful enough, the equilibrium with credible contracts is stable. If the employer does not trust the union, then the latter has an incentive to deprive the employer of profits. Consequently, the employer loses nothing if it trusts a strong union.

It is shown that credibility is an issue only at medium levels of union power: with a weak union, the pay parameters are competitively determined; with a strong union, there is a reputational equilibrium with credible contracts; and with a union of medium strength, there is unemployment in the absence of credible contracts. Consequently, any marginal attempt to undermine the power of a strong union causes a loss of credibility of contracts and, consequently, a fall in investment and welfare.

Chapter 6 considers a situation where the game is repeated continuously in time. For technical reasons, we consider only the case of a monopoly union. It is shown that if there is some investment going on, then there exists a reputational equilibrium where the union has no incentive to renege on its announced pay parameters. The interpretation is the same as in chapter 5: if the employer does not trust the union, then the latter can take all the profits by using two-part tariffs; so the firm loses nothing in trusting the union.

Chapter 7 extends the model of chapter 6 to the case of several unions. It is shown that a union can increase its members' income in two ways: by raising its members' real basic wage relative to the other workers, as above; or by extracting part of capital rent. If a union is small, it attempts to benefit at the expense of the other unions by raising the basic wage and ensures high capital stock and high employment in future by giving up any claim on capital income. When a union is big so that its basic wage considerably increases the price level, there is no incentive to rival the other unions and rent extraction is chosen. We conclude that at high levels of centralization, bargaining ends up with claims on capital income, while at low levels of centralization, it ends up with the use of ordinary wages. The substitution between labour and intermediate inputs only increases the likelihood of profit-sharing among the unions of medium size but it does not change the outcome.

Chapter 8 considers the effect of union power on economic growth. This is done by examining balanced growth in a closed (and fully unionized) economy. There are two categories of labour termed 'skilled' and 'unskilled', but the occupation of the workers is assumed to be flexible. It is assumed that when unskilled workers transform themselves into skilled workers, an increasing amount of unskilled labour is needed to produce one unit of skilled labour. The unions and the firms bargain simultaneously over the wages for skilled and unskilled labour and possibly over the workers' profit share. It is furthermore assumed that research employs only skilled labour, and that the producers of inter-mediate inputs are subject to monopolistic competition while those of final goods are subject to oligopolistic competition.

The first finding is that because an increase in R&D increases aggregate labour income, a union does not accept any agreement causing un-employment for its skilled members. If there were unemployment for both labour inputs, then both labour income and profits could be increased by producing more final goods, until either of the inputs became fully employed. This motivates a labour union and the corre-sponding firm to agree only on such wages for which either skilled or unskilled labour is fully employed. If skilled labour were less than fully employed, then employing more of this in research would increase the level of labour income. Consequently, the union has no incentive to start bargaining when the expected outcome of bargaining would yield full employment for unskilled, but unemployment for skilled labour. So in the case of growth, skilled labour must be fully employed.

Second, it is shown that union power speeds up growth: higher wages for unskilled labour increase research through decreased final output and the transfer of skilled labour from the production of final goods to research. The increase in the union's relative bargaining power increases both unemployment and the balanced growth rate. If the strengthening of union power increases the wage for unskilled labour so that there is unem-ployment for unskilled labour, then the final-goods sector employs less skilled labour. This fall in the demand for skilled labour decreases the wage for skilled labour and the unit cost of a new design. With a lower unit cost, the production of new designs expands, thereby speeding up economic growth.

Finally, it is shown that unemployment can be socially desirable: if a high growth rate is socially optimal, then the maintenance of it requires so much skilled labour in research that with the remaining skilled labour, only part of unskilled labour can be employed in ordinary production.

Chapter 9 examines the effect of union power on international specialization in a world where one economy is unionized but the rest of the world has competitive labour markets. Alternatively, the analysis holds for specialization in a closed economy which has both a unionized and a non-unionized sector. It is assumed that all economies produce both primary and refined goods, that technical change is based on international (or inter-sectoral) brand proliferation for refined goods, and that technology and preferences are everywhere the same. In other respects, the model is more or less similar to that in chapter 8.

Since there is perfect international competition in the market for the designs of new refined goods and since this sector employs only skilled labour, the wage for skilled labour is uniform all over the world. Consequently, the increase of union power in any economy decreases ordinary production and transfers resources to research in that economy. This means that countries with relatively high (low) union power export refined (primary) and import primary (refined) products. Brand proliferation increases the output of refined goods in all economies. Because the production of refined goods constitutes a relatively large share of economies with relatively high union power, it follows that real output growth is faster in countries with relatively high union power.

Finally, it is also shown that in an open economy unemployment can be socially desirable. When a large amount of skilled labour is needed to develop new designs for refined goods, such an amount must be taken from ordinary production. Then, in the production of the primary good, unit labour cost must be increased by so much that only part of unskilled labour is employed.

1 Basic concepts of game theory

1.1 Introduction

In order to obtain an extensive treatment of collective bargaining, one has to take game theory as a starting point. This chapter presents the elements of game theory that are needed in the rest of the book. The basic references are Nash (1950), Ståhl (1972), Rubinstein (1982), Binmore, Rubinstein and Wolinsky (1986), Sutton (1986) and Osborne and Rubinstein (1990, 1994).

In game theory the decision-makers, who are called *players*, pursue well-defined objectives (i.e. they are rational) and take into account their knowledge of other decision-makers' behaviour (i.e. they reason strategically). A *game* is a description of strategic interaction that includes the players' interests as well as the constraints on the actions that the players can take. The game does not specify the actions that the players do take. A *solution* of a game is a systematic description of the outcomes that may emerge. To find an equilibrium in a game, one must identify the patterns of each player's behaviour which are stable against selfish deviations by the other participants in the game. In this study, we ignore uncertainty, restrict ourselves to two-player situations and consider only games that are used in the later chapters. For convenience, the players are called 'the union' and 'the firm'.

1.2 The application of games to labour economics

In a (*non-cooperative*) *strategic game*, each player chooses its plan of action once and for all, and these choices are made simultaneously. A classical example of this is when the players must split a cake of fixed size knowing that the situation will not be repeated. The common solution concept in strategic games is a *Nash equilibrium*, which requires that no player can deviate and gain if the other sticks to its equilibrium behaviour.

Section 1.3 shows that a Nash equilibrium can be solved by the maximization of a simple function called the *Nash product* of the game. This function is the product of the players' gains in the equilibrium outcome over those in the outcome that corresponds to disagreement.

Many useful games in economics involve a sequential structure where the players have to take actions in some specified order. These are called *extensive games,* and in them each player considers its plan of action not only at the beginning of the game but also whenever it has to make a decision. In most extensive games, the players can make incredible threats that they themselves would prefer not to carry out. Section 1.4 eliminates this defect using the solution concept known as *subgame perfect equilibrium.* This says that the players' strategies must be the best responses not only at the beginning of the game but also in all parts of the game starting later.

An extensive game where the players take actions in two stages (and not simultaneously) is called a Stackelberg game. The player who acts first is called the (Stackelberg) leader and the one who reacts later is called the (Stackelberg) follower of the game. For instance, the common form of wage-bargaining, where the union sets the wage while the employer determines employment taking the wage as given, can be modelled as a Stackelberg game where the union's wage-setting is carried out strategically before the employment decision.[1] The outcome of such a game is that the union chooses its optimal wage–employment combination on the labour demand curve. The firm could warn that if the union increases the wage above the level corresponding to full employment, then it will stop production for good. Since everybody knows that in the event of this threat being implemented the firm will lose its profit, such a warning cannot be a relevant strategy in the game.

In economic applications, two special forms of extensive game are of special interest. First, when the same strategic game is repeated and the players have some sort of memory, we have a *repeated game.* This concept was created to explain the nature of long-term relationships. For instance, in the case where the firm is subject to adjustment costs in investment, the formation of reputation in collective bargaining can be modelled as a repeated game in which the firm will remember the union's cheating in the later stages of the game.[2] In such a game, it may be in the union's best interests to cheat, in which case wage-setting will be 'non-credible', or not to cheat, in which case it will be 'credible'. Since in the 'credible' case the wages are expected to be lower and the profits higher than in the

---

[1] This case is examined in section 2.2.
[2] This case is considered in chapters 6 and 7.

'non-credible' case, the credibility of wage-setting will encourage the firm to invest in capital.

A repeated game is *finite* if the bargaining is repeated only a fixed number of times, and *infinite* if it is repeated indefinitely. These two versions lead to different results. A model with an infinite horizon is appropriate if after each period the players believe that the game will continue for an additional period, while the model with a finite horizon is appropriate if the players clearly perceive a well-defined final period.[3] In the applications of this book, the fact that the players' lifetime is finite need not be important. If the game is played frequently so that the horizon approaches very slowly, then the players ignore the existence of the horizon entirely until its arrival is imminent. On the basis of this, we prefer the game with an infinite horizon to that with a finite horizon as the better approximation of reality for wage-bargaining. Infinitely repeated games are introduced in section 1.5.

In the second useful form of an extensive game, the players try to solve the conflict of their interests by committing themselves voluntarily to a course of action that is beneficial to both of them. This can be specified as an *alternating-offers game*: the players take turns to call out proposals for splitting a cake and the other party can decide whether or not to accept the offer as a basis for the agreement. A delay in agreement means welfare loss for both parties, so that in the long run they must end up with a solution. An example of this game is wage-bargaining in which the negotiators could in principle make each other a large number of offers in a very short time.

Section 1.6 shows that the outcome of the alternating-offers game is the following. Because of the losses associated with delays, one of the players immediately offers the final agreement and the other one accepts it.[4] If the time interval between successive offers is small, the outcome of any alternating-offers game can be approximated by the outcome of some strategic game. Given this result, any alternating-offers game can be solved through the maximization of the Nash product of the corresponding strategic game, i.e. through the maximization of the product of the players' gains over the outcome that corresponds to disagreement.

Section 1.7 generalizes the alternating-offers game to economically more interesting cases where the players are in an asymmetric position. Then the players share the cake in proportions that correspond to their

---

[3] See, for example, Osborne and Rubinstein (1994), p. 135.
[4] This is true only because we assume that the parties know perfectly the environment as well as each other's preferences. If, for example, the players were uncertain about each other's preferences, then there would be some 'learning' time without any agreement before the final offer was made.

relative bargaining power in the game. It is shown that this generalization can be transformed into the symmetric case so that the relative bargaining power of a player takes the form of a parameter. Consequently, the outcome of the game can be solved through the maximization of some weighted geometric average of the players' gains over the outcome with disagreement. This average is called a *generalized Nash product* of the game and its weights approximate the relative bargaining power of the parties. As an application of this property, it is possible to examine the problem of how the relative bargaining power of the union affects the general equilibrium of the economy.[5]

1.3 Strategic games

1.3.1 Bargaining problems

It is assumed that the union chooses its *action* x_u from a set $\mathcal{X}_u$ and the firm chooses its action x_f from a set $\mathcal{X}_f$. Then the pair

$$x = (x_u, x_f) \in \mathcal{X} = \mathcal{X}_u \times \mathcal{X}_f$$

of the players' actions can be called the *action of the game*. We denote the union's utility function by $u_u = U_u(x) \in \mathcal{R}$ and the firm's utility function by $u_f = U_f(x) \in \mathcal{R}$, where x belongs to set $\mathcal{X}$ and $\mathcal{R}$ is the set of real numbers. Game theory uses von Neumann–Morgenstern utility functions that were originally defined over lotteries.[6] One property of these functions is that the behaviour of an agent having such a utility function must be independent of the units in which we measure utility. This property can be formally presented as follows:

Assumption 1.1: Let U_u (U_f) be the utility function that is generated by the preferences of the union (firm). Then for any strictly increasing linear transformation Λ, the utility function $\Lambda(U_u)$ ($\Lambda(U_f)$) is generated by the same preferences of the union (firm).

Each player has to take into account the fact that the other player's behaviour may cause negotiations to break down. Therefore, in line with Nash (1950), we assume that the union and the firm either reach an *agreement* in some set X or fail to reach an agreement, in which case the *disagreement event D* occurs. It is furthermore assumed, for simplicity, that event D is unique. It follows that the set of the union's actions is

---

[5] This case is considered in chapters 5, 8 and 9.
[6] von Neumann and Morgenstern (1944).

given by $\mathcal{X}_u \doteq X_u \cup \{D\}$, and the set of the firm's actions is given by $\mathcal{X}_f \doteq X_f \cup \{D\}$.

We call the pair (u_u, u_f) of the players' utilities the *outcome of bargaining*. The set of the outcomes $(U_u(x), U_f(x))$ that are associated with possible agreements $x \in X$ is given by

$$S \doteq \cup_{x \in X} \{(U_u(x), U_f(x))\} \subset \mathcal{R}^2.$$

We assume that the set S is compact (i.e. closed and bounded) and convex, and that it is possible to make an agreement that yields the same utility for the players as the disagreement event D does. This latter assumption means that the disagreement outcome belongs to set S:

$$d = (\bar{u}_u, \bar{u}_f) = (U_u(D), U_f(D)) \in S.$$

When there exists some agreement $(u_u, u_f) \in S$ that is preferred by both players to the disagreement outcome, $u_u > \bar{u}_u$ and $u_f > \bar{u}_f$, a pair $\langle S, d \rangle$ that consists of both the set S of possible agreements and the disagreement point d is called a *bargaining problem*. Denoting the set of all bargaining problems by $\mathcal{B}$, we define a *bargaining solution* as a function $\theta : \mathcal{B} \to \mathcal{R}^2$ that assigns to each bargaining problem $\langle S, d \rangle \in \mathcal{B}$ a unique outcome $(\theta_u, \theta_f) \in S$. Since the players can agree to disagree, $d \in S$, and there is some agreement preferred by both of them to the disagreement outcome, they have a mutual interest in reaching an agreement.

1.3.2 Nash axioms

Later on, we will find that the following definition is very useful in proofs:

Definition 1.1: If the disagreement utilities are the same for both players, $\bar{u}_u = \bar{u}_f$, and if for any agreement $(u_u, u_f) \in S$ there exists a reversed agreement $(u_f, u_u) \in S$ so that the players' places are switched, then the bargaining problem $\langle S, d \rangle$ is termed symmetric.

Nash imposed three axioms concerning a bargaining solution $\theta : \mathcal{B} \to \mathcal{R}^2$.[7] The first of these is the following:

Axiom 1 (Symmetry): In the symmetric case, switching the players' places does not affect the solution, $\theta_u(S, d) = \theta_f(S, d)$.

---

[7] There was also a fourth axiom in Nash (1950) but this was the same as assumption 1.1 above.

Second, it is required that adding irrelevant alternatives to the problem does not affect the solution:

Axiom 2 (Independence of irrelevant alternatives): If $\langle S, d \rangle$ and $\langle T, d \rangle$ are bargaining problems so that the possible agreements in the former belong to those in the latter, $S \subset T$, and that the solution of the latter belongs to the possible agreements in the former, $\theta(T, d) \in S$, then both problems have the same solution, $\theta(S, d) = \theta(T, d)$.

Finally, it is assumed that the players never agree on an outcome (u_u, u_f) when there is available an outcome $(\hat{u}_u, \hat{u}_f)$ in which they both are better off:

Axiom 3 (Pareto efficiency): If $(u_u, u_f) \in S$, $(\hat{u}_u, \hat{u}_f) \in S$, $\hat{u}_u > u_u$ and $\hat{u}_f > u_f$, then the pair (u_u, u_f) cannot be a bargaining solution of the problem $\langle S, d \rangle$, $(u_u, u_f) \neq \theta(S, d)$.

Since there is an agreement preferred by both players to the disagreement point d, the players never disagree.

1.3.3 The Nash product

Axioms 1–3 fully characterize the Nash solution in a very simple form: they select solutions (u_u, u_f) that maximize the product of the players' gains in utility over the disagreement outcome. This leads to the following result:

Proposition 1.1: There exists a unique bargaining solution $G : \mathcal{B} \to \mathcal{R}^2$ satisfying axioms 1–3. This solution is given by the maximization of the *Nash product*

$$(u_u - \bar{u}_u)(u_f - \bar{u}_f) \tag{1.1}$$

over the feasible outcomes:

$$G(S, d) = \underset{(\bar{u}_u, \bar{u}_f) \leq (u_u, u_f) \in S}{\arg\max} \ (u_u - \bar{u}_u)(u_f - \bar{u}_f). \tag{1.2}$$

We refer to 1.2 as the *Nash solution* of the bargaining problem $\langle S, d \rangle$. Since the proof of this proposition is very complex, we place it in appendix 1a and replace it here by the following intuitive explanation. Assume, for simplicity, that the players share a fixed revenue. Furthermore, choose the units so that one unit of each player's utility is produced by one unit of currency. Since both players get an exogenous income $\bar{u}_u$ or $\bar{u}_f$ in the case of no agreement, there is no way that one player could hurt or punish the other. Therefore, in the case of no agreement, both players will lose their income over and above this outside option, $u_u - \bar{u}_u$ or $u_f - \bar{u}_f$. If the union (firm) benefits relatively more from an agreement,

$$u_u - \bar{u}_u > u_f - \bar{u}_f \quad (u_u - \bar{u}_u < u_f - \bar{u}_f),$$

then it loses more if the other player refuses to make an agreement. Therefore, it is plausible that the players divide their aggregate income in the case of an agreement, $u_u + u_f$, 'fairly' among themselves, $u_u - \bar{u}_u = u_f - \bar{u}_f$. Mathematically, such a fair division is obtained through the maximization of the product

$$(u_u - \bar{u}_u)(u_f - \bar{u}_f)$$

by the choice of the levels of income, u_u and u_f, while holding aggregate income $u_u + u_f$ constant. The advantage of using this optimization is that no matter in which units the players' utilities are defined, the outcome will be found directly.

The optimization 1.2 is presented graphically in figure 1.1. The optimum is defined by the tangency of the isoquant corresponding to the function (1.1) and the set S of the feasible outcomes. The strong Pareto frontier of S can be defined as

$$\{(u_u, u_f) \in S | \text{there is no } (\hat{u}_u, \hat{u}_f) \in S \text{ with } \hat{u}_u \geq u_u, \hat{u}_f \geq u_f,$$
$$\text{and } (\hat{u}_u, \hat{u}_f) \neq (u_u, u_f)\},$$

and it specifies the function

$$u_f = y(u_u), \quad \text{for which } y' < 0 \text{ holds when } y \text{ is differentiable.}$$

$$(1.3)$$

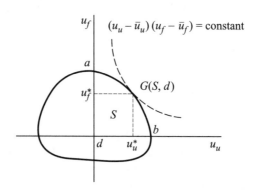

Figure 1.1 The Nash solution of the bargaining problem $\langle S, d \rangle$.

In figure 1.1, the function (1.1) is given by the frontier ab of the set S. The utility pair (u_u^*, u_f^*) is the Nash solution of $\langle S, d \rangle$ if and only if $u_f^* = y(u_u^*)$ and u_u maximizes

$$(u_u - \bar{u}_u)[y(u_u) - \bar{u}_f].$$

If the strong Pareto frontier (1.3) is differentiable at the point u^*, then the second condition is equivalent to

$$(u_f^* - \bar{u}_f)/(u_u^* - \bar{u}_u) = -y'(u_u^*).$$

1.4 Extensive games

1.4.1 Definitions

In a strategic game, the union or the firm chooses its plan of action once and for all, so that it has no possibility of reconsidering its plan after some events in the game have unfolded. To correct this defect, we now assume that there is a number k of successive periods or occasions in which the players determine their actions. The number k can be finite or infinite. We extend the players' utility functions as follows: the union evaluates the sequence (u_{ui}) of its utilities by

$$\mathcal{U}_u = \sum_{i=1}^{k} \delta_u^i u_{ui}, \quad \delta_u \in (0, 1], \tag{1.4}$$

and the firm evaluates the sequence (u_{fi}) of its utilities by

$$\mathcal{U}_f = \sum_{i=1}^{k} \delta_f^i u_{fi}, \quad \delta_f \in (0, 1], \tag{1.5}$$

where the discount factors of both the union and the firm, δ_u and δ_f, are constants.

Let us denote the actions of the union and the firm in period i by a_i. Then the sequence of actions, a_i $(i = 1, 2, ..., k)$, forms a *history* of the extensive game. In this study, we consider only extensive games with perfect information: when the union or the firm is making any decision, then it is perfectly informed of all the events that have previously occurred. Let us denote by h a history of length k,

$$a_i \quad (i = 1, ..., k),$$

and by $\hat{h}$ a history of length $\hat{k}$,

$$a_i \quad (i = 1, ..., \hat{k}).$$

Furthermore, let us denote the difference of these histories,

$$a_i \ (i = k+1, ..., \hat{k}),$$

by $(h, \hat{h})$, for convenience, and assume that the set H of possible histories satisfies the following properties:

- The empty sequence $\varnothing$ is a history as well, $\varnothing \in H$.[8]
- A history remains a history even without some of its latest actions: if $\hat{h} \in H$, then $h \in H$ for $\hat{k} > k$.
- If a finite sequence of actions, $a_i \ (i = 1, 2, ..., k)$, is a history for all integers k, then the infinite sequence of actions,

$$a_i \ (i = 1, 2, ...),$$

  is a history as well.

A *strategy* of the union (firm) is a plan that specifies the action of the union (firm) whenever it is the union's (firm's) turn to move. Now we denote the strategy of the union by u_u and that of the firm by u_f, for convenience. The *player function* $P(h)$ specifies the player who has to take an action after the history h. Then $P(h) = u$, if it is only the union's, $P(h) = f$, if it is only the firm's turn to take an action, and $P(h) = \{u, f\}$, if both players have to take an action simultaneously. If history $h \in H$ is such that there are actions to be made,[9] player $P(h)$ chooses an action from the set

$$A(h) = \{(h, \hat{h}) : \hat{h} \in H\}.$$

1.4.2 Concepts of equilibria

The set H of possible histories, the player function $P(h)$ and the discount factors of the players, δ_u and δ_f, specify the extensive game

$$\Gamma \doteq \langle H, P, \delta_u, \delta_f \rangle. \tag{1.6}$$

To eliminate irrelevant outcomes, two concepts of equilibria are introduced. The first of these is the following:

Definition 1.2: A pair (u_u^*, u_f^*) of the strategies is a Nash equilibrium of the extensive game $\Gamma = \langle H, P, \delta_u, \delta_f \rangle$, if, given the strategy of the

---

[8] The history at the beginning of the game must be empty.
[9] This means that the length of the history, k, is finite and there is a_{k+1} such that a_i $(i = 1, ..., k, k+1)$ is a history as well.

union (firm), no strategy of the firm (union) results in an outcome that the union (firm) prefers to the outcome that is generated by the equilibrium strategies (u_u^*, u_f^*).

In playing out an extensive game, there are certain moments such that from those moments onward, the remainder of the game is itself an extensive game. Such a game is called a *subgame* of the original game. Let us denote by H_h the set of sequences $(h, \hat{h})$ of actions for which $\hat{h} \in H$, and define $P_h(\hat{h})$ for each $(h, \hat{h}) \in H_h$. Then

$$\Gamma(h) \doteq \langle H_h, P_h, \delta_u, \delta_f \rangle$$

is the subgame which corresponds to the extensive game (1.6) and which follows the history h.

The Nash equilibrium of the extensive game is an appropriate solution if the players are rational, experienced, and have played the same game (or similar games) many times. Unfortunately, it evaluates the desirability of a strategy only at the beginning of the game. Therefore, to rule out the use of 'incredible threats' which in the long run hurt also the player itself, Selten (1975) proposed the concept of subgame perfectness, as follows. If for each subgame in the extensive game a player's strategy is the best reply to any strategy of the other, then there is a *subgame perfect equilibrium*. Neither of the players can then improve its outcome by a one-shot deviation from the equilibrium strategy, and the behaviour of the players would be unchanged for the rest of the game although they would lose their memories of the past. Given the pair (u_u, u_f) of strategies and a history h in the extensive game Γ, we can denote by $u_u(h)$ or $u_f(h)$ the strategy that u_u or u_f induces in the subgame $\Gamma(h)$. This and definition 1.2 enable the formal definition of the equilibrium as follows:

Definition 1.3: A pair of strategies (u_u^*, u_f^*) is a subgame perfect equilibrium of an extensive game $\Gamma = \langle H, P, \delta_u, \delta_f \rangle$ if and only if, for any history h, the pair $(u_u^*(h), u_f^*(h))$ of strategies is a Nash equilibrium of the subgame $\Gamma(h)$.

If the extensive game is finite, its subgame perfect equilibrium is easily found by dynamic programming as follows. One first finds a Nash equilibrium for the last period of the extensive game. Then, given the Nash equilibrium for the final period, that for the second last period is found. Proceeding in this manner period by period, the subgame perfect equilibrium is obtained when the whole extensive game has been analysed.

1.5 Repeated games

The model of an *infinitely repeated game* captures a situation in which players repeatedly engage in a strategic game M. Then M is called the *constituent game*. It is assumed that the action sets $\mathcal{X}_u$ and $\mathcal{X}_f$ of the players are compact and that there is no limit on the number of times that M is played. When taking an action, a player knows the actions that have previously been chosen by all players.

The union's (firm's) *minmax payoff* v_u (v_f) in the constituent game M is the lowest utility that the firm (union) can force upon the union (firm):

$$v_u \doteq \min_{x_f \in \mathcal{X}_f} \max_{x_u \in \mathcal{X}_u} U_u(x), \quad v_f \doteq \min_{x_u \in \mathcal{X}_u} \max_{x_f \in \mathcal{X}_f} U_f(x).$$

In the constituent game M, an outcome (w_u, w_f) for which conditions

$$w_u \geq v_u, \quad w_f \geq v_f,$$

hold is termed *enforceable*. If conditions

$$w_u > v_u, \quad w_f > v_f$$

hold, then (w_u, w_f) is *strictly enforceable*. If the outcome is not enforceable, either of the players has an incentive to reject it. This means that the possible equilibria of the repeated game must be chosen from the set of enforceable outcomes. If the outcome is strictly enforceable, both parties have an incentive to accept it.

To support an outcome that is not repetitions of Nash equilibria of the constituent game M, the union or the firm must be deterred from deviating from the outcome by some sort of 'punishment'. Most of the results in the literature of repeated games consist of various 'folk theorems' which give conditions, such as rules of 'punishment', under which the set of equilibrium strategies consists of nearly all enforceable strategies.[10] This means that in models of a repeated game, the notion of equilibrium has no more predictive power than in the models of other games in general. To obtain a unique solution, the structure of the repeated game must be so specific that there is at most one enforceable outcome. Fortunately, in our applications this will be the case.

---

[10] See Osborne and Rubinstein (1994), ch. 8.

1.6 Bargaining with alternating offers

1.6.1 The players

In models of bargaining with alternating offers, the problem is how to make an agreement between the union and the firm which take turns to call out proposals for splitting the income. If a proposal of one player is accepted by the other, the game ends; but otherwise no one gets anything for one period and the game proceeds to the other player's turn.

It is assumed that each period has fixed length $\Delta > 0$, so that a sequence of periods is given by $\{0, \Delta, 2\Delta, \ldots\}$. Then the union's and firm's objective functions (1.4) and (1.5) take the form

$$\mathcal{U}_u = \sum_{i=1}^{\infty} \delta_u^{\Delta i} U_u(x_i), \quad \mathcal{U}_f = \sum_{i=1}^{\infty} \delta_f^{\Delta i} U_f(x_i), \quad 0 < \delta_u, \delta_f < 1, \quad (1.7)$$

where δ_u (δ_f) is the discount factor per unit of time, and δ_u^{Δ} (δ_f^{Δ}) that per period, for the union (firm) and where x^i is the action of the game in period i.

1.6.2 Equal discount rates

In the simplest case, there is one call per period and both players have the same discount factor $\delta_u = \delta_f = \delta$. Then the game can be presented as

Period	Caller	Payoff for the union	Payoff for the firm
0	Union	u_u^0	u_f^0
1	Firm	$\delta^{\Delta} u_u^1$	$\delta^{\Delta} u_f^1$
2	Union	$\delta^{2\Delta} u_u^0$	$\delta^{2\Delta} u_f^0$

follows:

Let us transform, for convenience, the utility functions of the players so that the disagreement point d is at the origin: $\bar{u}_u = 0$ and $\bar{u}_f = 0$. Given assumption 1.1, this will have no effect on the results. The union starts the game in period 0 by making a proposal.[11] Let x^0 be the action of the game that results from its call, and let the corresponding levels of instantaneous utilities for the union and the firm be $u_u^0 = U_u(x^0)$ and $u_f^0 = U_f(x^0)$. Since the structure of the game remains identical over time, x^0 must also be the optimal strategy for the union in every even round.

---

[11] Since we later assume $\Delta \to 0$, the assumption of the firm starting the game would not make any difference to the results.

If there is no agreement in period 0, then in period 1 the firm makes a proposal. Let x^1 be the action of the game that results from this call, and let the corresponding levels of instantaneous utilities for the union and the firm be $u_u^1 = U_u(x^1)$ and $u_f^1 = U_f(x^1)$. Since the structure of the game remains identical over time, x^1 must also be the optimal strategy for the firm in every odd round. The payoffs differ because they entail income streams starting at different points in time. Hence to compare the payoffs, we measure these in terms of permanent income streams that begin in period 0 and have the same present value as these.

It is clear that all the payoffs attainable from period 2 onwards are dominated by those attainable in the first two rounds. The firm will then accept the opening offer of the union provided that it exceeds the maximum the firm can obtain by the best strategy the firm can play at the union's first call in period 2. Thus the best strategy of the union is to aim for the largest utility for itself consistent with the firm being prepared to accept it. In other words, the union maximizes $u_u^0 = U_u(x^0)$ within the inequality

$$u_f^0 = U_f(x^0) \geq \delta^\Delta u_f^1,$$

but it evaluates this requirement knowing that the firm, following the same strategy, will maximize $u_f^1 = U_f(x^1)$ within the inequality

$$u_u^1 = U_u(x^1) \geq \delta^\Delta u_u^0.$$

Since the utility functions U_u and U_f are differentiable, the optimal strategy satisfies

$$u_f^0 = \delta^\Delta u_f^1, \quad u_u^1 = \delta^\Delta u_u^0. \tag{1.8}$$

The actual bargain is determined by the original offer x^0 of the union, so that, noting (1.3), the outcome of the game is

$$u_u^0 = U_u(x^0) \text{ for the union;} \quad u_f^0 = y(u_u^0) \text{ for the firm.} \tag{1.9}$$

Since the function $u_u y(u_u)$ is concave by (1.3), there exists a value u_u^* for u_u such that it maximizes the product $u_u u_f$:

$$u_u^* \doteq \operatorname{argmax}[u_u u_f] = \operatorname{argmax}[u_u y(u_u)]. \tag{1.10}$$

Now, from (1.9) and (1.3), we obtain

$$\begin{aligned}
u_u^0 < u_u^* < u_u^1, \quad & \lim_{\Delta \to 0} u_u^0 = u_u^* -, \quad \lim_{\Delta \to 0} u_u^1 = u_u^* +, \\
u_f^0 > u_f^* > u_f^1, \quad & \lim_{\Delta \to 0} u_f^0 = u_f^* +, \quad \lim_{\Delta \to 0} u_f^1 = u_f^* -,
\end{aligned} \tag{1.11}$$

and the following result:

Proposition 1.2: If the length of the periods becomes very small, $(\Delta \to 0)$, then with equal discount rates $\delta_u = \delta_f = \delta$, the outcome of the subgame perfect equilibrium is the same as the outcome from the maximization of the product of the players' utilities for making an agreement, $u_u u_f$.

In proposition 1.2, the utility functions were transformed so that the disagreement point d is in the origin. If $d = (\bar{u}_u, \bar{u}_f)$ differs from the origin, then the union's (firm's) utility from making an agreement is equal to the difference $U_u(x) - \bar{u}_u$ $(U_f(x) - \bar{u}_f)$. In such a case, the same analysis can be carried out by substituting

$$u_u^0 - \bar{u}_u, \quad u_u^1 - \bar{u}_u, \quad u_f^0 - \bar{u}_f \quad \text{and} \quad u_f^1 - \bar{u}_f$$

for u_u^0, u_u^1, u_f^0 and u_f^1, respectively, so that the outcome of the game is obtained by the maximization of the Nash product (1.2) rather than by the maximization of $u_u u_f$. This means that when the length of the periods becomes insignificantly small, $(\Delta \to 0)$, the outcome of an extensive game with alternating offers can be approximated by that of a Nash game, in which the levels of instantaneous utilities u_u and u_f in the former are taken as the levels of utilities.

The proof of the result is illustrated in figure 1.2. If the union starts the game, the equilibrium is (u_u^0, u_f^0), and if the firm starts the game, it is (u_u^1, u_f^1). The shorter is the length Δ of the periods, the smaller is the distance between points (u_u^0, u_f^0) and (u_u^1, u_f^1). Therefore in the limit $\delta \to 0$, the case in figure 1.1 must hold.

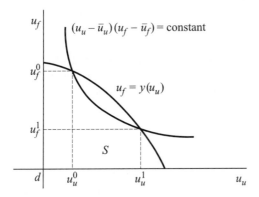

Figure 1.2 The proof of proposition 1.2.

1.7 Asymmetric bargaining with alternating offers

1.7.1 Unequal discount rates

If the players have different discount rates, the game is no longer symmetric and the optimal calls of the two players will differ. Now define

$$w \doteq u_u - \bar{u}_u = U_u(x) - \bar{u}_u,$$
$$v \doteq [u_f - \bar{u}_f]^{\log \delta_u / \log \delta_f} = [U_f(x) - \bar{u}_f]^{\log \delta_u / \log \delta_f}. \tag{1.12}$$

Then given (1.12) and proposition 1.2, we obtain

$$\lim_{\Delta \to 0} [u_u^0 - u_u] = \lim_{\Delta \to 0} w^0 = \mathrm{argmax}[wv]$$

$$= \mathrm{argmax}\left\{ [u_u - \bar{u}_u][u_f - \bar{u}_f]^{\log \delta_u / \log \delta_f} \right\}$$

$$= \mathrm{argmax}\left\{ [u_u - \bar{u}_u]^{\alpha}[u_f - \bar{u}_f]^{1-\alpha} \right\}^{1+\log \delta_u / \log \delta_f}$$

$$= \mathrm{argmax}\left\{ [u_u - \bar{u}_u]^{\alpha}[u_f - \bar{u}_f]^{1-\alpha} \right\},$$

where

$$\alpha \doteq \log \delta_f / [\log \delta_u + \log \delta_f] \in (0, 1). \tag{1.13}$$

Now it is possible to extend proposition 1.2 as follows:

Proposition 1.3: If the length of the periods becomes very small, $(\Delta \to 0)$, then the outcome of the subgame perfect equilibrium is the same as the outcome from the maximization of the weighted product of the two players' utilities from making an agreement,

$$[u_u - \bar{u}_u]^{\alpha}[u_f - \bar{u}_f]^{1-\alpha},$$

where $(\bar{u}_u, \bar{u}_f)$ is the disagreement point, and where the relative bargaining power of the union, α, is constant and given by (1.13)

In other words, the more patient the union is relative to the firm (i.e. the lower is the ratio of the discount factors δ_u / δ_f), the greater influence it has on the outcome of bargaining (i.e. the closer α is to one).

1.7.2 Unequal times of response

Another source of asymmetry may be embedded in the structure of the game: the amount of time that elapses between a rejection and an offer may be different for the union and the firm. Let this time be $\eta\Delta$ for the union and $\gamma\Delta$ for the firm, where $\eta > 0$ and $\gamma > 0$ are constants. Then, as

Δ converges to zero, the length of time between any rejection and counter-offer diminishes, while the ratio of these times for the players remains constant η/γ. For simplicity, we assume that the discount rates are equal, $\delta_u = \delta_f = \delta$. Following the analysis in the preceding subsection, the results can be easily generalized to the case where discount rates differ.

Transforming the utility functions so that the disagreement point d becomes $(0,0)$, the game can be represented as follows:

Period	Caller	Payoff for the union	Payoff for the firm
0	Union	u_u^0	u_f^0
1	Firm	$\delta^{\eta\Delta} u_u^1$	$\delta^{\eta\Delta} u_f^1$
2	Union	$\delta^{(\eta+\gamma)\Delta} u_u^0$	$\delta^{(\eta+\gamma)\Delta} u_f^0$

The best strategy of the union is to aim for the largest utility for itself consistent with the firm being prepared to accept it. In other words, the union maximizes $u_u^0 = U_u(x^0)$ within the inequality $u_f^0 = U_f(x^0) \geq \delta^{\eta\Delta} u_f^1$, but it evaluates this requirement knowing that the firm, following the same strategy, will maximize $u_f^1 = U_f(x^1)$ within the inequality $u_u^1 \geq \delta^{\gamma\Delta} u_u^0$. Since the utility functions are differentiable, the optimal strategy satisfies

$$u_f^0 = \delta^{\eta\Delta} u_f^1, \quad u_u^1 = \delta^{\gamma\Delta} u_u^0. \tag{1.14}$$

The actual bargain is determined by the original offer x^0 of the union, so that, noting (1.3), the outcome of the game is

$$u_u^0 = U_u(x^0) \text{ for the union; } \quad u_f^0 = y(u_u^0) \text{ for the firm.} \tag{1.15}$$

Now define

$$w \doteq u_u, \quad v \doteq u_f^{\eta/\gamma}. \tag{1.16}$$

Then, given (1.16) and proposition 1.2, we obtain

$$\lim_{\Delta \to 0} u_u^0 = \lim_{\Delta \to 0} w^0 = \text{argmax}[wv] = \text{argmax}[u_u u_f^{\eta/\gamma}]$$
$$= \text{argmax}[u_u^\alpha u_f^{1-\alpha}]^{1+\eta/\gamma} = \text{argmax}[u_u^\alpha u_f^{1-\alpha}], \tag{1.17}$$

where $\alpha = \gamma/(\eta + \gamma)$. If the disagreement point d is arbitrary, then by substituting

$$u_u^0 - \bar{u}_u, \quad u_u^1 - \bar{u}_u, \quad u_f^0 - \bar{u}_f \text{ and } u_f^1 - \bar{u}_f,$$

for u_u^0, u_u^1, u_f^0 and u_f^1, respectively, and by defining

$$w \doteq u_u - \bar{u}_u, \quad v \doteq [u_f - \bar{u}_f]^{\eta/\gamma},$$

the same analysis as above can be carried out. In such a case, the result (1.17) takes the form

$$\lim_{\Delta \to 0} [u_u^0 - \bar{u}_u] = \lim_{\Delta \to 0} w^0 = \text{argmax}[wv]$$

$$= \text{argmax}\left\{[u_u - \bar{u}_u][u_f - \bar{u}_f]^{\eta/\gamma}\right\}$$

$$= \text{argmax}\left\{[u_u - \bar{u}_u]^\alpha [u_f - \bar{u}_f]^{1-\alpha}\right\}^{1+\eta/\gamma}$$

$$= \text{argmax}\left\{[u_u - \bar{u}_u]^\alpha [u_f - \bar{u}_f]^{1-\alpha}\right\}.$$

So we obtain the second extension of proposition 1.2 as follows:

Proposition 1.4: Assume that the discount rates are equal $\delta_u = \delta_f = \delta$, and that the amount of time that elapses between a rejection and an offer is $\eta\Delta$ for the union and $\gamma\Delta$ for the firm, where η and γ are positive constants. Now, if the length of the periods becomes very small, $(\Delta \to 0)$, then the outcome of the subgame perfect equilibrium is the same as the outcome from the maximization of the weighted product of the two players' utilities,

$$[u_u - \bar{u}_u]^\alpha [u_f - \bar{u}_f]^{1-\alpha},$$

where the relative weight of the union's bargaining power is given by $\alpha = \gamma/(\eta + \gamma)$.

In other words, the quicker the union can respond relative to the firm (i.e. the smaller is the ratio η/γ), the greater influence it has on the outcome of bargaining (i.e. the closer α is to one).

1.7.3 The generalized Nash product

In the models that are presented in subsections 1.7.1 and 1.7.2, there are two types of asymmetry. First, there is a slight procedural asymmetry which gives the advantage to the party which makes the first proposal. However, when the time difference between successive offers converges to zero, this advantage disappears. The parties differ also with respect to their preferences (including time preferences), their times of response and their disagreement points. The theory captures these latter asymmetries as follows. We call the function

$$[u_u - \bar{u}_u]^\alpha [u_f - \bar{u}_f]^{1-\alpha} \tag{1.18}$$

where $d = (\bar{u}_u, \bar{u}_f)$ is the disagreement point, α the relative bargaining power of the union and $1 - \alpha$ that of the firm, the *generalized Nash product* of the game. According to propositions 1.3 and 1.4, the outcome of an alternating-offers game can be approximated by the maximization of the product (1.18) provided that the time difference between successive offers is insignificant. The union's relative weight α in bargaining is exogenously determined by the players' time preferences and times of response. The more patient the player is, or the quicker the player is to respond, the more influence it has on the outcome of the game.

1.8 Conclusions

In order to apply game theory in economics, one has to choose the economic elements that correspond to the properties of the game. On the basis of the results of this chapter, the following remarks can be made. First, the solution of a strategic game must be obtained through the maximization of the product of the parties' gains in utility over the disagreement outcome. This means that in the models of collective bargaining, the disagreement outcome must be specified for both parties in bargaining.

In an extensive game, we can construct a subgame perfect equilibrium through the principle of dynamic programming, as follows. First find the optimal choices of the agents for the last stage of the game. Then, taking these optimal choices into account, find the optimal choice of the agents for the second last stage of the game. This procedure is continued until one arrives at the beginning of the extensive game. A repeated game leads very probably to multiple equilibria. Therefore, to preserve the predictive power of the model, a repeated game must be specified such that there exists at most one enforceable outcome, i.e. that the parties have an incentive to reject the other outcomes.

Earlier in game theory, the disagreement point was commonly identified with the income streams available to the parties if they abandoned the attempt to reach an agreement and took up the best permanent alternative elsewhere. For an employee, this could be his/her income stream in an alternative job, and for the employer, it could be the income stream derived from using a less skilled worker. In the model with alternating offers, however, this specification is incompatible with the basic structure: here, the disagreement point should be identified with the streams of income accruing to the two parties in the course of the dispute. For instance, if the dispute involves a strike, these income streams would be the employee's income from temporary work or union strike funds, while the employer's income might be due to temporary arrangements that keep the business running.

Furthermore, the model with alternating offers suggests that the instantaneous preferences of the players – i.e. the players' preferences concerning the states of the world within the same period – cannot be a source of asymmetry in bargaining. After impatience is assumed to be the driving force for reaching an agreement, the differences in the parties' subjective discount rates is one source of asymmetry. The other sources are associated with the structure of the bargaining process. From all this it follows that the relative bargaining power of the parties is exogenously determined.

Appendix 1a. *The proof of proposition 1.1*

This proof follows Osborne and Rubinstein (1990). First, we show that the maximizer G is unique. Given that the set

$$\{(u_u, u_f) \in S : u_u \geq \bar{u}_u, u_f \geq \bar{u}_f\} \tag{1a.1}$$

is compact and that the function

$$H(u_u, u_f, \bar{u}_u, \bar{u}_f) = (u_u - \bar{u}_u)(u_f - \bar{u}_f) \tag{1a.2}$$

is continuous, there is a solution to the maximization problem (1.2). Furthermore, given that the function (1a.2) is strictly quasi-concave on the set (1a.1), there exists $(u_u, u_f) \in S$ such that $u_u > \bar{u}_u$ and $u_f > \bar{u}_f$. Finally, since the set S is convex, the maximizer G is unique.

Second, we prove that the strictly increasing linear transformation of the utility functions of the players has no effect on the outcome of the game. Let this transformation be

$$u'_u = \lambda_u u_u + \mu_u, \quad \lambda_u > 0, \quad u'_f = \lambda_f u_f + \mu_f, \quad \lambda_f > 0, \tag{1a.3}$$

where λ_u, μ_u, λ_f and μ_f are parameters, and let u_u and u_f denote the levels of instantaneous utilities before the transformation, and u'_u and u'_f after it. Transformation (1a.3) changes the set of feasible utilities S into S' and the disagreement point $d = (\bar{u}_u, \bar{u}_f)$ into $d' = (\bar{u}'_u, \bar{u}'_f)$. Now given (1a.2) and (1a.3), we obtain

$$H(u'_u, u'_f, \bar{u}_u, \bar{u}_f) = \lambda_u \lambda_f (u_u - \bar{u}_u)(u_f - \bar{u}_f)$$
$$= \lambda_u \lambda_f H(u_u, u_f, \bar{u}_u, \bar{u}_f).$$

Since the pair (u_u', u_f') maximizes $H(u_u', u_f', \bar{u}_u, \bar{u}_f)$ over S' if and only if the pair (u_u, u_f) maximizes $H(u_u, u_f, \bar{u}_u, \bar{u}_f)$ over S, then given (1.2) and (1a.2), we obtain

$$G(S', d') = \underset{\bar{u}_u \leq u_u', \bar{u}_f \leq u_f' \in S}{\arg\max} \ H(u_u', u_f', \bar{u}_u, \bar{u}_f)$$

$$= \underset{\bar{u}_u \leq u_u, \bar{u}_f \leq u_f \in S}{\arg\max} \ H(u_u, u_f, \bar{u}_u, \bar{u}_f) = G(S, d).$$

Since the value of the maximand G is the same before and after the transformation, the outcome of the game is unchanged.

Third, we ensure that the function G satisfies the three axioms.

Axiom 1: Given (1a.2), the function H is symmetric over its arguments u_u and u_f. Therefore, if the game $\langle S, d \rangle$ is symmetric and the pair (u_u^*, u_f^*) maximizes the function H over the set S, then the pair (u_f^*, u_u^*) also maximizes H over S. Since the maximizer is shown above to be unique, there must be $u_u^* = u_f^*$.

Axiom 2: If $S \subset T$ and the pair $(u_u^*, u_f^*) \in S$ maximizes the function H over the set T, then the pair (u_u^*, u_f^*) also maximizes the same function H over the set S.

Axiom 3: Since the function H or (1a.2) is increasing in each of its arguments, the pair (u_u, u_f) cannot maximize the function H over the set S if there exists a pair $(u_u', u_f') \in S$ such that $u_u' > u_u$ and $u_f' > u_f$.

Finally, we show that G is the only bargaining solution that satisfies all three axioms. Suppose that G^* is a bargaining solution that satisfies all the three axioms. We will show that equality $G^*(S, d) = G(S, d)$ holds for any bargaining problem $\langle S, d \rangle$.

Stage 1: Let us denote

$$G(S, d) = (z_u, z_f), \quad G^*(S, d) = (z_u^*, z_f^*).$$

Since there exists $(u_u, u_f) \in S$ such that $u_u > \bar{u}_u$ and $u_f > \bar{u}_f$, there must be $z_u > \bar{u}_u$ and $z_f > \bar{u}_f$. Now we make a transformation which moves the disagreement point $d = (\bar{u}_u, \bar{u}_f)$ to the origin $(0, 0)$ and the solution $G(S, d) = (z_u, z_f)$ to the point $(\frac{1}{2}, \frac{1}{2})$. This transformation changes the set S into $\hat{S}$ and the solution $G^*(S, d) = (z_u^*, z_f^*)$ into $(\hat{z}_u^*, \hat{z}_f^*)$. Since both G^* and G satisfy axiom 1, we have

$$\hat{z}_u^* = \lambda_u z_u^* + \mu_u, \quad \hat{z}_f^* = \lambda_f z_f^* + \mu_f, \quad \tfrac{1}{2} = \lambda_u z_u + \mu_u, \quad \tfrac{1}{2} = \lambda_f z_f + \mu_f.$$

Hence $G^*(S, d) = G(S, d)$ if and only if $(z_u^*, z_f^*) = (\frac{1}{2}, \frac{1}{2})$.

Stage 2: We claim that

$$\hat{z}_u + \hat{z}_f \leq 1 \quad \text{for all } (\hat{z}_u, \hat{z}_f) \in \hat{S}. \tag{1a.4}$$

Assume on the contrary that there exists such a point $(\hat{z}_u, \hat{z}_f) \in \hat{S}$ for which $\hat{z}_u + \hat{z}_f > 1$. Now define

$$t_u = (1 - \varepsilon)\tfrac{1}{2} + \varepsilon\hat{z}_u, \quad t_f = (1 - \varepsilon)\tfrac{1}{2} + \varepsilon\hat{z}_f,$$

where $0 < \varepsilon < 1$ is a constant. Since the set $\hat{S}$ is convex, the point (t_u, t_f) belongs to the set $\hat{S}$. Then for ε being small enough, we have $t_u t_f > \tfrac{1}{4}$. This is in contradiction to $(\hat{z}_u, \hat{z}_f) = (\tfrac{1}{2}, \tfrac{1}{2})$, so that relation (1a.4) is true.

Stage 3: Since $\hat{S}$ is bounded, the result (1a.4) ensures that we can find such a rectangle T that is symmetric about the $45°$ line and that contains the set $\hat{S}$, on the boundary of which there is the point $(\tfrac{1}{2}, \tfrac{1}{2})$. This is illustrated in figure 1a.1.

Stage 4: By axioms 1 and 3 we have $G^*(T, 0) = (\tfrac{1}{2}, \tfrac{1}{2})$.

Stage 5: By axiom 2 we have $G^*(\hat{S}, 0) = G^*(T, 0)$. Given this and the result in stage 4, there must be

$$G^*(\hat{S}, 0) = (\tfrac{1}{2}, \tfrac{1}{2}) = G(\hat{S}, 0).$$

Since the transformation has no effect on the outcome, we obtain

$$G^*(S, d) = G^*(\hat{S}, 0) = G(\hat{S}, 0) = G(S, d).$$

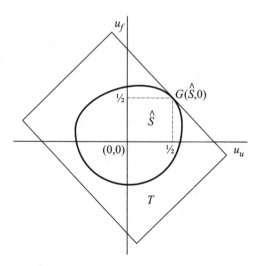

Figure 1a.1 The sets $\hat{S}$ and T in the proof.

2 Collective bargaining without investment

2.1 Introduction

This chapter attempts to construct an integrated framework in which many interesting issues of wage-setting – such as labour taxation, central vs. local bargaining, the credibility of labour contracts, and profit-sharing – could be analysed. For convenience, we start from the basic model where labour is the only productive input. One can assume, for instance, that there is no investment in real capital. Equivalently, one can assume that investment in real capital is not subject to adjustment costs. Then, at given prices for investment goods, a firm will adjust its capital stock to the optimal level so that output will be a function of labour input only. In the rest of the book, this one-input model is then extended and used to solve different problems that are associated with collective bargaining. We proceed here as follows.

Section 2.2 introduces the model of a monopoly union which sets the wage for its members given the employer's anticipated response.[1] Nowadays this model – with all of its extensions concerning more complicated interplay between the union and the employer[2] – is the one that is the most commonly used to explain wage-setting. One of the critical points in this book is that there is no plausible reason for why bargaining should be only over the wage. Therefore, in sections 2.3–2.5, we consider how the model of wage-bargaining can be extended into one where two parameters, the base wage and the workers' share of profit, are simultaneously determined.

In the basic model of the monopoly union, it is assumed that each union takes the level of consumer prices as well as the prices for intermediate

---

[1] The current form of this model is established in McDonald and Solow (1981) and Oswald (1979, 1982).
[2] These are commonly known and fairly well surveyed, for example in Oswald (1985), Farber (1986), Layard, Nickell and Jackman (1991) and Booth (1995).

inputs as given. This is very convenient, for it makes different unions strategically independent: each of these can ignore wage-setting by the others. In section 2.6, this assumption is relaxed and product differentiation is introduced. Consequently, the prices are endogenous, the unions are strategically interlinked through the price level and each union, when making its wage-setting decision, must also consider the response of the other unions. Given this framework, we analyse the degree of centralization in collective bargaining and other related issues.

2.2 The agents

2.2.1 The employees

We assume that a firm is a profit-maximizer and that the workers have standard utility functions of the sort that economic theory usually employs in the analysis of individual behaviour. A labour union is then a group of workers who bargain collectively with employers regarding the terms and conditions of employment. They do not generally bargain themselves, but they elect union leaders as their representatives both in the bargaining and in the administration of the contract. Since union leaders are constrained by the political process of the union, it is plausible to assume that the union has a utility function which is somehow related to the preferences of its members.

It is common to specify union utility U as a function of the total pay per employed worker (here the wage) w and the level of employment l for the members of the union:[3]

$$U(w,l), \quad U_w \doteq \partial U/\partial w > 0, \quad U_l \doteq \partial U/\partial l, \quad U(w,0) = 0. \qquad (2.1)$$

We assume, for simplicity, that the number of union members, L, is fixed. Then the full-employment constraint is given by

$$l \leq L. \qquad (2.2)$$

Given the utility function (2.1), it is possible to employ the standard techniques of indifference curve analysis to study the union's wage–employment objectives. Although in practice unions may be concerned with a variety of other issues as well, this simple two-variable formulation serves to illustrate the nature of the trade-offs and constraints faced by the union.

---

[3] The union's first-order condition will ensure that, in the neighbourhood of the equilibrium, $U_l > 0$.

Where the workers have the same fixed value for spare time (e.g. in the form of unemployment benefits) and the same likelihood of being employed, the function (2.1) takes the form where union utility U is in fixed proportion to employment l:

$$U(w,l) = u(w)l, \quad u > 0, \quad u' > 0, \quad u'' < 0. \tag{2.3}$$

The utility function (2.3) can be further simplified by either of the following two assumptions (or any combination of these): (i) the government supports each unemployed worker with benefit b and both the employed and unemployed workers are subject to the same preferences; or (ii) spare time yields utility and a worker's labour time is fixed. In both of these cases, union utility is determined by

$$U(w,l) = (w - b)l, \tag{2.4}$$

where the disutility of employment, b, is constant.

2.2.2 The employer

We characterize a firm by a revenue function $R(l)$ for which there is no revenue without labour input, $R(0) = 0$, and the marginal product of labour is positive and decreasing, $R' > 0$ and $R'' < 0$. To obtain this function, one can assume, for example, that there exists neoclassical technology and some firm-specific input (e.g. land) which is held fixed, or that the firm faces a downward-sloping demand curve for its output.

Given the revenue function $R(l)$, the profit Π of the firm is a function of the wage w and the level of employment l as follows:

$$\Pi(w,l) = R(l) - wl, \quad \Pi_w \doteq \partial\Pi/\partial w = -l < 0,$$
$$\Pi_l \doteq \partial\Pi/\partial l = R'(l) - w, \quad \Pi(w,0) = R(0) = 0. \tag{2.5}$$

The profit function (2.5) produces a family of iso-profit curves (figure 2.1). The slope of a single iso-profit curve is given by

$$\Pi_l(w,l)/\Pi_w(w,l) = [w - R'(l)]/l. \tag{2.6}$$

When the level l of employment increases, the slope (2.6) is positive until the marginal product of labour, $R'(l)$, reaches the wage w, then negative. Therefore, the firm's equilibrium is characterized by the first-order condition $w = R'(l)$. Since $R'' < 0$, this condition can be transformed into the labour demand

$$l(w), \quad l' \doteq 1/R'' < 0, \quad \gamma \doteq -wl'/l > 0, \tag{2.7}$$

where γ is the wage elasticity of labour demand.

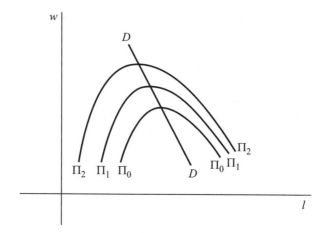

Figure 2.1 The iso-profit curves $\Pi_0\Pi_0$, $\Pi_1\Pi_1$ and $\Pi_2\Pi_2$ and the labour demand curve DD.

For any level of employment l, a smaller wage creates a bigger profit, so that in the (w, l)-plane, lower iso-profit curves are better for the firm. If the firm is a wage-taker, then in the (w, l)-plane, its equilibrium condition $w = R'(l)$ goes through the maximum points of its iso-profit curves, and this function is decreasing since R is strictly concave (see figure 2.1).

2.2.3 Efficiency wages

This theory originates from Shapiro and Stiglitz (1984). Its basic idea is that the employer pays 'extra' to his/her workers to make them work harder. Then the possibility of losing one's job acts as a discipline device.

To extend the model that was presented above, we specify labour input l as an *effective* input and the wage w as that per *physical* input (i.e. per worker). Let ν be expected income outside the firm and let a worker's productivity e in the firm be an increasing and concave function of his/her wage relative to outside income, w/ν:

$$e(w/\nu), \quad e' > 0, \quad e'' < 0. \tag{2.8}$$

If a worker earns relatively more in the firm, then to preserve his/her job in the firm he/she is willing to work harder. The wage per effective input is given by w/e, the full-employment constraint (2.2) takes the form $l/e \leq L$, and the firm's profit (2.5) the form

$$\Pi(w/e, l) = R(l) - (w/e)l. \tag{2.9}$$

In this study, it is assumed that wages are determined by collective bargaining. However, by allowing the firm to determine the wage w, we obtain the lower limit $\underline{w}$ for the wage in bargaining. Taking outside income ν and effective input l as fixed, the maximization of the profit (2.9) by the choice of w is equivalent to the minimization of labour cost per effective input, w/e, by the choice of w. Given this and the function (2.8), we obtain the Solow condition that the wage elasticity of a worker's efficiency must be equal to one:

$$\underline{w}e'(\underline{w}/\nu)/e(\underline{w}/\nu) = 1. \tag{2.10}$$

Now the feasible union wages are given by $w \geq \underline{w}(\nu)$, where $\underline{w}(\nu)$ is solved from condition (2.10).

The function (2.8) must be derived from a worker's preferences. This means that a worker's utility is a function of outside income ν as well, and that the union's target function (2.3) takes the form

$$U(w,l,\nu), \quad U_w > 0, \quad U(w,0,\nu) = 0.$$

The effect of outside income ν on union utility U forms an additional strategic dependence between the unions but in other respects, there is no qualitative change in a single union's behaviour:[4] as long as there is unemployment, $l/e < L$, and the union wage w is above the minimum level $\underline{w}(\nu)$ satisfying condition (2.10), the same analysis holds as above.[5] So because the theory of efficiency wages does not add much to our understanding of collective bargaining, we prefer to ignore it in the analysis.

2.2.4 The monopoly union

The simplest case of determination of the wage is the union setting the wage unilaterally subject to the firm's labour demand. Once the wage is set by the union, the firm then employs workers until a worker's marginal product becomes equal to the wage. The monopoly union model can be illustrated graphically, with the union seeking the highest level of utility (2.1) on the labour demand curve DD (figure 2.2). Since in the employment–wage plane the utility function (2.1) is represented by a family of decreasing and convex indifference curves, the equilibrium is found by the point of tangency between the labour demand curve DD and some indifference curve UU. The level of the firm's profit corresponding to this equilibrium is given by the iso-profit curve $\Pi\Pi$.

---

[4] In section 2.6, it is shown that the unions are strategically interlinked through the consumer price level of the economy. The use of efficiency wages would only make these links more complex.
[5] If $U_w \leq 0$, there cannot be a union wage that is above the minimum level $\underline{w}$.

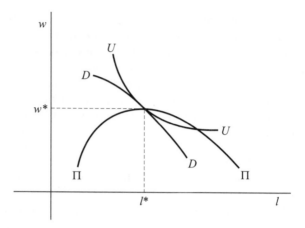

Figure 2.2   The monopoly union outcome.

Substituting the labour demand curve (2.7) into the union's utility function (2.1) yields $U(w, l(w))$. The maximization of this by the choice of the wage w leads to the following equilibrium for the monopoly union:

Proposition 2.1: The monopoly union determines the wage w so that the wage elasticity of employment on its indifference curve, $wU_w/(lU_l)$, is equal to that on the labour demand curve, γ.

Given this proposition, the only information that the union needs to know about the firm's behaviour is the elasticity of employment with respect to the wage on the labour demand curve, γ. Such an elasticity can be easily estimated by the past behaviour of the wage and the level of employment. The result in the proposition can be interpreted as follows: a higher wage leads to a lower level of employment and, consequently, each worker faces a greater risk of being unemployed. On the other hand, any employed member will receive a higher wage. Therefore, in the equilibrium of a monopoly union, the marginal benefit from a higher wage must be equal to the marginal cost from a lower level of employment.

2.3 The use of two-part wages

2.3.1 Profit-sharing

In the basic model of the monopoly union that was presented in section 2.2, it was assumed that the only instrument is the wage w

that is paid per unit of labour. The literature of collective bargaining too has almost one-sidedly concentrated on models where only the base wage is negotiated. A consistent theory should, however, at least explain why there are no other instruments of bargaining. Game theory, which was surveyed in chapter 1, suggests that the parties normally share the cake directly in proportion to their relative bargaining power. Thus it is worth examining whether such a share could be used as an instrument of bargaining.

The two-parameter bargain is most commonly specified in the form of profit-sharing where, on top of a base wage, the workers get some share of the firm's profit. Weitzman (1984, 1985, 1987) suggested that conversion from an ordinary wage to a profit-sharing system is a remedy for inflation and unemployment: if the base wage is reduced to keep a worker's income at the same level as before profit-sharing, each firm will expand employment and output so that prices will fall. Weitzman, however, considered profit-sharing only as a part of public policy: he assumed that the determination of the wage is endogenous but the workers' profit share is 'statutorily fixed by the government'.[6] In contrast, we find it more interesting to assume that both the base wage and the profit share are endogenously determined.

Some authors assume that the firms have discretion over choosing either a pure wage system or a profit-sharing system.[7] From the viewpoint of game theory, however, this would mean that the firm could *credibly* commit itself to the policy that it will always accept the union's claims on base wages but never those on profit shares. Since it is hard to justify such asymmetry between the two kinds of claims, we assume, to the contrary, that the base wage and the workers' profit share are simultaneously determined.

2.3.2 The limits of union power

In the basic model of a monopoly union, profit-sharing leads very easily to the unappealing conclusion that the union extracts the whole of the firm's profit: there is no evidence for such behaviour. This book will present three causes of why the union has to leave some of the profit for the owners of the firm.

(1) The firm accumulates real capital and uses this as a productive input. Then, if the union extracts too much profit, the rate of return

[6] Weitzman (1987), p. 91.
[7] See, for example, Steward (1989), Fung (1989) and Sorensen (1992).

paid to capital falls, resulting in a lower level of investment, capital and employment. Since low employment harms the interests of the union as well, there must be some optimal profit share for the union.

(2) The firm can hide profit from the union at some cost. This is the case in particular when the union cannot distinguish between productive inputs and non-productive expenditure. The union's claims must be based on observable profit. Because a higher share of the profit for the workers leads to a smaller observable profit, there must be an optimal profit-sharing ratio for the union.

(3) The union does not unilaterally determine the pay parameters but negotiates these with the employer. In this case, which is called the *right-to-manage model* of bargaining, the union cannot extract all the profit.

Since cause 1 involves a complex dynamic model, we exclude it here and consider it in chapters 6 and 7. Causes 2 and 3 are examined in the following two sections.

2.4 Hidden profits

2.4.1 Costs of hiding

Now we extend the basic model of the monopoly union for the case where the firm is able to hide profit at some cost. Let Π be total profit, $q\Pi$ hidden profit and $(1-q)\Pi$ observed profit, where $0 \leq q \leq 1$. We assume that the size of the firm does not affect its ability to conceal profit, but that such activity is subject to increasing costs. This means that the administrative cost of hiding profit, E, is linear homogeneous with respect to total profit Π but increasing and strictly convex with respect to the ratio q of hidden to total profit. Finally, it is obvious that with all profits revealed, $q = 1$, there is no cost, $E = 0$. Given these assumptions, we obtain the cost function

$$E = z(q)\Pi, \quad z' > 0, \quad z'' > 0, \quad z(0) = 0, \tag{2.11}$$

where z is the ratio of administrative cost to total profit.

Alternatively, it is possible to assume that the firm hides total revenue R rather than total profit $\Pi = R - wl$. In this case, the cost function (2.11) would take the form $E = zR$, where z would now be the ratio of administrative cost to total revenue. This specification would, however, yield exactly the same results as the one above but through a more complicated model.

2.4.2 The firm

Let $0 \leq h \leq 1$ be the share of observed profit $(1 - q)\Pi$ that is distributed over the workers, where constraint $h \geq 0$ means that a worker cannot directly support the firm. Then, reducing the workers' profit share $h(1 - q)\Pi$ and administrative cost E from total profit Π, we obtain the owner's income:

$$\pi(w, h, l, q) \doteq \Pi - h(1 - q)\Pi - E = [1 + (q - 1)h - z(q)]\Pi(w, l),$$

where $(1 - q)h + z < 1$. \hfill (2.12)

The union is in the position to determine both the wage w and the profit-sharing ratio h unilaterally. Therefore, taking the wage w and the ratio h as given, the firm chooses labour input l and the ratio q of hidden to total profit to maximize the owner's income (2.12) within the limits $0 \leq q \leq 1$. Given (2.5), the choice of input l again leads to the condition that the firm is on the labour demand curve $\Pi_l = 0$ or $w = R'(l)$. The choice of the ratio q leads to the function (see appendix 2a)

$$q(h) = \begin{cases} 1 & \text{for } h > z'(1), \\ 0 & \text{for } h < z'(0), \\ q^*(h) \text{ with } dq^*/dh > 0 & \text{for } z'(0) \leq h \leq z'(1). \end{cases}$$

\hfill (2.13)

Given (2.5), $\Pi_l = 0$ and $\Pi(w, 0) = R(0) = 0$, the application of l'Hôpital's rule yields

$$\lim_{l \to 0} [\Pi(w, l)/l] = \lim_{l \to 0} \Pi_l(w, l) = \lim_{l \to 0} [R'(l) - w] = 0.$$ \hfill (2.14)

2.4.3 The union

Assume that the workers' total share of profit $h(1 - q)\Pi$ is evenly distributed over labour input l. Then each employed worker obtains the amount $h(1 - q)\Pi/l$ on top of the base wage w. Then, given (2.13), the total pay per employed worker W is

$$W = w + h(1 - q)\Pi/l = w + [1 - q(h)]h\Pi(w, l)/l.$$ \hfill (2.15)

Since now the total pay per employed worker W differs from the wage w, the union's utility function (2.1) must be modified as follows:

$$U = \mathcal{U}(W, l), \quad \mathcal{U}_W \doteq \partial \mathcal{U}/\partial W > 0, \quad \mathcal{U}_l \doteq \partial \mathcal{U}/\partial l > 0, \quad \mathcal{U}(W, 0) = 0.$$

\hfill (2.16)

The monopoly union maximizes utility (2.16) by the choice of the wage w and the profit-sharing ratio h. Given (2.13) and (2.15), this optimization leads to the following result (see appendix 2b):

Proposition 2.2: The workers' profit-sharing ratio h, the ratio of hidden to total profit, q, and the administrative cost of hiding profit, z, are all fixed. The union will always prefer profit-sharing to the ordinary wage system with no profit-sharing, $h > 0$.

This result can be explained as follows. Since the profit-sharing ratio h, the ratio of hidden to total profit, q, and the administrative cost $z(q)$ are all defined in proportion to total profit Π, then the equilibrium values of these must be constants. If the union can choose the profit-sharing ratio as an additional instrument, then its welfare must improve. Finally, where the firm can hide profits at a very low cost, any attempt to claim a significant share of profit will make the observed profit disappear.

2.4.4 Wage-setting

Given the function (2.15), we obtain

$$\partial W/\partial w = 1 + (1 - q)h\Pi_w/l = 1 + (q - 1)h > 0,$$

$$\partial W/\partial l = (q - 1)h\Pi/l^2 = (w - W)/l. \tag{2.17}$$

Substituting (2.15) into (2.16) and noting result (2.14), we obtain the union's utility as a function of the wage w and the level of employment l only:

$$U(w,l) \doteq \mathcal{U}(W(w,l),l), \quad U_w = \mathcal{U}_W[\partial W/\partial w] > 0,$$

$$U(w,0) = \mathcal{U}(w,0) = 0.$$

Since this function U has exactly the same properties as the function U in (2.1), and since the firm's equilibrium condition $w = R'(l)$ is the same as before, we obtain the same analysis and the same results as in section 2.2.

Finally, if the union's utility function is of specific form (2.4), then substituting (2.17) into $U = (W - b)l$ and also noting the partial derivatives in (2.17), we obtain

$$U = \mathcal{U}(W,l) = [W(w,l) - b]l,$$

$$U_w \doteq \partial U/\partial w = l[\partial W/\partial w] = [1 + (q - 1)h]l,$$

$$U_l \doteq \partial U/\partial l = W - b + l[\partial W/\partial l] = w - b.$$

All these findings can be summarized as follows:

Proposition 2.3: With profit-sharing, the monopoly union behaves as if it chooses the optimal wage–employment combination on
the labour demand curve according to preferences that are similar to
(2.1). If the marginal disutility of employment in terms of income, b, is
constant, then $U_w = [1 + (q - 1)h]l > 0$, $U_l = w - b$ and $1 + (q - 1)h > z$.

This result means that in a monopoly union model with no investment,
profit-sharing can, on fairly general conditions, be ignored. This is due
to the union's two-stage behaviour: it chooses first the optimal sharing
ratio for its members; and then it finds the optimal wage–employment
combination on the labour demand curve.

2.5 The right-to-manage model

2.5.1 Labour income and profit

Suppose that the union and the firm bargain about the wage w and the
workers profit income x.[8] When this income is deducted from total profit
Π, the owner's revenue is equal to $\pi = \Pi - x$. We assume that profit
income x is evenly distributed over labour input, so that the total pay
per employed worker is determined by

$$W = w + x/l. \tag{2.18}$$

We define, for convenience, the union's utility function to be similar
to (2.3). Since total pay W differs from the wage w, the union's utility
function (2.3) takes the form

$$U(W, l) = u(W)l, \quad u > 0, \quad u' > 0, \quad u'' < 0. \tag{2.19}$$

Solving x from (2.18) and noting the profit function (2.5), the owner's
profit can be transformed into the form

$$\pi = \Pi(w, l) - x = R(l) - wl - x = R(l) - Wl = \Pi(W, l). \tag{2.20}$$

2.5.2 Collective bargaining

Assume that the union attempts to maximize its utility (2.19) while the
firm attempts to maximize the owner's profit (2.20). Define a status quo

---

[8] The alternative specification that the union claims a share s of total profit Π would yield
exactly the same results but through a more complex model.

point for each party as its position when no bargain is reached. We assume that without an agreement either of the parties can prevent production from taking place, so that the firm's status quo position is given by $\Pi(\cdot, 0) = 0$, and the union's status quo position is given by $U(\cdot, 0) = 0$. Then, according to the results of chapter 1, the outcome of the bargaining is obtained through the maximization of the Nash product G of the parties' targets: noting (2.18), (2.19) and (2.20), we obtain

$$G(W, l, \alpha) = U(W, l)^{\alpha} \Pi(W, l)^{1-\alpha} = u(W)^{\alpha} l^{\alpha} [R(l) - Wl]^{1-\alpha},$$

$$0 < \alpha < 1, \quad G_W \doteq \partial G / \partial W, \quad G_l \doteq \partial G / \partial l, \tag{2.21}$$

where α is the union's relative bargaining power. Given the definitions (2.1) and (2.5), the Nash product (2.21) is strictly quasi-concave in the domain of its arguments. This means that in the (W, l)-plane, the Nash product (2.21) corresponds to a family of decreasing and convex indifference curves.

It is assumed that decisions on employment and pay parameters are not made simultaneously. Manning (1987) justifies this sequential feature of the bargaining model as follows. First, because there is uncertainty and complete contingent contracts are impossible, the parties agree on the pay parameters first and then vary employment in response to a changing environment. Second, because it is impossible to specify employment throughout a whole industry (or even through a large enterprise), negotiations on the pay parameters are commonly conducted at a higher level (e.g. at the level of the industry or the whole enterprise) than those on employment, which generally occur at the workplace level.

2.5.3 The game

Now we have an extensive game with two stages: first, the union and the firm bargain over the wage w while second, the firm chooses its labour input l. This extensive game must be solved recursively backwards. Thus, at the second stage, the firm maximizes its profit by setting the marginal product of labour equal to the wage, which leads to the labour demand schedule $\Pi_l = 0$, $w = R'(l)$ or $l(w)$ with $l' \doteq 1/R'' < 0$. For this reason, employment will always lie on the labour demand curve DD: the marginal product $R'(l)$ will be equal to the wage w.

At the first stage, the parties determine the wage w and the workers' profit share x through the maximization of the Nash product (2.21). Since, however, given the definition (2.18) and the labour demand curve $w = R'(l)$, there is one-to-one correspondence from (x, w) to (W, l), we replace the wage w and x by W and l as the instruments of optimization.

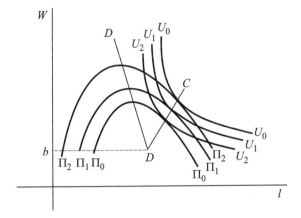

Figure 2.3 Indifference curves $U_0 U_0$, $U_1 U_1$ and $U_2 U_2$, iso-profit curves $\Pi_0 \Pi_0$, $\Pi_1 \Pi_1$ and $\Pi_2 \Pi_2$, the labour demand curve DD, the contract curve CD, and the lowest possible pay per worker b satisfying $u(b) = 0$.

Thus the right-to-manage bargaining with profit-sharing is equivalent to *efficient bargaining*, where the parties choose the total pay per employed worker W and the level of employment l simultaneously.

2.5.4 Solution

The maximization of the generalized Nash product (2.21) by the choice of (W, l) gives us the conditions

$$\frac{\partial G}{\partial W} = \frac{\alpha u'}{u} - \frac{(1 - \alpha)l}{R - Wl} = 0, \quad \frac{\partial G}{\partial l} = \frac{\alpha}{l} + (1 - \alpha)\frac{R' - W}{R - Wl} = 0.$$

$$(2.22)$$

From these conditions, it follows that the *contract curve* which in the (l, W)-plane corresponds to the tangency points of the union's indifference curves and the firm's iso-profit curves (figure 2.3) is given by:

$$\frac{\partial U}{\partial W} \bigg/ \frac{\partial U}{\partial l} \doteq \frac{u' l}{u} = -\frac{(1 - \alpha)l^2}{\alpha[R - Wl]} = -\frac{l}{R' - W} \doteq \frac{\partial \Pi}{\partial W} \bigg/ \frac{\partial \Pi}{\partial l}.$$

Rearranging this, we obtain the contract curve in the form

$$W = R'(l) + u(W)/u'(W). \tag{2.23}$$

This result says that it is in the interests of both parties to bargaining to set the total pay per employed worker W equal to the marginal product of

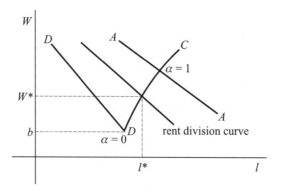

Figure 2.4 The efficient bargaining outcome.

labour, $R'(l)$, plus the value of a new job in terms of consumption for the union, $u(W)/u'(W)$.

Finally, multiplying the second equation in (2.22) by $R(l) - Wl$, we obtain the following result of Pohjola (1987):

> **Proposition 2.4:** In efficient bargaining, the equilibrium is chosen on the contract curve (2.23) so that the total pay per employed worker W is equal to the weighted sum of the average product $R(l)/l$ and the marginal product $R'(l)$ of labour where the weights are respectively the union's and the firm's relative bargaining power:
>
> $$W = \alpha R(l)/l + (1 - \alpha)R'(l). \tag{2.24}$$

Proposition (2.4) is illustrated in figure 2.4.[9] The parties share total profit $R - wl$ in proportion to their relative bargaining power. The equilibrium is the point (l^*, W^*) on the contract curve CD. If the union has no power, $\alpha = 0$, then the rent division curve is the same as the labour demand curve DD or $W = w = R'(l)$. If the firm has no power, $\alpha = 1$, then the union takes all revenue from the owners of the firm to its members and the rent division curve is the same as the average-productivity-of-labour curve AA or $W = R(l)/l$. Between these two extreme cases, $0 < \alpha < 1$, both the wage and the level of employment increase together with the union's relative bargaining power α: a stronger union claims higher wages and better employment.

---

[9] This figure is the same as in Booth (1995), p. 133.

2.6 The case of many unions

2.6.1 The background

We assume now that there are several unions and that product markets are differentiated. Then a strategic dependence will arise between the unions, and the outcome of wage-setting will be significantly dependent on the organization of collective bargaining. Technically, product differentiation can take two forms. First, final goods can be differentiated, in which case the unions are interlinked through the output prices of the goods. Second, intermediate goods can be differentiated in which case the interplay of the unions arises through the substitution of labour and intermediate inputs. We shall show that these two forms of product differentiation have different effects on the organization of collective bargaining.

In this kind of framework, one important issue is at what level of centralization the wages should be determined. On the basis of cross country evidence, Calmfors and Driffill (1988) claimed that 'extremes work best' in collective bargaining: either highly centralized systems with national bargaining, or highly decentralized systems with wage-setting at the level of individual firms seem to perform well in employment while the worst outcomes are found in systems with an intermediate degree of centralization. This assertion is illustrated in figure 2.5. Let us denote the level of employment by l, the degree of centralization in wage-setting by g and the interdependence of these by curve EE. When $g = g_{max}$, wage-setting is agreed at the level of the whole economy, and when $g = g_{min}$, it is agreed at the level of the workplace. The Calmfors–Driffill assertion is that in these two extreme cases employment is better than at any intermediate level g_0, so that curve EE is U-shaped. If the labour supply L is exogenous, it forms an upper limit for employment but does not change this basic shape of curve EE.

Calmfors and Driffill did not give any formal proof for their result but Hoel (1991) and Calmfors (1993) have presented the following explanation. Assume first that the consumer real wage is increased in a single price-taking firm. Since this firm cannot raise its output price relative to the other prices, such a wage increase leaves the relative prices in the economy unchanged. Second, assume that the consumer real wage is increased in all firms in the economy. Again in this case the relative prices in the economy are unchanged. Only when the consumption real wages are increased at some 'medium' level can the wage increases lead to changes in the relative prices. In such a case, a labour union faces a lower wage elasticity of employment than in the two extreme cases above. Therefore, wage claims by the unions will be more moderate and

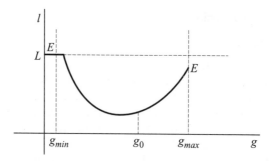

Figure 2.5 The U-shaped employment curve.

employment higher when bargaining is carried out at the level of a single firm or the whole economy than when this is carried out, for example, at the level of industries.

The reasoning of Hoel (1991) and Calmfors (1993) implicitly assumes that if a firm is a price-taker, then the union facing this firm has no effect on the output price. Consequently, the outcome with this union is the same as with a single all-encompassing union. Now we examine a different case where one union controls several price-taking firms but where the union is aware of aggregate demand for the output of these firms. We show that, even in this case, the lower tail of the U-shaped curve exists: the decentralization of bargaining leads to lower wages and a higher level of employment.

Two other papers have directly supported the Calmfors–Driffill assertion. The first one is Driffill and Van der Ploeg (1993), but this does so only because of the role played by the flexible exchange rate. Examining a many-economy world, these authors showed that because national centralized unions can take account of the effect of raising domestic wages on the country's real exchange rate and price level, they will aim at higher wages and lower employment than either decentralized or international unions. The second paper is Palokangas (1997) which presents a growth model. The model in this section is originally a part of this growth model, but it is here simplified and transferred into a static framework.

2.6.2 The differentiation of final goods

We examine an economy which is closed. The same analysis holds for an open economy with the modification that the world is taken as the basic economy and a single country is taken as a sector of that economy. Here central bargaining means bargaining at the level of the whole world and national bargaining is equivalent to bargaining at some intermediate level of centralization. Furthermore, we assume that there are no public goods and no government. The existence of these would introduce the authorities as an additional player into the game of collective bargaining.

Let there be a fixed number m of industries each of which produces a different good and faces a different monopoly union. We assume, for tractability, that there is perfect symmetry over these industries. The goods $i = 1, \ldots, m$ form a composite product using Cobb–Douglas technology, which, by a proper choice of units, can be expressed as follows:[10]

$$y = m y_1^{1/m} y_2^{1/m} \ldots y_m^{1/m}, \tag{2.25}$$

where y is the output of the composite good and y_i the output of good i. The price p of the composite good is chosen as the numeraire, $p = 1$. The producer of the composite good (=the representative consumer) sets marginal product $\partial y / \partial y_i$ equal to input price p_i for each good i. Given (2.25), this leads to the inverse demand function

$$p_i(y_1, \ldots, y_m) = \frac{\partial y}{\partial y_i} = \frac{y}{m y_i} \quad \text{with} \quad \frac{y_i}{p_i} \frac{\partial p_i}{\partial y_i} = \frac{p_i y_i}{y} - 1 \quad \text{and}$$

$$[p_1 p_2 \ldots p_m]^{1/m} = (y/m)[y_1 y_2 \ldots y_m]^{-1/m} = 1. \tag{2.26}$$

2.6.3 The differentiation of intermediate goods

The firms buy intermediate products from each other. The larger is the part of the production sector that is considered, the smaller is the share of production costs this part spends on intermediate products that are purchased from the rest of the economy. Noting the assumed perfect symmetry among the industries $i = 1, \ldots, m$, we specify this property as follows: industry i produces output y_i from labour l_i and an intermediate input that consists of the composite product of all goods. The industries are subject to the same CES technology. This specification yields the unit cost function[11]

---

[10] With the assumption of *CES* technology, the derivation of the price function (2.31) would become very complicated.

[11] When $\phi \to 1$, this function yields the Cobb–Douglas unit cost function as a special case.

$$s(w_i) \doteq [(1/m)w_i^{1-\phi} + (1 - 1/m)\delta p^{1-\phi}]^{1/(1-\phi)}$$
$$= [w_i^{1-\phi}/m + (1 - 1/m)\delta]^{1/(1-\phi)} \text{ with } \phi > 0 \text{ and } \phi \neq 1,$$

$$(2.27)$$

where w_i is the wage for industry i, $p = 1$ the price for the intermediate input and ϕ is the elasticity of substitution between labour and the intermediate input. The unit cost function (2.27) has the following useful properties:

$$0 < \eta \doteq s'(w_i)w_i/s(w_i) = 1/[1 + (m - 1)\delta w_i^{\phi-1}] < 1,$$
$$w_i s''(w_i)/s'(w_i) = \phi[w_i s'(w_i)/s(w_i) - 1] = (\eta - 1)\phi,$$

$$(2.28)$$

where η is the expenditure share falling on labour.

2.6.4 The production of goods

Assume that all firms produce output y_i from the composite input of labour l_i and intermediate input Z_i through similar Cobb–Douglas technology with decreasing returns to scale. By a proper choice of units, this technology can be expressed as follows:

$$y_i = [\beta/(\beta - 1)]Z_i^{1-1/\beta} \text{ with } \beta > 1, \tag{2.29}$$

where constant β is the elasticity of the demand for input Z_i. Decreasing returns to scale are necessary to ensure a profit. Otherwise, the unions would have nothing to bargain over. We assume that the firms in each industry i are price-takers, so that they set marginal product $p_i dy_i/dZ_i$ equal to unit cost $s(w_i)$:

$$Z_i^{-1/\beta} = dy_i/dZ_i = s(w_i)/p_i.$$

Using this and the properties of the unit cost function $s(w_i)$, we obtain inputs Z_i and l_i as follows:

$$Z_i = s(w_i)^{-\beta}p_i^{\beta}, \quad l_i = Z_i s'(w_i). \tag{2.30}$$

Substituting outputs y and y_i from (2.25) and (2.29) and inputs Z_i from (2.30) into the inverse demand functions (2.26), the prices can be expressed as functions of the wages (see appendix 2c):

$$p_i(w_1,\dots,w_m) \text{ with } \frac{1}{p_i}\frac{\partial p_i}{\partial w_i} = \left(1 - \frac{1}{\beta}\right)\left(1 - \frac{1}{m}\right)\frac{s'(w_i)}{s(w_i)} > 0.$$

$$(2.31)$$

2.6.5 The unions

We assume, for simplicity, that the workers consume the composite good the price of which is $p = 1$, and that the union's utility function takes the form (2.4) so that the marginal disutility of employment is given by constant b. In this case, according to proposition 2.3, profit-sharing would not make any difference. More specifically, from the labour demand function l_i in (2.30) and proposition 2.3, it follows that the objective function for union i takes the form

$$U_i = U(w_i, l_i) \text{ with } \partial U(w_i, l_i)/\partial w_i = \gamma l_i, \quad \partial U(w_i, l_i)/\partial l_i = w_i - b,$$

$$0 < \gamma \leq 1 \text{ and } l_i = s'(w_i)s(w_i)^{-\beta}p_i(w_1, \ldots, w_n)^{\beta}, \tag{2.32}$$

where γ is constant. Union i maximizes its objective (2.32) subject to the full-employment constraint $l_i \leq L$ for its members. We assume that the union has a unique equilibrium and ignore the constraint $l_i \leq L$ for the moment. Then the union's first-order and second-order conditions are given by

$$\partial U_i/\partial w_i = \partial U(w_i, l_i)/\partial w_i + [\partial U(w_i, l_i)/\partial l_i]\partial l_i/\partial w_i$$

$$= \gamma l_i + (w_i - b)\partial l_i/\partial w_i = 0$$

and $\partial^2 U_i/\partial w_i^2 < 0$, which are equivalent to

$$\frac{1}{(w_i - b)l_i}\frac{\partial U_i}{\partial w_i} = \frac{\gamma}{w_i - b} + \frac{s''(w_i)}{s'(w_i)} - \beta\frac{s'(w_i)}{s(w_i)} + \frac{\beta}{p_i}\frac{\partial p_i}{\partial w_i} = 0,$$

$$\frac{\partial}{\partial w_i}\left[\frac{1}{(w_i - b)l_i}\frac{\partial U_i}{\partial w_i}\right] < 0. \tag{2.33}$$

2.6.6 Local versus central bargaining

Since there is perfect symmetry over the industries $i = 1, \ldots, m$, the equilibrium levels for the wage and employment must be the same for all industries, $w_i = w$ and $l_i = l$. This symmetry in the model makes it easy to compare wage-setting at different levels of centralization. Given that there is one union for each industry i, the inverse of the number of industries, $g = 1/m$, is used as a measure for the degree of centralization in collective bargaining. Central bargaining, in which wages are agreed at the level of the whole economy, is equivalent to the case where there is only one industry, $m = 1$ and $g = 1$. On the other hand, if bargaining is carried out locally, then m is large and $g \approx 0$. In terms of figure 2.5, we have $g_{max} = 1$ and $g_{min} = 0$.

Now we examine the effect of the degree of centralization, $g = 1/m$, on the wage w. Since the level of employment l is a decreasing function of the wage w, the effect of g on l will be reversed. From conditions (2.33), $l_i = l$ and $w_i = w$ it follows that the wage w is a function of the degree of centralization g and the elasticity of substitution ϕ. In appendix 2d, given relations (2.28), (2.31) and (2.33) as well as the symmetry over $i = 1, \ldots, m$, we prove the following result:

Proposition 2.5: If $0 < \phi \leq 1$, then an increase in the degree of centralization decreases the wage w. Furthermore, if $\phi \to \infty$, then a decrease in the degree of centralization decreases the wage w.

The explanation of proposition 2.5 is the following. When the intermediate inputs are bad substitutes for labour, $0 < \phi \leq 1$, the wage elasticity of labour demand is steeper, the smaller the union is and the more the employers facing the union purchase intermediate inputs from the rest of the economy. This means that in figure 2.5, curve EE is increasing rather than U-shaped for $0 < \phi \leq 1$. On the other hand, when the intermediate inputs are close enough substitutes for labour, $\phi \to \infty$, then the wage elasticity of the demand for labour is steeper, the larger the union is and the less the employers facing the union purchase intermediate inputs. Consequently, for $\phi \to \infty$, larger unions set higher wages which yields a lower level of employment for the whole economy. This means that in figure 2.5, curve EE is decreasing rather than U-shaped for $\phi \to \infty$.

Now assume that labour and intermediate inputs are not bad substitutes (i.e. that $\phi > 1$ holds), but not too close substitutes either, so that there exists an interior solution $0 < g_0 < 1$ that maximizes the wage and minimizes employment. Given this interpretation, we obtain the following result:

Proposition 2.6: If labour and intermediate inputs are close substitutes (i.e. if $\phi > 1$) but the elasticity of substitution is not very high, then central bargaining ($m = 1$ and $g = g_{max} = 1$) as well as local bargaining (m large, $g \approx g_{min} = 0$) lead to a lower wage w and a higher level of employment than bargaining at the medium level of centralization.

This result corresponds directly to the case in figure 2.5. Above we assumed that the full-employment constraint $l \leq L$ is non-binding and we obtained some optimal level of employment, l^*, for each union. If the full-employment constraint $l \leq L$ is taken into account, then by defining $l = \min[L, l^*]$, propositions 2.5 and 2.6 still hold as they stand.

This means that in figure 2.5, the horizontal line corresponding to full employment, $l = L$, may cut either tail or both tails of the employment curve EE, but still employment is at a lower level at some middle point g_0 than at the extreme points g_{min} and g_{max}.

The degree of centralization has two opposing impacts on wages: one through the internalization of the macroeconomic effects of a single union's wage policy, and the other through the elasticity of the labour demand that a single union faces. Since large unions can more easily internalize the benefit of a lower price level due to lower wages for their members, they are more willing to moderate their wage claims than small unions. On the other hand, the smaller is the part of the production sector in which bargaining is carried out, the smaller the share of production costs this part spends on labour and the larger the share of these it spends on intermediate inputs that are purchased from the rest of the economy. Therefore, a union facing a small part of the production sector observes a high elasticity of demand and sets low wages.

If the elasticity of substitution between labour and intermediate products is low enough, then the effect through the internalization outweighs the effect through the elasticity of labour demand, and central bargaining at the level of the whole economy provides the lowest wage and the highest level of employment. If the elasticity of substitution between labour and intermediate products is high enough, then the effect through the elasticity of demand outweighs the effect through the internalization, and local bargaining at the level of a single firm provides the lowest wage and the highest level of employment. If the elasticity of substitution between labour and intermediate inputs is between these two extremes, then at the medium level of centralization, a single union is too small to observe the macroeconomic consequences of its wage policy but large enough to face a low elasticity of demand. Consequently, the unions at the medium level of centralization set higher wages and accept a lower level of employment than those at the low or high levels of centralization.

2.7 Conclusions

In this chapter, we examined models that are characterized by collective bargaining and the absence of real investment and we arrived at the following conclusions. The first of these is that a plausible equilibrium with involuntary unemployment can be constructed on the assumption that the workers are organized in a labour union. This union is able to determine the base wage only by observing the elasticity of labour demand.

Second, assuming that the firm can hide profit or revenue at some cost, the results of the monopoly union model can be extended to this case of profit-sharing as well. In such a case, the union chooses the profit-sharing ratio for its members optimally, but otherwise, it behaves in the same way as in the absence of profit-sharing. Third, right-to-manage bargaining, in which the union and the firm bargain over the two pay parameters while the firm alone chooses the level of employment, is shown to be equivalent to efficient bargaining, in which the parties bargain the level of employment and the total pay per worker simultaneously: through the pay parameters, the parties can fully control employment and a worker's income.

The fourth result concerns the degree of centralization in collective bargaining. When there are several unions in the economy, the relative prices of the economy change so that the unions become strategically dependent. It was shown that in such a case – provided that labour and intermediate inputs are substitutes and the elasticity of substitution between them is not very high – employment is better when wage-setting is done at the central or local level than when it is made at some medium level of centralization. The reason for this is the coexistence of two opposite effects: one through the elasticity of the labour demand, and the other through the internalization of the consumer price.

When collective bargaining is decentralized, each union controls only a small fraction of the economy. Then the firms in that fraction purchase a large share of their inputs from the rest of the economy and consequently, the union in that fraction faces a high wage elasticity of employment. When, on the other hand, collective bargaining is centralized, each union controls a large fraction of the economy. Then the union is aware that wage increases lead to an increase in the consumer price. Consequently, at both extremes of centralization in collective bargaining, the unions have an incentive to set low wages, which leads to a high level of employment.

Appendix 2a.   *The proof of relations* (2.13)

The maximization of the owner's income (2.12) s.t. $0 \le q \le 1$ by the choice of the ratio q is equivalent to the maximization of

$$1 + (q - 1)h - z(q)$$

s.t. $0 \le q \le 1$ by the choice of q. Since

$$\partial[1 + (q - 1)h - z]/\partial q = h - z'(q),$$

this optimization leads to the first-order condition

$$q = \begin{cases} 1 & \text{for } \partial[1 + (q-1)h - z]/\partial q > 0, \\ 0 & \text{for } \partial[1 + (q-1)h - z]/\partial q < 0, \\ (z')^{-1}(h) & \text{for } \partial[1 + (q-1)h - z]/\partial q = 0 \end{cases}$$

or

$$q = \begin{cases} 1 & \text{for } h > z'(q) = z'(1), \\ 0 & \text{for } h < z'(q) = z'(0), \\ q^*(h) \doteq (z')^{-1}(h) & \text{for } z'(0) \leq h \leq z'(1), \end{cases}$$

where $(z')^{-1}$ is the inverse function of $z'(q)$. Because from (2.12) it follows that

$$\partial^2 \pi / [\partial q \partial l] = 0, \quad \partial^2 \pi / \partial q^2 = -z'' \Pi < 0,$$

$$\partial^2 \pi / \partial l^2 = [1 + (q-1)h - z(q)]\Pi_{ll}$$

$$= [1 + (q-1)h - z(q)]R'' < 0,$$

the firm's optimum is unique.

Appendix 2b. *The proof of proposition* 2.2

From (2.13) it follows that

$$[1 - q(h)]h = \left. \begin{cases} 0 & \text{for } h > z'(1), \\ h & \text{for } h < z'(0), \\ [1 - q^*(h)]h & \text{for } z'(0) \leq h \leq z'(1). \end{cases} \right\}$$

(2b.1)

Now let us choose the ratio h optimally, holding the wage w constant. Then given the firm's equilibrium condition $w = R'(l)$, the level of employment, l, will be constant as well. In such a case, given (2.15), the maximization of union utility (2.16) so that $0 \leq h \leq 1$ by the choice of the ratio h is equivalent to the maximization of (2b.1) by the choice of h. Since $z'(1) > z'(0) > 0$, this leads to the first-order condition

$$h = \text{argmax}\{[1 - q(h)]h\}$$

$$= \max[z'(0), \ \text{argmax}\{[1 - q^*(h)]h \,|\, z'(0) \leq h \leq z'(1)\}].$$

This shows that h must be a constant, which means that $q(h)$ and $z(q)$ are constants as well.

Appendix 2c. *The proof of functions* (2.31)

Substituting Z_i from (2.30) into (2.25) and (2.29), we obtain

$$y_i = [\beta/(\beta - 1)]s(w_i)^{1-\beta}p_i^{\beta-1} = [\beta/(\beta - 1)][s(w_i)/p_i]^{1-\beta},$$

$$y = m\prod_{j=1}^{m}y_j^{1/m} = [\beta/(\beta - 1)]m\prod_{j=1}^{m}[s(w_j)/p_j]^{(1-\beta)/m}.$$

Substituting these into (2.26), we obtain m equations

$$p_i = \frac{y}{my_i}$$

$$= \left[s(w_i)^{1/m-1}p_i^{1-1/m}\prod_{j\neq i}s(w_j)^{1/m}p_j^{-1/m}\right]^{1-\beta} \quad \text{for } i = 1,\ldots,m,$$

with m endogenous variables $p_1,\ldots,p_m$. Finally, rearranging terms and noting (2.26), we obtain

$$p_i^\beta = \left\{s(w_i)^{1/m-1}\left[\prod_{j\neq i}s(w_j)\right]^{1/m}\left[\prod_{j=1}^{m}p_j\right]^{-1/m}\right\}^{1-\beta}$$

$$= \left\{s(w_i)^{1/m-1}\left[\prod_{j\neq i}s(w_j)\right]^{1/m}\right\}^{1-\beta}.$$

Differentiating the logarithm of this system totally yields

$$\beta\frac{dp_i}{p_i} = (1 - \beta)\left[\left(\frac{1}{m} - 1\right)\frac{s'(w_i)}{s(w_i)}dw_i + \frac{1}{m}\sum_{j\neq i}\frac{s'(w_j)}{s(w_j)}dw_j\right].$$

Transforming this into partial derivatives leads to the functions (2.31).

Appendix 2d. *The proof of proposition* 2.5

Since there is perfect symmetry over $i = 1,\ldots,m$ in the model, given (2.25), (2.26) and (2.33), then in equilibrium there must be

$$y_i = y/m, \quad p_i = p = 1, \quad l_i = l, \quad w_i = w > b. \tag{2d.1}$$

Given this and $0 < g \leq 1$, relations (2.28) and (2.31) become

$$0 < \eta(w,g) = ws'(w)/s(w) = g/[g + (1-g)\delta w^{\phi-1}] < 1,$$

$$(1/p_i)\partial p_i/\partial w_i = (1-g)(1-1/\beta)s'/s = (1-g)(1-1/\beta)\eta/w,$$

$$ws''(w)/s'(w) = (\eta - 1)\phi < 0. \tag{2d.2}$$

From (2d.2) and $0 < g \le 1$ it follows that

$$\partial\eta/\partial g = \delta w^{\phi-1}/[g + (1-g)\delta w^{\phi-1}]^2$$

$$= \frac{\eta}{g}\frac{\delta w^{\phi-1}}{g + (1-g)\delta w^{\phi-1}} \ge \frac{\eta\delta w^{\phi-1}}{g + (1-g)\delta w^{\phi-1}}$$

$$> \frac{\eta\delta w^{\phi-1}}{g + \delta w^{\phi-1}} \ge \frac{\eta\delta w^{\phi-1}}{1 + \delta w^{\phi-1}} > \frac{\eta\delta}{w^{1-\phi} + \delta} > 0. \tag{2d.3}$$

From relations (2d.1) and (2d.2) as well as the first-order condition (2.33), we obtain the equilibrium condition

$$\Psi(w,g) \doteq \frac{w}{(w_i - b)l_i}\frac{\partial U_i}{\partial w_i} = \frac{\gamma w}{w - b} + \frac{s''w}{s'} - \beta\frac{s'w}{s} + \frac{w\beta}{p_i}\frac{\partial p_i}{\partial w_i}$$

$$= \gamma w/(w - b) + (\eta - 1)\phi - \beta\eta + (\beta - 1)(1 - g)\eta$$

$$= \gamma w/(w - b) - \phi + \eta[\phi - \beta + (\beta - 1)(1 - g)]$$

$$= \gamma w/(w - b) - \phi + \eta[\phi - 1 + (1 - \beta)g] = 0. \tag{2d.4}$$

Relation (2d.4) defines the (symmetric) equilibrium of the economy as a function of the degree of centralization, g, and the elasticity of substitution between labour and intermediate products, ϕ.

From relations (2.31) and (2.33) it follows that

$$\frac{\partial}{\partial w_j}\left[\frac{1}{p_i}\frac{\partial p_i}{\partial w_i}\right] = 0 \text{ and } \frac{\partial}{\partial w_j}\left[\frac{1}{(w_i - b)l_i}\frac{\partial U_i}{\partial w_i}\right] = 0 \text{ for } j \ne i.$$

Given this, $0 < g \le 1$, $\beta > 1$, (2d.3), (2d.4) and the second-order condition in (2.33), we obtain the following properties:

$$\frac{\partial\Psi}{\partial w} = w\frac{\partial}{\partial w_i}\left[\frac{1}{(w_i - b)l_i}\frac{\partial U_i}{\partial w_i}\right] < 0,$$

$$\frac{\partial\Psi}{\partial g} = (1 - \beta)\eta + [\phi - 1 + (1 - \beta)g]\partial\eta/\partial g, \tag{2d.5}$$

$$\frac{\partial\Psi}{\partial g} < (\phi - 1)\partial\eta/\partial g < 0 \text{ for } \phi \le 1.$$

It remains to be proven that $\lim_{\phi \to \infty} \partial \Psi / \partial g > 0$. Assuming $\phi > \beta$ and noting $0 < g \leq 1$, $\beta > 1$, (2d.3) and (2d.5), we obtain

$$\phi - 1 + (1 - \beta)g > \phi - 1 + (1 - \phi)g = (\phi - 1)(1 - g) \geq 0$$

and

$$\partial \Psi / \partial g > (1 - \beta)\eta + (\phi - 1)(1 - g)\partial \eta / \partial g$$

$$> (1 - \beta)\eta + (\phi - 1)(1 - g)\eta \delta / (w^{1-\phi} + \delta)$$

$$= \eta \phi [(1 - \beta)/\phi + (1 - 1/\phi)(1 - g)\delta / (w^{1-\phi} + \delta)].$$

Given that $(1 - g)\delta / (w^{1-\phi} + \delta) \leq \delta / (w^{1-\phi} + \delta) < 1$, we obtain

$$\lim_{\phi \to \infty} [(1 - \beta)/\phi + (1 - 1/\phi)(1 - g)\delta / (w^{1-\phi} + \delta)]$$

$$= (1 - g)\delta / (w^{1-\phi} + \delta) \geq 0$$

and $\lim_{\phi \to \infty} \partial \Psi / \partial g > 0$. This and results (2d.5) lead to the following dependence between w and g:

$$\left. \frac{\partial w}{\partial g} \right|_{\Psi=0} = - \frac{\partial \Psi}{\partial g} \bigg/ \frac{\partial \Psi}{\partial w} < 0 \text{ for } \phi \leq 1,$$

$$\lim_{\phi \to \infty} \left. \frac{\partial w}{\partial g} \right|_{\Psi=0} = - \lim_{\phi \to \infty} \frac{\partial \Psi}{\partial g} \bigg/ \frac{\partial \Psi}{\partial w} > 0.$$

3 The use of corrective taxes and subsidies

3.1 Introduction

Subsidies are frequently used to improve domestic employment and to assist domestic firms in their competition with foreign rivals. This chapter examines the case where the government uses some subsidies (or taxes) as policy instruments but balances its budget with other 'revenue-raising' taxes, and where the parties in collective bargaining take this government behaviour as given. In contrast to the optimal taxation approach being applied in chapter 4, it is assumed that only small subsidies (taxes) are used starting from the initial position of free trade.

The idea of corrective subsidies arises from Bhagwati and Srinivasan's (1983) assertion that if wages are not competitively fixed, then the distortions resulting from this should be corrected by subsidies. The defect of their analysis was, however, that wages were taken as exogenously fixed: there was no theory as to how they are determined. Palokangas (1991b) examined government intervention in a framework that was in many respects the opposite of Bhagwati and Srinivasan's approach: it was assumed that the wages of the whole economy are simultaneously set by one all-encompassing monopoly union, and that this union observes the need to balance the government budget. Assuming, furthermore, that all industries are subject to decreasing returns to scale, so that a tax on one industry is effectively a subsidy to the others, Palokangas (1991b) arrived at the following conclusions.

Since the expansion of one industry is carried out by depriving the others of resources, the industries should be divided into two groups: 'high wage' industries for which the ratio of the wage to the wage elasticity of employment is above some index, and 'low wage' industries for which this wage/elasticity ratio is below the index. The government should encourage employment in the 'high wage' industries by a tax (a subsidy) if marginal labour income in these depends negatively (positively) on the level of employment. Correspondingly, the government should discourage employment in the 'low wage' industries by a subsidy (a tax) if marginal labour income in these depends negatively (positively) on the level of employment. These measures substitute 'better paid' for 'worse paid' jobs, so welfare will increase.

The model we are using in this chapter differs from that of Palokangas (1991b) in two respects. First, it is assumed that the marginal disutility of employment is fixed for a worker.[1] In return for this simplification there can be unions of any size, so that we can compare public policy for different levels of centralization of collective bargaining. The second difference is that this chapter considers public policy also in the case of profit-sharing.

In the literature of employment policy, the strategic relationship between the government and a wage-setting union has inspired some British and Scandinavian economists. Using particular utility functions for the government, Hersoug (1985), Driffill (1985) and Gylfason and Lindbeck (1986) showed that employment policy may increase wages and thereby reduce employment in the private sector. Extending the same framework, Sampson (1983), Calmfors and Horn (1985, 1986), Gylfason and Lindbeck (1986) and Rodseth (1995) showed that if a union is large enough to observe the government's budget constraint, then employment policy will be less counterproductive. Our study differs from these authors in the following respects: we focus on welfare rather than employment changes, consider all degrees of centralization in collective bargaining, use industry-specific subsidies (taxes, if negative) and assume that the government budget is balanced by the income tax. This will give a direct answer to the question of whether it is worthwhile to tax or subsidize a particular industry.

The plan of this chapter is the following. In section 3.2, we introduce a model which focuses on the issue of central concern, i.e. policy towards industries which compete with foreign producers and face a monopoly union at home. Section 3.3 presents the fine details of the behaviour of the workers, firms and labour unions. For reference, section 3.4 reconstructs the classical policy rules on the assumption that the wages are held fixed. Section 3.5 examines bargaining over the basic wages and, using its results, section 3.6 constructs public policy rules

---

[1] For this assumption, see section 2.2.1 of the preceding chapter.

for the case where the wages are endogenously determined. Finally, section 3.7 extends the results for the case of profit-sharing.

3.2 The structure of the economy

3.2.1 Industries

This study considers an open economy where the labour markets are non-competitive. We assume that there is (at least) one traded good the price of which is given from abroad. We choose such a good as the numeraire and label it 0. The economy consists of a fixed number of industries $i = 1, \ldots, n$. Each industry i produces a separate good being labelled as i and faces a separate labour union also labelled i. We assume, for simplicity, that this union represents all workers in the industry.

The products $i = 1, \ldots, n$ of the industries can be traded or non-traded goods. The producers of non-traded goods are price-makers but those of traded goods can be both price-makers and price-takers. We specify that each industry i composes its output y_i from labour l_i according to the twice differentiable production function

$$y_i = f_i(l_i) \text{ with } f_i' > 0. \tag{3.1}$$

In addition to unionized industries $i = 1, \ldots, n$, there could be a non-unionized sector in which the wages are competitively determined and which produces traded goods at given world market prices. The model will in any case assume that the marginal disutility of employment is fixed (see subsection 3.2.3). Then the competitive wages of this sector are fixed as being equal to the marginal disutility of employment. Because the wages and prices are thus given for the non-unionized sector, revenue from this sector is wholly exogenous income for a household. From this it follows that the introduction of a non-unionized sector into the model would not make any difference in the results.

3.2.2 Foreign trade

Let p_i be the output price, c_i the domestic demand and x_i the net export demand for good $i \neq 0$. We assume that the utility functions of the foreign consumers as well as the production functions of the foreign firms are additive over goods $i = 1, \ldots, n$, and that the economy is small enough relative to the rest of the world. Then the effects of domestic trade policy on the foreign demands can be ignored, and the net export of each product i, x_i, can be taken as a decreasing function of its product price p_i only.[2]

Given this property, the equilibrium conditions of the markets for goods $i = 1, \ldots, n$ can be written as follows:

$$y_i - c_i = x_i = X_i(p_i) \text{ with } X_i' < 0 \text{ for } i = 1, \ldots, n. \tag{3.2}$$

The model thus specified is general enough for our purposes. First, the production functions (3.1) for all i may be subject to any returns to scale. The only constraint is that the firm's revenue function is concave. Second, the model is also flexible enough in the sense that it also contains the following two special cases: if $X_i \to 0$ and $X_i' \to 0$, then product i is a non-tradable, i.e. there is no import or export of this product, and if $X_i' \to -\infty$, then the price elasticity of foreign demand is infinite and the economy is a price-taker in the world market for product i.

3.2.3 Domestic demand

In order to make the model tractable, we eliminate the cross and income elasticities from the domestic demand functions as well. This is done with the following two assumptions. First, a representative worker in any industry i has a utility function which is additive over all commodities and linear in the numeraire. Second, products $i = 1, \ldots, n$ are either wage or export goods, so that domestic profits are used solely in the consumption of the numeraire. One can think, for instance, that the profits are spent abroad or that the domestic capitalists purchase only 'luxuries' in the world markets of which the economy is a price-taker. Now the domestic demand c_j for good $j \neq 0$ is determined by

$$c_j = \sum_{i=0}^{n} c_{ij} \text{ for } j = 0, 1, \ldots, n, \tag{3.3}$$

where c_{ij} is the demand for good j by the workers in industry i.

Finally, for simplicity, we assume that a worker's marginal disutility of employment, b, is fixed.[3] From all the assumptions made in this

---

[2] See, for example, Deaton and Muellbauer (1980), pp. 137–42. A differentiable function $F(x_1, \ldots, x_n)$ is additive if it can be written in the form $F(x_1, \ldots, x_n) = \mathcal{F}(F_1(x_1) + \cdots + F_n(x_n))$, where $\mathcal{F}$ and F_i are differentiable functions. For instance, the CES and Cobb–Douglas functions satisfy this property. Given additivity, the demand functions of the products take the form $p_i = \lambda_i F_i'(x_i)$, where the producer of good i takes the level of demand, λ_i, as given if its products comprise a small share of the customers' expenditure.

[3] This assumption is motivated in subsection 2.2.1 and it is useful in the following respects. First, a union behaves qualitatively in the same way at all levels of centralization in collective bargaining. Second, when profit-sharing is examined in section 3.7, we can construct propositions 3.6 and 3.7.

subsection, it follows that the utility function of the representative worker in industry i takes the form

$$U_i = c_{i0} + \sum_{j=1}^{n} u_j(c_{ij}) - bl_i \text{ with } b > 0, u_j' > 0 \text{ and } u_j < 0. \quad (3.4)$$

It is assumed for the moment that there is no profit-sharing. This assumption will be relaxed in section 3.7.

3.2.4 The exercise of public policy

When unemployment is incorporated into the economy, the government, whose objective is to maximize national welfare, is influenced by the employment consequences of taxation. Brecher (1974) has shown that if unemployment is induced by a minimum wage, then the optimal policy involves a wage subsidy. On the other hand, the least distorting way to finance corrective subsidies would be to tax pure profits. However, we rule out both wage subsidies and profit taxes as feasible policy tools for the reason that they are incentive-incompatible. This can be justified as follows. Only the management of the firm knows which expenditures are necessary for production and which ones provide services to the owners or the management of the firm. Thus, in the presence of a wage subsidy, profits will be announced as wages, and in the presence of a profit tax they will be presented as expenditures. Given this problem of incentive incompatibility, policy tools are restricted to *ad valorem* taxes and subsidies on output.

Let s_i be the *ad valorem* subsidy to the domestic production of good $i \neq 0$ (good 0 is only imported). If $s_i < 0$, then $-s_i$ is a tax. The crucial strategic assumption of public policy is that the government can credibly commit itself to the payment of the industry-specific subsidies $s_1, \ldots, s_n$. In the presence of such a commitment, there must be some source of public finance from which the government budget will be balanced (and everybody expects it to be balanced). In an open economy, there are many reasons why it is difficult to keep profits in the income tax base. One of these is the problem of incentive incompatibility that was mentioned above. Another is transfer pricing: a firm hides its profit by purchasing inputs from its foreign agent at prices that are higher than the marginal costs of these inputs. With reference to these problems, we make the extreme assumption that the government's ultimate source of finance is the tax on wage income.

3.2.5 Welfare measures

There still remains the problem of how to construct the social welfare function for the exercise of public policy. The standard procedure is to postulate a utilitarian welfare function $\Phi(\phi_1, \phi_2, \ldots, \phi_N)$, which is increasing and differentiable with respect to all individual utilities $\phi_1, \phi_2, \ldots, \phi_N$. This function is consistent with the Pareto criterion that social welfare is increased if at least one person is better off and no one is worse off.

In this chapter, however, we are interested only in the improvement of efficiency by industry-specific taxes and subsidies. Therefore, the comparison of individual utilities would add very little to our understanding of the problem and so we can sacrifice it in favour of simplicity. For this reason, we measure social welfare by the maximum value of the utilitarian welfare function when the government can freely choose lump-sum transfers between households. In doing this, we do not assume that lump-sum transfers are feasible in reality, only that such a specification of the social welfare function is chosen that ignores utility comparisons. Any attempt to introduce realistic constraints on government transfers would lead to policy rules that were more complex but that were nevertheless based on the same principles as our results.

3.2.6 Revenue-raising taxation

For industry i, let the wage be denoted by w_i, labour input or the level of employment by l_i, output by y_i and the output price by p_i. Then for this industry, the total wage bill is given by $w_i l_i$ and the total (pre-tax or pre-subsidy) sales revenue by $r_i = p_i y_i$. It was assumed earlier that the government budget is balanced by a (proportional) tax on wage income. Then the tax base is the sum of the wages over all industries, $\sum_j w_j l_j$, and the share of the tax burden falling on the workers in industry i, T_i, is equal to the relative wage bill of the industry:

$$T_i \doteq w_i l_i \bigg/ \sum_{j=1}^{n} w_j l_j. \tag{3.5}$$

The subsidy to industry i, s_i, is based on total revenue r_i. Then the cost of all industry-specific subsidies is equal to $\sum_{j=1}^{n} s_j r_j$, so that the total tax burden for the workers in industry i is given by

$$T_i \sum_{j=1}^{n} s_j r_j = w_i l_i \sum_{j=1}^{n} s_j r_j \bigg/ \sum_{j=1}^{n} w_j l_j. \tag{3.6}$$

Since the workers in industry i earn the wage bill $w_i l_i$ and pay taxes (3.6), they receive labour income

$$I_i \doteq w_i l_i - T_i \sum_{j=1}^{n} s_j r_j = \left[1 - \sum_{j=1}^{n} s_j r_j \Big/ \sum_{j=1}^{n} w_j l_j \right] w_i l_i. \tag{3.7}$$

3.3 The private agents

3.3.1 The workers

Because the workers in industry i earn after-tax income (3.7) and consume the amount c_{ij} of each good j, they face the budget constraint

$$I_i = c_{i0} + \sum_{j=1}^{n} p_j c_{ij}, \tag{3.8}$$

where p_j is the price for good $j \neq 0$. The workers set their marginal utilities equal to prices. Thus, given the utility function (3.4), we obtain the equilibrium conditions

$$u_j'(c_{ij}) \doteq \partial U_i / \partial c_{ij} = p_j \text{ for } i = 1, \ldots, n \text{ and } j = 1, \ldots, n. \tag{3.9}$$

From (3.3) and (3.9) it follows that

$$c_{ij} = c_j / n \text{ for } i = 0, 1, \ldots, n \text{ and } j = 1, \ldots, n. \tag{3.10}$$

Solving c_{i0} from the budget constraint (3.8) and substituting it into (3.4), we obtain the utility of the representative worker in industry i as follows:

$$U_i = I_i - b l_i + \sum_{j=1}^{n} [u_j(c_{ij}^*) - p_j c_{ij}^*], \tag{3.11}$$

where, by duality and by (3.9), the optimal levels of consumption, c_{ij}^*, can be taken as being held constant.

3.3.2 The firms

Differentiating the production function (3.1) as well as equations (3.2), (3.9) and (3.10) totally yields

$$dy_i = f_i' dl_i, \quad dp_i = u_i'' dc_{ii}, \quad X_i' dp_i = dy_i - dc_i = dy_i - n dc_{ii}. \tag{3.12}$$

On the assumption that a firm's sales revenue $r_i \doteq p_i y_i$ is an increasing and concave function of the level of employment l_i, equations (3.12) lead to the following consumption, price and revenue functions:

$c_{ii}(l_i)$ with $c_{ii}' = f_i'/[n + X_i'u_i''] > 0$,

$p_i(l_i)$ with $p_i' = nu_i''c_{ii}' < 0$,

$r_i(l_i) = p_i(l_i)f_i(l_i)$ with $r_i > 0, r_i' > 0$ and $r_i'' < 0$ for $i = 1, \ldots, n$.

$$(3.13)$$

It is easy to see that if industry i is a price-taker in the world market, i.e. if $X_i' \to -\infty$, then we obtain $c_{ii}' \to 0$ and $p_i' \to 0$.

Given (3.13), the representative firm in industry i receives profit

$$\Pi_i \doteq (1 + s_i)r_i(l_i) - w_il_i, \qquad (3.14)$$

where $(1 + s_i)r_i$ is sales revenue after subsidy and w_il_i labour cost. The maximization of profit (3.14) by the choice of labour input l_i yields the inverse demand function for labour:

$$w_i = (1 + s_i)r_i'(l_i). \qquad (3.15)$$

3.3.3 Some definitions

Given (3.15), the wage elasticity of employment in industry $i \neq 0$, when the subsidy s_i is held constant, is defined by

$$E_i(l_i) \doteq -(w_i/l_i)\partial l_i/\partial w_i = -r_i'(l_i)/[l_ir_i''(l_i)] > 0. \qquad (3.16)$$

The unions know the elasticities (3.16) for all i by experience.

Finally, given (3.7), (3.11), (3.13), (3.15) and (3.16), it is shown in appendix 3a that the marginal utility of employment for the workers in industry i, m_i, has the following properties:

$$m_i(l_1, \ldots, l_n, s_1, \ldots, s_n) \doteq \partial U_i/\partial l_i = \partial I_i/\partial l_i - b - p_i'c_{ii} \text{ with}$$

$$m_i|_{s_1=\cdots=s_n=0} = w_i + l_ir_i'' - b - p_i'c_{ii}$$

$$= (1 - 1/E_i)w_i - b - p_i'c_{ii},$$

$$\partial m_i/\partial s_i|_{s_1=\cdots=s_n=0} = (1 - 1/E_i - T_i)w_i$$

$$+ (1/E_i - 1)(1 - T_i)T_ir_i/l_i,$$

$$\partial m_i/\partial s_j|_{s_1=\cdots=s_n=0} = (1/E_i - 1)(1 - T_i)T_ir_j/l_i < 0 \text{ for } j \neq i,$$

$$\partial m_i/\partial l_j|_{s_1=\cdots=s_n=0} \equiv 0 \text{ for } j \neq i. \qquad (3.17)$$

3.3.4 Social welfare

The workers' utility function (3.11) is linear in the consumption of numeraire good 0 and the capitalists' utilities are equal to their profits (3.14), which are wholly spent on numeraire good 0. We assume, as explained in subsection 3.2.5, that social welfare is an increasing and differentiable function of all individual utilities but that the government uses this target on the assumption that all lump-sum transfers between households are feasible. Here, it follows that the government's behaviour is equivalent to the maximization of the sum of the workers' and capitalists' utilities in terms of income, i.e. the sum of the functions (3.11) and (3.14) over all industries $i = 1, \ldots, n$. Noting (3.5) and (3.13), we obtain this measure of social welfare in the form

$$W(l_1, \ldots, l_n) \doteq \sum_{i=1}^{n} [U_i + \Pi_i]$$

$$= \sum_{i=1}^{n} \left\{ r_i(l_i) + \sum_{j=1}^{n} [u_i(c_{ij}^*) - c_{ij}^* p_j(l_j)] - bl_i \right\}, \quad (3.18)$$

where, by duality and by (3.9), the optimal levels of consumption, c_{ij}^*, can be taken as given.

It is now possible to consider various issues involving the choice of public policy. Unfortunately, the model is too complex for an explicit global welfare evaluation, so we pay attention to small changes in the subsidy rates from an initial position of free trade: $s_i \approx 0$ for $i = 1, \ldots, n$.

3.4 Exogenous wages

As a reference point, let us examine first the case where the consumer wages w_j are held fixed for some industries $j \in J$. Given (3.15), this leads to the minimum wage constraints

$$(1 + s_j) r_j'(l_j) = w_j > b \text{ for } j \in J. \quad (3.19)$$

In the other 'competitive' industries $j \notin J$, the wage will be equal to the marginal disutility of employment:

$$(1 + s_j) r_j'(l_j) = w_j = b \text{ for } j \notin J. \quad (3.20)$$

Although the assumption of exogenous wages is too unrealistic, this exercise allows us to integrate the results in this chapter into those in the literature.

Differentiating conditions (3.19) and (3.20) totally and noting $s_k \approx 0$, we obtain that a subsidy to any industry i increases employment both in that industry and in the whole economy:

$$dl_j = -(r_j'/r_j'')ds_j \text{ and } \frac{\partial}{\partial s_j} \sum_{k=1}^{n} l_k = \partial l_j/\partial s_j$$

$$= -r_j'/r_j'' > 0 \text{ for all } j. \tag{3.21}$$

Furthermore, differentiating social welfare (3.18) totally and noting $s_k \approx 0$ and (3.19)–(3.21), we obtain

$$dW = \sum_{j=1}^{n} [r_j' - c_j p_j' - b]dl_j = \sum_{j=1}^{n} [w_j - c_j p_j' - b]dl_j$$

$$= \sum_{j \in J} [w_j - c_j p_j' - b]dl_j - \sum_{j \notin J} c_j p_j' dl_j$$

$$= \sum_{j \in J} [c_j p_j' + b - w_j](r_j'/r_j'')ds_j + \sum_{j \notin J} c_j p_j'(r_j'/r_j'')ds_j.$$

This equation and relations (3.19) and (3.13) lead to the outcome that subsidy to any industry is, in general, welfare-enhancing:

$$\frac{\partial W}{\partial s_j} = \begin{cases} [c_j p_j' + b - w_j]r_j'/r_j'' > 0 & \text{for } j \in J, \\ c_j p_j' r_j'/r_j'' > 0 & \text{for } j \notin J. \end{cases}$$

There is only one possibility that a subsidy is ineffective: if industry j has no minimum wage (i.e. if $j \notin J$) and if it is a price-taker in the world market (i.e. if $p_j' \approx 0$), then $\partial W/\partial s_j \approx 0$. So we have arrived at the following result:

Proposition 3.1: Assume that in some markets there are exogenous minimum wages but in others the wages are competitively determined. Then, it is desirable to provide a subsidy to such industries which either face a downward-sloping demand curve from abroad or which are subject to exogenous minimum wages.

Proposition 3.1 can be explained as follows. A subsidy increases output and decreases the output price. A lower consumer price leads to a higher level of welfare. On the other hand, in line with Bhagwati and Srinivasan (1983), it is welfare-enhancing to subsidize industries having high wages, for this will bring marginal products of labour closer to wages. The problem with these results is that there is no theory for the determination of the wages. When the wage bargain is properly incorporated into the model, then the wages will somehow adjust to the existence of the subsidies $s_1, \ldots, s_n$. It is instructive to see how this modification will change the policy rules that are given in proposition 3.1.

3.5 Endogenous wages

3.5.1 General equilibrium

There is a single monopoly union for each industry. This is a flexible framework since the industry can be of any size: at one extreme, the whole economy can be considered as a single industry and at the other, each firm can be treated as a separate industry.

The unions behave in a Cournot manner, taking each other's wages as given. Because the government balances its budget with the wage income tax, it can credibly commit itself to the payment of subsidies $s_1, \ldots, s_n$ and the unions take these as given. It follows that union i maximizes the representative worker's utility (3.11) by the choice of the wage w_i for its members, assuming that the other wages, w_j for $j \neq i$, as well as the subsidies $s_1, \ldots, s_n$ are held constant. Since the functions (3.15) can be transformed into

$$l_j = (r_j')^{-1}(w_j/[1 + s_j]) \text{ for } i = 1, \ldots, n,$$

where $(r_j')^{-1}$ is the inverse function of r_j', the union's problem can be equivalently presented as follows: maximize (3.11) by the choice of labour input in industry i, l_i, assuming that labour inputs in the other industries, l_j for $j \neq i$, as well as the subsidies $s_1, \ldots, s_n$ are held constant. Noting the definition (3.17), this optimization yields the first-order conditions

$$\partial U_i/\partial l_i = m_i(l_1, \ldots, l_n, s_1, \ldots, s_n) = 0. \tag{3.22}$$

Given (3.17) and (3.22), we can define marginal labour income for industry i in real terms as $\partial I_i/\partial l_i - p_i'c_{ii} = m_i + b = b$, where $\partial I_i/\partial l_i$ is its nominal value and $|p_i'c_{ii}| = -p_i'c_{ii}$ is the fall in the value of a worker's consumption basket due to the increase in the level of employment in the worker's own trade. Because there are many goods, we can assume that $|p_i'c_{ii}|$ is smaller than marginal labour income b. Now, from (3.17) and (3.22) it follows that the wage elasticity of employment, E_i, is greater than one:

$$(1 - 1/E_i)w_i = b + p_i'c_{ii} > 0 \text{ and } E_i > 1 \text{ for } i \neq 0. \tag{3.23}$$

Furthermore, we define the elasticity of marginal labour income $m_i + b$ with respect to employment l_i for industry i – when all the subsidies and the levels of employment for the other industries $j \neq i$ are held constant – as

$$e_i \doteq |[l_i/(m_i + b)]\partial(m_i + b)/\partial l_i|.$$

When conditions (3.22) hold for industries $i = 1, \ldots, n$, the economy is in equilibrium. Assuming that the second-order condition $\partial^2 U_i/\partial l_i^2 = \partial m_i/\partial l_i < 0$ holds as well for each industry i, the equilibrium is unique and we obtain

$$e_i = -[l_i/(m_i + b)]\partial(m_i + b)/\partial l_i = -(l_i/b)\partial m_i/\partial l_i > 0. \quad (3.24)$$

3.5.2 The employment effects

Differentiating the first-order conditions (3.22) and noting (3.17), (3.24) and $s_i \approx 0$, we obtain

$$\sum_{j=1}^{n}(\partial m_i/\partial s_j)ds_j = -(\partial m_i/\partial l_i)dl_i = (be_i/l_i)dl_i.$$

Given this, $s_i \approx 0$, $0 < T_i \leq 1$, (3.17) and (3.23), we obtain the levels of employment, l_i, as functions of the subsidies $s_1, \ldots, s_n$:

$$\partial l_i/\partial s_j = (\partial m_i/\partial s_j)l_i/(be_i)$$
$$= (1/E_i - 1)(1 - T_i)T_i r_j/(be_i) < 0 \text{ for } j \neq i, \quad (3.25)$$
$$\partial l_i/\partial s_i = (\partial m_i/\partial s_i)l_i/(be_i)$$
$$= (1 - 1/E_i - T_i)w_i l_i/(be_i) + (1/E_i - 1)(1 - T_i)T_i r_i/(be_i)$$
$$< 0 \text{ for } T_i > 1 - 1/E_i, \quad \partial l_i/\partial s_i > 0 \text{ for } T_i \to 0, \quad (3.26)$$

The explanation of result (3.25) is straightforward: it shows that a subsidy to any industry i reduces employment in the other industries $j \neq i$. To finance a subsidy the wage tax must be increased. With a higher wage tax the unions increase their wage claims, letting the level of employment for their members fall. Result (3.26) can be written as follows:

Proposition 3.2: A subsidy to a small industry for which $T_i \approx 0$ or a tax on a large industry i for which $T_i > 1 - 1/E_i$ increases the level of employment in that industry.

In any industry, a subsidy makes the union increase the level of employment. On the other hand, the increase of the wage tax that is needed to finance this subsidy makes the union decrease the level of employment. The increase of the wage tax and the resulting fall in employment are the greater, the larger the share of the tax burden which falls on the members of the union. It follows that for a small union the members' tax burden is small and a subsidy is better, while for a large union the members' tax burden is high and a tax is better for boosting employment.

3.6 Public policy

3.6.1 Targeted subsidies

Assume that there is initially free trade, $s_k \approx 0$, and that the levels of employment, l_j, for the other unionized industries $j \neq 0, i$ are held constant. Then given conditions $s_k \approx 0$, (3.15), (3.17) and (3.22), we obtain the marginal social benefit of employment in industry i as follows:

$$r_i' - c_{ii}p_i' - b = w_i/E_i. \tag{3.27}$$

Alternatively, one can call the ratio w_i/E_i or (3.27) the wage margin for union i, since it tells how much union i raises its members' real wage above marginal labour income, $m_i + b = b$.

Differentiating the welfare function (3.18) totally and substituting (3.27) yields

$$dW = \sum_{i=1}^{n} [r_i' - c_{ii}p_i' - b]dl_i = \sum_{i=1}^{n} (w_i/E_i)dl_i. \tag{3.28}$$

Substituting (3.26) and (3.25) into this and noting the definition (3.5), we obtain (see appendix 3b)

$$\partial W/\partial s_i = [l_i w_i^2/(be_i E_i)](T_i^* - T_i), \tag{3.29}$$

where

$$T_i^* \doteq 1 - 1/E_i + [r_i e_i E_i/(w_i^2 l_i)] \sum_{j=1}^{n} (1/E_j - 1)(1 - T_j)T_j. \tag{3.30}$$

A subsidy increases social welfare W for $\partial W/\partial s_i > 0$, and a tax does the same for $\partial W/\partial s_i < 0$. Since the multiplier of $T_i^* - T_i$ in (3.29) is positive, the outcome can be written as follows:

Proposition 3.3: There exists a critical level T_i^*, defined in (3.30), such that to increase social welfare W, the government should tax large industries i with $T_i > T_i^*$ and subsidize small industries i with $T_i < T_i^*$.

The interpretation of proposition 3.3 is as follows. There is involuntary unemployment in the sense that union wages exceed a worker's marginal disutility of employment b, and a higher level of employment for unionized industries means higher social welfare. Since, according to proposition 3.2, a tax on a large industry or a subsidy to a small industry raises the level of employment, such a tax or subsidy also increases the level of social welfare.

3.6.2 Special cases

Now we clarify the meaning of proposition 3.3 by examining it in some well-known special cases. The first of these is full centralization in collective bargaining: all wages are determined at the level of the whole economy. In our model, this means that there is only one industry and one union in the economy. Then $n = 1$ and $T_1 \equiv 1$ by definition (3.5), and from (3.29) and (3.30) it follows that $T_1^* = 1 - 1/E_1$ and

$$\partial W/\partial s_1 = [l_1 w_1^2/(be_1 E_1)](T_1^* - 1) = -l_1 w_1^2/(be_1 E_1^2) < 0.$$

This means that a tax is welfare-enhancing.

The other extreme is the case of full decentralization (or local bargaining): all wages are determined at the level of the single firm, which is small relative to the whole economy. In our model, this means that the number of industries and unions, n, is very large and each industry i is small. Then, by definition (3.5), the tax burden for the members of union j is insignificant, $T_j \approx 0$. Letting $T_j \to 0$ for all j in (3.29) and (3.30) yields $T_i^* = 1 - 1/E_i$ and

$$\partial W/\partial s_i = [l_i w_i^2/(be_i E_i)]T_i^* = (1 - 1/E_i)l_i w_i^2/(be_i E_i) > 0,$$

and a subsidy to any industry i improves welfare.

3.6.3 A uniform subsidy

Sometimes in practice, the government is constrained to choosing a common rate of subsidy, $s_i = s$, to all industries i. To investigate this issue in the case of asymmetric industries, take $ds_i = ds$ for all $i = 1, \ldots, n$. Given (3.5) and (3.29), we obtain $dW/ds = \sum_i \partial W/\partial s_i$ and

$$b\left(\sum_{k=1}^{n} w_k l_k\right)^{-1} dW/ds = b\left(\sum_{k=1}^{n} w_k l_k\right)^{-1} \sum_{i=1}^{n} \partial W/\partial s_i$$

$$= \sum_{i=1}^{n} \frac{w_i^2 l_i}{e_i E_i}(T_i^* - T_i) \Big/ \sum_{k=1}^{n} w_k l_k$$

$$= \sum_{i=1}^{n}(T_i^* - T_i)(T_i/e_i)w_i/E_i.$$

Since $b/\sum_k w_k l_k > 0$, this leads to the following result:

Proposition 3.4: If, on the average, the term $(T_i/e_i)(w_i/E_i)$ is relatively low (high) for small industries i with $T_i < T_i^*$ and relatively high (low) for large industries with $T_i > T_i^*$, where T_i^* is given by (3.30), then a uniform tax on (a uniform subsidy to) all industries $i = 1, \ldots, n$ will raise welfare, $\partial W/\partial s < 0 \ (> 0)$.

Proposition 3.4 can be explained as follows. According to proposition 3.3, a subsidy to a small industry i with $T_i < T_i^*$ and a tax on a large industry i with $T_i > T_i^*$ will increase welfare. Now if the weighted average of $T_i^* - T_i$ over small industries outweighs the weighted average of $T_i - T_i^*$ over large industries, a uniform subsidy $s = s_i$ improves welfare; and if vice versa, a uniform tax is welfare-enhancing. It remains to be shown how the weights of $T_i^* - T_i$ are determined. The subsidy s increases the wage w_i and marginal labour income in industry i. Since $1/e_i$ is the elasticity of employment with respect to marginal labour income, a subsidy s to industry i will increase employment in industry i by the amount $1/e_i$. Because, from the welfare point of view, large industries having a high share of labour income (i.e. having high T_i), industries showing stronger employment effects of public policy (i.e. having high $1/e_i$) as well as 'better-paid' industries having high real-wage margins w_i/E_i (or (3.27)) are more important, the terms $T_i^* - T_i$ must be weighted by the product of the terms T_i, $1/e_i$ and w_i/E_i.

3.7 Profit-sharing

Finally, we extend the model to the case where each union sets the basic wage and the profit-sharing ratio for its members. We suppose that the only reason that prevents the unions from taking all the profits is the possibility that the firms can hide their profits.

In line with section 2.4, we denote the ratio of hidden to total profit by q, the ratio of the administrative cost of hiding income to total profit by z and the workers' profit-sharing ratio by h. On the assumption that the technology of hiding profits is the same for all industries, it follows that the ratios q, z and h are fixed at the same level for all industries. It is already assumed that the marginal disutility of employment, b, is constant. Then there will be no changes in the behaviour of the firms but, according to proposition 2.3, the representative worker's utility (3.11) in industry i must be modified as follows:

$$U_i = \mathcal{U}_i(w_i, l_i) + \sum_{j=1}^{n}[u_j(c_{ij}^*) - p_j(l_j)c_{ij}^*] - T_i\sum_{j=1}^{n}s_jr_j, \qquad (3.31)$$

in which

$$\partial\mathcal{U}_i/\partial w_i = \rho l_i, \quad \partial\mathcal{U}_i/\partial l_i = w_i - b, \quad \text{where } \rho \doteq 1 + (q-1)h > z. \qquad (3.32)$$

Given (3.14), (3.15) and (3.16), we can define the profit in industry i as a function of subsidy s_i and employment, l_i:

$$\Pi_i(l_i, s_i) = (1 + s_i)r_i - w_il_i = (1 + s_i)[r_i(l_i) - r_i'(l_i)l_i],$$
$$\partial\Pi_i/\partial s_i|_{s_i=0} = \Pi_i, \quad \partial\Pi_i/\partial l_i|_{s_i=0} = -r_i''l_i = w_i/E_i. \qquad (3.33)$$

Finally, since the capitalists in industry i pay administrative costs $z\Pi_i$, their net income is given by $(1 - z)\Pi_i$. This means that the measure of social welfare (3.18) changes into the form

$$W \doteq \sum_{i=1}^{n}[U_i + (1 - z)\Pi_i]$$

$$= \sum_{i=1}^{n}\left\{r_i(l_i) + \sum_{j=1}^{n}[u_j(c_{ij}^*) - c_{ij}^*p_j(l_j)] - bl_i - z\Pi_i(l_i, s_i)\right\}. \qquad (3.34)$$

In Appendix 3c, we obtain from condition $s_i \approx 0$ and equations (3.5), (3.15), (3.16), (3.17), (3.26), (3.28) and (3.31)–(3.34) that result (3.29) changes into the form

$$\partial W/\partial s_i = [l_iw_i^2/(be_iE_i)](T_i^0 - T_i), \qquad (3.35)$$

where

$$T_i^0 \doteq \frac{r_ie_iE_i}{w_i^2l_i}\sum_{j=1}^{n}(1/E_i - 1)(1 - T_j)T_j$$

$$- bze_iE_i\Pi_i/[(\rho - z)l_iw_i^2] + 1 - \rho/E_i. \qquad (3.36)$$

Given the partial derivatives (3.35), we see that proposition 3.3 holds as it stands if the critical level T_i^* of the tax burden T_i is replaced by T_i^0 or (3.36). This shows that even with the introduction of profit-sharing the result is qualitatively similar: large industries should be taxed and small industries subsidized.

3.8 Conclusions

This chapter examined the prospects of public policy in an open economy where the industries face monopoly unions at home. The policy instruments consist of small taxes and subsidies which are used starting from the initial position of free trade. The government budget is balanced by imposing a uniform tax on labour income. In this framework, the labour unions are able to internalize the effects through the government budget when they are determining the wages (and possibly the profit shares) for their members.

Standard results – as surveyed by Bhagwati and Srinivasan (1983) and reconstructed in section 3.4 – suggest that if wages are fixed arbitrarily high in some part of the economy, it is desirable to provide a subsidy to counteract the resulting distortion. This study shows, however, that the effect through the government budget on the workers' tax burden very commonly outweighs the direct effect of the subsidies, so that a tax is more likely to be preferable for this purpose.

The lower the wage elasticity of employment for an industry, or the larger the share of the tax burden which falls on the members of the union controlling the industry, the more likely a tax on this industry will increase employment and social welfare. This outcome can be explained as follows. Since in the unionized industries the wages exceed the marginal disutility of employment, social welfare increases if the level of employment in these industries increases. A subsidy to an industry benefits both the workers and the profit-earners in that industry. The less elastic the demand for labour in that industry, the larger is the workers' relative share of this subsidy and the more the subsidy encourages the union in the industry to increase employment. On the other hand, the subsidy is financed by an income tax which encourages the union to increase wages and to decrease employment. The larger the part of this income tax that falls on the workers of the industry (i.e. on the members of the union), the more likely from the viewpoint of the union that the defects of the income tax will outweigh the benefits of the subsidy. Therefore, it is more likely that employment in that industry and social welfare will fall.

Assume that the government cannot discriminate among industries in setting the tax and subsidy rates. Assume, furthermore, that there is a correlation such that, on the average, the workers are worse paid in industries having a low tax burden (i.e. have a low share of aggregate labour income) and better paid in those having a high tax burden. If this correlation is strong enough, a uniform *ad valorem* tax on all industries will raise welfare. The explanation of this result is the following. According to the result being reviewed above, a uniform tax increases employment in industries with a high tax burden relative to those with a low tax burden. Then, given the assumed correlation, the tax replaces worse-paid by better-paid jobs, the workers are better off and social welfare will increase. Correspondingly, if, on the average, the workers are better paid in industries having a low tax burden and worse paid in those having a high tax burden, a subsidy is welfare-enhancing.

Appendix 3a. *The proof of function* (3.17)

Substituting (3.13) and (3.15) into the function (3.7) yields

$$I_i(l_1, \ldots, l_n, s_1, \ldots, s_n)$$

$$= (1 + s_i)\left[1 - \sum_{j=1}^{n} s_j r_j(l_j) \middle/ \sum_{k=1}^{n}(1 + s_k)r_k'(l_k)l_k\right] r_i'(l_i)l_i.$$

Taking a partial derivative of this function with respect to l_i and noting (3.5), (3.15) and the definition (3.16), we obtain

$$\frac{\partial I_i}{\partial l_i} = (1 + s_i)\left\{\left[1 - \sum_{j=1}^{n} s_j r_j(l_j) \middle/ \sum_{k=1}^{n}(1 + s_k)r_k'(l_k)l_k\right]\right.$$

$$\times [r_i'(l_i) + r_i''(l_i)l_i] - s_i r_i'(l_i)^2 l_i \middle/ \sum_{k=1}^{n}(1 + s_k)r_k'(l_k)l_k$$

$$+ (1 + s_i)r_i'(l_i)l_i[r_i''(l_i)l_i + r_i'(l_i)]$$

$$\left. \times \sum_{j=1}^{n} s_j r_j(l_j) \middle/ \left[\sum_{k=1}^{n}(1 + s_k)r_k'(l_k)l_k\right]^2\right\}$$

$$= (1 + s_i)r_i'(l_i)\left\{\left[1 - \sum_{j=1}^{n} s_j r_j(l_j)\middle/ \sum_{k=1}^{n}(1 + s_k)r_k'(l_k)l_k\right]\right.$$

$$\times [1 - 1/E_i(l_i)] - s_i r_i'(l_i)l_i\middle/ \sum_{k=1}^{n}(1 + s_k)r_k'(l_k)l_k$$

$$+ (1 + s_i)r_i'(l_i)l_i[1 - 1/E_i(l_i)]$$

$$\left.\times \sum_{j=1}^{n} s_j r_j(l_j)\middle/ \left[\sum_{k=1}^{n}(1 + s_k)r_k'(l_k)l_k\right]^2\right\} \qquad (3a.1)$$

and

$$\left.\partial I_i/\partial l_i\right|_{s_1=\cdots=s_n=0} = r_i'(1 - 1/E_i) = (1 - 1/E_i)w_i, \qquad (3a.2)$$

$$\left.\partial^2 I_i/(\partial l_i \partial s_i)\right|_{s_1=\cdots=s_n=0}$$

$$= (1 + s_i)r_i'\left\{(1/E_i - 1)r_i\middle/ \sum_{k=1}^{n}(1 + s_k)r_k'(l_k)l_k\right.$$

$$-r_i'l_i\middle/ \sum_{k=1}^{n}(1 + s_k)r_k'(l_k)l_k$$

$$\left.+ (1 + s_i)(1 - 1/E_i)r_i'l_i r_i\middle/ \left[\sum_{k=1}^{n}(1 + s_k)r_k'(l_k)l_k\right]^2\right\}$$

$$+ (1 + s_i)^{-1}\partial I_i/\partial l_i$$

$$= r_i'\left[(1 - T_i)(1/E_i - 1)r_i\middle/ \sum_{k=1}^{n} r_k'(l_k)l_k - T_i\right] + \partial I_i/\partial l_i$$

$$= \left[(1 - T_i)(1/E_i - 1)r_i\middle/ \sum_{k=1}^{n} w_k l_k + 1 - 1/E_i - T_i\right]w_i$$

$$= \left[(1 - T_i)(1/E_i - 1)r_i T_i/(w_i l_i) + 1 - 1/E_i - T_i\right]w_i$$

$$= (1 - T_i)(1/E_i - 1)T_i r_i/l_i + (1 - 1/E_i - T_i)w_i, \qquad (3a.3)$$

$$\left. \partial^2 I_i/(\partial l_i \partial s_j) \right|_{s_1=\cdots=s_n=0}$$

$$= (1 + s_i)r_i' \left\{ (1/E_i - 1)r_j \middle/ \sum_{k=1}^{n}(1 + s_k)r_k'(l_k)l_k \right.$$

$$\left. + (1 + s_i)(1 - 1/E_i)r_i'l_i r_j \middle/ \left[\sum_{k=1}^{n}(1 + s_k)r_k'(l_k)l_k \right]^2 \right\}$$

$$= (1 - T_i)(1/E_i - 1)r_j w_i \middle/ \sum_{k=1}^{n} r_k'(l_k)l_k$$

$$= (1 - T_i)(1/E_i - 1)T_i r_j/l_i \quad \text{for } j \neq i. \tag{3a.4}$$

Substituting the functions (3a.1)–(3a.4) into the definition of m_i and noting (3.13), (3.10) and (3.16), we obtain

$$m_i\big|_{s_1=\cdots=s_n=0} = \partial I_i/\partial l_i\big|_{s_1=\cdots=s_n=0} - b - p_i'c_{ii}$$

$$= (1 - 1/E_i)w_i - b - p_i'c_{ii}$$

$$= [1 - 1/E_i(l_i)]r_i'(l_i) - b - p_i(l_i)c_i(l_i)/n,$$

$$\partial m_i/\partial s_i\big|_{s_1=\cdots=s_n=0} = \partial^2 I_i/(\partial l_i \partial s_i)\big|_{s_1=\cdots=s_n=0}$$

$$= (1 - T_i)(1/E_i - 1)T_i r_i/l_i + (1 - 1/E_i - T_i)w_i,$$

$$\partial m_i/\partial s_j\big|_{s_1=\cdots=s_n=0} = \partial^2 I_i/(\partial l_i \partial s_j)\big|_{s_1=\cdots=s_n=0}$$

$$= (1 - T_i)(1/E_i - 1)T_i r_j/l_i \quad \text{for } j \neq i,$$

$$\partial m_i/\partial l_j\big|_{s_1=\cdots=s_n=0} = \partial^2 I_i/(\partial l_i \partial l_j)\big|_{s_1=\cdots=s_n=0} \equiv 0 \quad \text{for } j \neq i.$$

Appendix 3b. *The proof of result* (3.29)

Differentiating the employment functions (3.25) totally and substituting into (3.28), we obtain

$$b\,dW = b\sum_{i=1}^{n}\frac{w_i}{E_i}dl_i = \sum_{i=1}^{n}\frac{w_i}{E_i}\sum_{j=1}^{n}b\frac{\partial l_i}{\partial s_j}ds_j. \tag{3b.1}$$

Substituting (3.26), (3.25) and (3.30) in equation (3b.1) yields

$$b\,dW = \sum_{i=1}^{n}\left[\frac{w_i}{E_i}b\frac{\partial l_i}{\partial s_i}ds_i + \frac{w_i}{E_i}\sum_{j\neq i}b\frac{\partial l_i}{\partial s_j}ds_j\right]$$

$$= \sum_{i=1}^{n}\frac{w_i}{E_i}\left\{[(1-T_i-1/E_i)w_il_i/e_i\right.$$

$$+ (1/E_i-1)(1-T_i)T_ir_i/e_i]ds_i$$

$$\left. + (1/E_i-1)(1-T_i)(T_i/e_i)\sum_{j\neq i}r_jds_j\right\}$$

$$= \sum_{i=1}^{n}\frac{w_i}{E_i}\left\{(1-T_i-1/E_i)(w_il_i/e_i)ds_i\right.$$

$$\left. + (1/E_i-1)(1-T_i)(T_i/e_i)\sum_{j=1}^{n}r_jds_j\right\}$$

$$= \sum_{i=1}^{n}\frac{w_i}{E_i}(1-T_i-1/E_i)(w_il_i/e_i)ds_i$$

$$+ \sum_{i=1}^{n}\frac{w_i}{E_i}(1/E_i-1)(1-T_i)(T_i/e_i)\sum_{j=1}^{n}r_jds_j$$

$$= \sum_{i=1}^{n}\frac{w_i}{E_i}(1-T_i-1/E_i)(w_il_i/e_i)ds_i$$

$$+ \sum_{j=1}^{n}\frac{w_j}{E_j}(1/E_j-1)(1-T_j)(T_j/e_j)\sum_{i=1}^{n}r_ids_i$$

$$= \sum_{i=1}^{n}\left\{\frac{w_i}{E_i}(1-T_i-1/E_i)w_il_i/e_i\right.$$

$$\left. + r_i\sum_{j=1}^{n}\frac{w_j}{E_j}(1/E_j-1)(1-T_j)T_j/e_j\right\}ds_i$$

$$= \sum_{i=1}^{n}\frac{w_i^2l_i}{e_iE_i}\left\{1-T_i-1/E_i\right.$$

$$\left. + \frac{r_ie_iE_i}{w_i^2l_i}\sum_{j=1}^{n}\frac{w_j}{E_j}(1/E_j-1)(1-T_j)T_j/e_j\right\}ds_i$$

$$= \sum_{i=1}^{n}\frac{w_i^2l_i}{e_iE_i}(T_i^*-T_i)ds_i.$$

In terms of partial derivatives, this result takes the form (3.29).

Appendix 3c. *The proof of result* (3.35)

Given (3.31), (3.32) and (3a.2), the marginal utility of employment (3.17) changes into

$$m_i(l_1, \ldots, l_n, s_1, \ldots, s_n) = \partial U_i / \partial l_i$$

$$= (\partial U_i / \partial w_i)\partial w_i / \partial l_i + \partial U_i / \partial l_i - b$$

$$- p_i' c_{ii} - T_i s_i r_i' - \left(\sum_{j=1}^{n} s_j r_j \right) \partial T_i / \partial l_i$$

$$= (1 + s_i)(\rho l_i r_i'' + r_i') - b$$

$$- p_i' c_{ii} - T_i s_i r_i' - \left(\sum_{j=1}^{n} s_j r_j \right) \partial T_i / \partial l_i$$

$$= (1 + s_i)(\rho - 1)l_i r_i''(l_i)$$

$$+ \partial I_i / \partial l_i - b - p_i' c_{ii} = 0. \tag{3c.1}$$

Noting this, (3.15), (3.16) and $s_i \approx 0$, we obtain

$$r_i' - b - p_i' c_{ii} - \rho w_i / E_i = \rho l_i r_i'' + r_i' - b - p_i' c_{ii} = 0. \tag{3c.2}$$

Finally, from (3c.1) it follows that the partial derivatives $\partial m_i / \partial s_i$ and $\partial l_i / \partial s_i$ in (3.17) and (3.26) must be modified as follows:

$$\partial m_i / \partial s_i |_{s_1 = \cdots = s_n = 0} = \partial^2 I_i / (\partial l_i \partial s_i) |_{s_1 = \cdots = s_n = 0} + (\rho - 1)l_i r_i''$$

$$= (1 - T_i)(1/E_i - 1)T_i r_i / l_i$$

$$+ (1 - 1/E_i - T_i)w_i + (1 - \rho)w_i / E_i$$

$$= (1 - T_i)(1/E_i - 1)T_i r_i / l_i$$

$$+ (1 - \rho/E_i - T_i)w_i,$$

$$\partial l_i / \partial s_i = -(\partial m_i / \partial s_i)/(\partial m_i / \partial l_i)$$

$$= [(1 - T_i - \rho/E_i)w_i l_i / r_i$$

$$+ (1/E_i - 1)(1 - T_i)T_i r_i / (be_i). \tag{3c.3}$$

The rest of the partial derivatives in (3.17) and (3.26) remain the same as before.

Noting $s_i \approx 0$, (3.28), (3c.2) and (3.33), and differentiating the welfare function (3.34) totally, we obtain

$$dW = \sum_{i=1}^{n}\{[r'_i - c_{ii}p'_i - b]dl_i - z[\Pi_i ds_i + (w_i/E_i)dl_i]\}$$

$$= \sum_{i=1}^{n}\{(\rho w_i/E_i)dl_i - z[\Pi_i ds_i + (w_i/E_i)dl_i]\}$$

$$= (\rho - z)\sum_{i=1}^{n}(w_i/E_i)dl_i - z\sum_{i=1}^{n}\Pi_i ds_i. \tag{3c.4}$$

Substituting the properties of the employment function (3c.3) into (3c.4) and noting (3.5), (3.29) and (3.36) yields

$$\frac{b\,dW}{\rho - z} = \sum_{i=1}^{n}\left[\frac{w_i}{E_i}b\frac{\partial l_i}{\partial s_i}ds_i + \frac{w_i}{E_i}\sum_{j\neq i}b\frac{\partial l_i}{\partial s_j}ds_j\right]$$

$$- [z/(\rho - z)]\sum_{i=1}^{n}\Pi_i ds_i$$

$$= \sum_{i=1}^{n}\frac{w_i}{E_i}\left\{[(1 - T_i - \rho/E_i)w_i l_i/e_i\right.$$

$$+ (1/E_i - 1)(1 - T_i)T_i r_i/e_i]ds_i$$

$$+ (1/E_i - 1)(1 - T_i)(T_i/e_i)\sum_{j\neq i}r_j ds_j\Bigg\}$$

$$- [z/(\rho - z)]\sum_{i=1}^{n}\Pi_i ds_i$$

$$= \sum_{i=1}^{n}\frac{w_i}{E_i}\left\{(1 - T_i - \rho/E_i)(w_i l_i/e_i)ds_i\right.$$

$$+ (1/E_i - 1)(1 - T_i)(T_i/e_i)\sum_{j=1}^{n}r_j ds_j\Bigg\}$$

$$- [z/(\rho - z)]\sum_{i=1}^{n}\Pi_i ds_i$$

$$= \sum_{i=1}^{n} \frac{w_i}{E_i}(1 - T_i - \rho/E_i)(w_i l_i/e_i)ds_i$$

$$+ \sum_{i=1}^{n} \frac{w_i}{E_i}(1/E_i - 1)(1 - T_i)(T_i/e_i) \sum_{j=1}^{n} r_j ds_j$$

$$- [z/(\rho - z)] \sum_{i=1}^{n} \Pi_i ds_i$$

$$= \sum_{i=1}^{n} \frac{w_i}{E_i}(1 - T_i - \rho/E_i)(w_i l_i/e_i)ds_i$$

$$+ \sum_{j=1}^{n} \frac{w_j}{E_j}(1/E_j - 1)(1 - T_j)(T_j/e_j)$$

$$\times \sum_{i=1}^{n} r_i ds_i - [z/(\rho - z)] \sum_{i=1}^{n} \Pi_i ds_i$$

$$= \sum_{i=1}^{n} \left\{ \frac{w_i}{E_i}(1 - T_i - \rho/E_i)(w_i l_i/e_i) \right.$$

$$\left. + r_i \sum_{j=1}^{n} \frac{w_j}{E_j}(1/E_j - 1)(1 - T_j)(T_j/e_j) - [z/(\rho - z)]\Pi_i \right\} ds_i$$

$$= \sum_{i=1}^{n} \frac{w_i^2 l_i}{e_i E_i} \left\{ 1 - T_i - \rho/E_i + \frac{r_i e_i E_i}{w_i^2 l_i} \right.$$

$$\times \sum_{j=1}^{n} \frac{w_j}{E_j}(1/E_j - 1)(1 - T_j)(T_j/e_j)$$

$$\left. - z e_i E_i \Pi_i / [(\rho - z)w_i^2 l_i] \right\} ds_i$$

$$= \sum_{i=1}^{n} \frac{w_i^2 l_i}{e_i E_i}(T_i^o - T_i).$$

In terms of partial derivatives, this gives the result (3.35).

4 Taxation and production efficiency

4.1 Introduction

In the preceding chapter, we used the 'partial improvements' approach to public policy. This makes rather realistic assumptions on the feasibility of government instruments and attempts to find out how, by the use of partial changes, the existing tax structure should be reformed. Now it is instructive to take the 'optimal taxation' approach to public policy as a reference point.[1] This assumes rather boldly that the government has enough information to set taxes and subsidies at any level, and attempts to find out the potentials for public policy. In such a framework, the government could easily eliminate unemployment, for example by paying wage subsidies or by decreasing unemployment benefits. We shall see, however, that such measures may not be socially optimal.

To be specific, we apply the theory of optimal commodity taxation, which excludes non-linear taxes from the analysis and assumes a general equilibrium where the government budget is always balanced, as distinct from the theory of optimal income taxation which uses non-linear tax instruments in a partial equilibrium framework. However, in contrast to the 'partial improvements' approach of the preceding chapter, it is assumed that the government determines all policy instruments simultaneously. Then there will be no instruments which are used solely for policy purposes as distinct from those which are used for revenue-raising purposes.

In the framework of optimal commodity taxation, it is also easy to analyse public production and the provision of public services. In such a case, it is instructive to see whether the government sector should, for employment reasons, depart from private-sector prices. If the resources are Pareto optimally allocated, i.e. if producer prices are uniform all over the economy, then it is said that there is aggregate production efficiency.

---

[1] For the basic principles of this theory, see, for example, Diamond and Mirrlees (1971) or Atkinson and Stiglitz (1980).

This chapter tries to find out how labour taxation could support such efficiency.

Although many economists have examined public policy with a centralized wage-setting,[2] so far very few have done so in the framework of optimal taxation. Traditionally, optimal tax theory considers competitive economies, but in some cases it has been applied also to economies with monopolistic producers[3] or a single monopoly.[4] In Palokangas (1987), optimal commodity taxation and public production were introduced into an economy where the wages were unilaterally set by labour unions but where the private sector was subject to constant returns to scale. We extend the analysis of that paper so that the constant-returns-to-scale assumption is relaxed and so that optimal taxation is also examined in association with the production of public goods.

The plan of the study is the following. Sections 4.2 and 4.3 present the institutional background and the general equilibrium of the model on which the analysis is based. Assuming a 100% profit tax and no public goods, section 4.4 examines production efficiency, constructs the basic principles of labour taxation and considers the possibility of unemployment with optimal taxation. In section 4.5, the model is extended for the case of public goods and in section 4.6, it is generalized for the case where the government cannot tax all private profits.

4.2 The framework

In contrast to the model of the preceding chapter, we consider here a closed economy with two sectors, one consisting of private producers, and the other being controlled by the government. Defining foreign trade as an industry of the private sector that produces imported goods from exported products, it is straightforward to generalize the results for an open economy.

To simplify the model, the following assumptions are made. The first is that some households are workers whose labour time is fixed, who supply labour and earn only labour income. It is furthermore assumed that all workers have the same preferences over the commodities, and that all households and private firms are price-takers. The substitution of consumption and spare time as well as the introduction of price-setting firms, together with wage-setting unions, would make the analysis of optimal taxation intractable. Because of these assumptions, and employing duality, we can consider the whole private sector as if it were

---

[2] See, for example Calmfors (1985), Calmfors and Horn (1985) and Hersoug (1985).
[3] Myles (1989).
[4] Palokangas (1994).

a single firm, and aggregate the commodities so that some index of the workers' consumption is the only wage-good in the economy. We choose the price of this wage-good as the numeraire.

There is a fixed number K of separate labour inputs, each of which is supplied by a different group of workers. We call these groups *trades*, for convenience. Some or all trades are organized in labour unions that set the wages for their members. These unions are, however, assumed to be Stackelberg followers with respect to the government so that they take taxes and the level of government employment as given. The private sector employs all labour inputs $k = 1, \ldots, K$ while the government sector employs some or all of these. The economy as a whole, i.e. the private and government sectors taken together, is subject to decreasing returns to scale and the Inada conditions, so that there is no output without the use of all K inputs.

In the basic model that is presented in sections 4.3 and 4.4, we make three simplifying assumptions that are later relaxed. The first of these is that the government sector produces the same wage-good as the private sector, i.e. government expenditure consists of publicly provided private goods. In section 4.5, we examine the government sector that also produces public goods for which there are no markets and no observable prices.

Second, it is assumed that in each trade k the workers of both sectors are organized in the same union, and that the union cannot discriminate between the sectors. This ensures that there will be the same wages for the same inputs all over the economy. In section 4.5, we consider the cases where the workers in the private and government sectors are organized in different unions, or where the unions are able to discriminate between the sectors.

Third, it is assumed that the government is able to set a 100% profit tax. The motive for this is that we want to deduce intermediate results in a simpler framework: if the households do not earn any profits, then consumption is wholly independent of producer prices. In section 4.6, this admittedly unrealistic assumption is relaxed. Then it is possible to examine the case where some unions also use the workers' profit share as the bargaining instrument.

4.3 General equilibrium

4.3.1 Notation

The basic model employs the following notation. For each trade k, we denote aggregate employment by l_k, private employment by m_k, government employment by n_k, the payroll tax by t_k, the employment tax by T_k, the consumer wage by w_k and the producer wage by h_k. Since labour time is fixed for a single worker and the number of workers supplying each input k is constant, the aggregate supply of labour by trade k, L_k, must be fixed. For convenience, we define the vectors

$$l = (l_1, \ldots, l_K), \qquad m = (m_1, \ldots, m_K), \qquad n = (n_1, \ldots, n_K),$$
$$t = (t_1, \ldots, t_K), \qquad w = (w_1, \ldots, w_K), \qquad h = (h_1, \ldots, h_K),$$
$$T = (T_1, \ldots, T_K), \qquad L = (L_1, \ldots, L_K).$$

4.3.2 The households

Because the model is fully static, the workers spend their whole income on the consumption of the numeraire good. Consequently, a worker's indirect utility function is increasing and concave with respect to income. Because there is no substitution between consumption and spare time, a worker is either employed or unemployed. Given that spare time yields utility, the same income must yield higher utility for the unemployed than for the employed. Thus a worker has two specifications of the indirect utility function:

$$v(\cdot), \;\; v' > 0, \;\; v'' < 0, \;\; V(\cdot), \;\; V' > 0, \;\; V'' < 0, \;\; v(\theta) < V(\theta),$$

where v (V) is the level of utility when employed (unemployed).

When employed, a worker in trade k receives the consumer wage w_k but when unemployed, he/she receives unemployment benefit b from the government. Therefore, the expected utility of a worker in trade k, u^k, is given by

$$u^k(w_k, l_k, b) \doteq v(w_k)l_k/L_k + V(b)(1 - l_k/L_k),$$
$$u_w^k \doteq \partial u^k/\partial w_k, \;\; u_l^k \doteq \partial u^k/\partial l_k, \;\; u_b^k \doteq \partial u^k/\partial b, \tag{4.1}$$

where l_k/L_k is the probability of being employed and $1 - l_k/L_k$ that of being unemployed. For each trade k, the value of a new job, i.e. the marginal utility of employment in income terms, can be defined as the difference between the employed's and unemployed's welfare divided by the marginal utility of income:

$$q_k \doteq [v(w_k) - V(b)]/v'(w_k) = l_k u_l^k/u_w^k. \tag{4.2}$$

4.3.3 Private production

The private sector as a whole behaves as if it were a single firm producing the single good from all labour inputs $k = 1, \ldots, K$. By duality, the profit of this firm is a function of producer wages h as follows:

$$\pi(h), \quad \partial\pi/\partial h_k < 0, \quad \partial^2\pi/\partial h_k^2 > 0. \tag{4.3}$$

We denote, for convenience, the first-order and second-order vector-valued derivatives of the profit function $\pi(h)$ by $\pi_h(h)$ and $\pi_{hh}(h)$. Then, by duality, private-sector labour demand m and private output y are determined by producer wages h as follows:

$$m(h) = -\partial\pi/\partial h \quad \text{or} \quad m_k(h) = -\partial\pi/\partial h_k \text{ for all } k,$$
$$\partial m_k/\partial h_k < 0, \quad y(h) = \pi - h\pi_h = \pi + hm. \tag{4.4}$$

Noting the demand function m in (4.4), the full-employment constraints of the economy take the form

$$l = n + m(h) \le L \quad \text{or} \quad l_k = n_k + m_k(h) \le L_k \text{ for all } k. \tag{4.5}$$

Given (4.3), (4.4) and (4.5), we obtain the wage elasticity of labour demand, when taxes (t, T) and government employment n are held fixed, as follows:

$$E_k \doteq -(h_k/l_k)\partial l_k/\partial h_k = -(h_k/l_k)\partial m_k/\partial h_k$$
$$= (h_k/l_k)\partial^2\pi/\partial h_k^2 > 0 \text{ for all } k. \tag{4.6}$$

4.3.4 The economy as a whole

Let g be government output and S the set of labour inputs that are employed by the government. The government has a differentiable production function $F(n)$, so that the production constraint of the public sector is

$$g \le F(n), \quad \text{where}$$

$$F_k \doteq \partial F/\partial n_k \begin{cases} > 0 & \text{for } k \in S, \\ \equiv 0 & \text{for } k \notin S, \end{cases} \quad n_k \equiv 0 \text{ for } k \notin S. \tag{4.7}$$

If there are decreasing returns to scale in the government sector, then there are profits from public production. Since by Walras' law, the government budget is always balanced, this profit will be delivered back to the population through government subsidies.

The producer wages h are determined by the consumer wages w and labour taxes (t, T) as follows:

$$h_k = (1 + t_k)(w_k + T_k) \text{ for all } k. \tag{4.8}$$

We assume, for convenience, that payroll taxes t_k are based on wages and employment taxes taken together, $w_k + T_k$, rather than on wages w_k alone, because in this manner we obtain simpler tax rules.

Every household consumes its whole income. In this basic model, it is assumed that all profits are taxed away. Then there are no households other than workers, and the goods market is cleared by the condition that the sum of private and public production, $y + g$, is equal to the workers' aggregate demand:

$$y + g = \sum_{k=1}^{K} [w_k l_k + (L_k - l_k)b], \tag{4.9}$$

where l_k is the number of employed, $L_k - l_k$ that of unemployed, w_k an employed person's consumption in trade k and b an unemployed person's consumption. We specify the measure of social welfare W as the direct sum of the workers' utilities: given (4.1), we obtain

$$W(w, l, b) = \sum_{k=1}^{K} L_k u^k(w_k, l_k, b). \tag{4.10}$$

4.3.5 The equilibrium of the labour market

We assume that each union k attempts to maximize its members' expected welfare (4.1). Since the union observes the determination of taxes (4.8) and employment (4.5), substituting these into (4.1) yields the following objective function for the union:

$$U^k(w, t, T, n, b) \doteq u^k(w_k, n_k + m_k(h), b), \tag{4.11}$$

where $h_k = (1 + t_k)(w_k + T_k)$. Union k maximizes its objective (4.11) by setting the wage w_k for its members, taking taxes (t, T), unemployment benefit b, public employment n and the wages set by the other unions, w_j for $j \neq k$, as fixed. Then, given (4.4) and (4.1), the equilibrium conditions for the labour market are

$$\partial U^k / \partial w_k = u_w^k + u_l^k (\partial m_k / \partial h_k) \partial h_k / \partial w_k$$
$$= u_w^k + (1 + t_k) u_l^k \partial m_k / \partial h_k$$
$$= 0 \text{ for } k \text{ with } l_k < L_k. \tag{4.12}$$

4.4 Public policy

4.4.1 Public production

We assume for the moment that for some unspecified reason, the unemployment benefit b is held constant. In subsection 4.4.3, this assumption is relaxed.

The government maximizes social welfare (4.10) by the choice of taxes (t, T) and public employment n within the limits of the government's production constraint (4.7), the constraints for producer wages (4.8), the full-employment constraints (4.5) as well as the equilibrium conditions for the goods and labour markets, (4.9) and (4.12). This optimization is presented in appendix 4a and the results are summarized in this and the following section. Where the equilibrium conditions for the goods market (4.9) and those for the labour market (4.12) simultaneously hold, by Walras' law, the government budget is always balanced.

The first result that is obtained from the government's optimal policy is the one associated with efficiency:

Proposition 4.1: Aggregate production efficiency is desirable, so the public sector must use the private-sector producer prices:

$$F_k(n) = h_k \text{ for } k \in S. \tag{4.13}$$

Diamond and Mirrlees (1971) presented the assertion of aggregate production efficiency for a competitive economy and they explained it as follows. With constant returns to scale in the private sector (or alternatively, with a 100% tax on profits), there are no private profits and consumption and production decisions are wholly independent. Consequently, in order to produce total output in the most efficient manner, marginal costs must be equal for the two sectors. We have shown this result to hold also in the case of non-competitive wage-setting. Since there is a payroll tax t_k and an employment tax T_k for each trade k, the government is able to control both the levels of employment and the workers' income by taxation. Consequently, also in this case, consumption and production decisions are wholly independent and marginal costs must be equal for the two sectors.

4.4.2 Taxes and subsidies

In appendix 4a, we obtain the second result for optimal public policy as follows:

Proposition 4.2: The total pay per employed worker must be uniform, $w_k = w_1$ for all k. The minimum producer wage for any labour input k, $\underline{h}$, must be equal to the consumer wage w_k minus unemployment benefit b minus the value of a new job in terms of income, $q_k = q = (v - V)/v'$. For trades k with unemployment $l_k < L_k$, the producer wage must be equal to this minimum, $h_k = \underline{h}$, but for trades k with full employment $l_k = L_k$, it exceeds this minimum, $h_k > \underline{h}$.

This result is explained as follows. Since the social welfare function (4.10) is utilitarian and every worker has similar preferences, it is desirable to have uniform consumer wages. When the government subsidizes labour with unemployment, it saves unemployment benefit b for each worker becoming employed and each such worker receives the benefit of a job, $q = (v - V)/v'$. Therefore, the aggregate subsidy to unemployed labour (=the difference of the consumer and producer wages), $w_k - h_k$, must be equal to the sum $b + q$.

Substituting definitions (4.6) and (4.2) into the definitions (4.8) and the equilibrium conditions (4.12), we obtain the following corollary of proposition 4.2 (see appendix 4a):

Proposition 4.3: The payroll subsidy $-t_k$ and the employment subsidy $-T_k$ must be determined as follows:

$$-t_k^* \doteq 1 - \underline{h}/(qE_k) \qquad \text{for } k \text{ with } l_k < L_k,$$

$$-T_k^* \doteq \begin{cases} w_1 - qE_k & \text{for } k \text{ with } l_k < L_k, \\ w_1 - h_k/(1 + t_k) & \text{for } k \text{ with } l_k = L_k, \end{cases} \qquad (4.14)$$

where $\underline{h}$ is defined by proposition 4.2. For fully employed labour inputs k with $l_k = L_k$, a payroll tax or subsidy is inefficient.

This shows the minimum set of tax instruments that are needed to maintain aggregate production efficiency. To apply the tax rules (4.14), the government must know the consumer wages w_k, the wage elasticities of labour demand, E_k, as well as the shapes of the utility functions v and V for the employed and unemployed. Then the value of a new job, q, and the desirable labour cost $\underline{h}$ can be estimated. The tax rules (4.14) say that for unemployed labour, the payroll subsidy $-t_k$ must be higher and the employment subsidy $-T_k$ lower, the greater is the wage elasticity of employment, E_k, and the higher the value of a new job, q_k. This will change the unions' choice-sets so that they set the same consumer wages $w_k = w_1$. Consequently, the value of a new job, q_k, is uniform for all trades k. For labour inputs k with full employment $l_k = L_k$, the payroll tax t_k is equivalent to the employment tax and can therefore be eschewed. For labour inputs with unemployment $l_k < L_k$, the upper rule in (4.14) sets the producer wages h_k at the target level $\underline{h}$.

4.4.3 Unemployment benefits

Above it was assumed that unemployment benefit b is held constant. The results above still hold when the benefit is fixed at the socially optimal level. In appendix 4a, we obtain the following result:

Proposition 4.4: The unemployment benefit b is optimal when the marginal utility of income for an unemployed person, $V'(b)$, is equal to that for an employed person, $v'(w_k)$.

Because the welfare function (4.10) is utilitarian, all workers (employed or not) should have the same marginal utility of income.

We demonstrate the coexistence of efficiency and involuntary unemployment by a commonly used structure of consumer preferences. Let the employed's and unemployed's utility functions be

$$v(w_k) = w_k^{1-\rho}/(1-\rho), \quad V = \eta^\rho b^{1-\rho}/(1-\rho), \quad \rho > 0, \quad \rho \neq 1,$$

where constant ρ is the degree of a consumer's risk aversion. On account of differing amounts of spare time, the same income offers a higher welfare for the unemployed than for the employed, and therefore $\eta < 1$. Now by the condition $v'(w_k) = V'(b)$ we obtain

$$w_k = b/\eta > b, \quad v(w_k) > V/\eta > V.$$

In other words, the wages exceed the unemployment benefit and welfare is higher for the employed than for the unemployed. Thus the incentive to work remains although the marginal utility of income is held uniform among the workers.

4.5 Wage-setting in the public sector

4.5.1 The public good

In the basic model above, the government produces the same good as the private sector. Now assume that the public sector also provides services that have no market but that improve productivity in the private sector (e.g. education, public roads). In the model, this market failure can be specified as follows. Let there be trade 0 which is employed only by the public sector. Then the full-employment constraint is $l_0 \leq L_0$, where l_0 is labour input and L_0 total labour force in trade 0. Because labour input l_0 increases private profit, the profit function (4.3) is replaced by the following modified form:

$$\pi(h, l_0), \quad \partial \pi / \partial h_k < 0, \quad \partial \pi / \partial l_0 > 0, \quad \partial^2 \pi / \partial h_k^2 > 0. \qquad (4.15)$$

Alternatively, one could assume that labour input l_0 produces public services for the households. If these services were included in the index of the workers' consumption which was chosen as the numeraire good, then the model would technically take the same form as above: labour input l_0 is included in the production constraint and the profit function of the private sector. Consequently, the results would be the same as here.

When the economy is taken as a whole, the marginal product of input 0 can be defined as the producer price of that input:

$$h_0 \doteq \partial \pi / \partial l_0 > 0. \qquad (4.16)$$

After the introduction of new trade 0 and new labour input 0, the equilibrium condition for the goods market (4.9) and the social welfare function (4.10) change into the forms:

$$y + g = \sum_{k=0}^{K} [w_k l_k + (L_k - l_k) b], \qquad (4.17)$$

$$W(w_0, w, l_0, l, b) = \sum_{k=0}^{K} L_k u^k(w_k, l_k, b). \qquad (4.18)$$

4.5.2 The labour market

Since the markets do not value labour input 0 at all, there is the problem of how the wage w_0 for labour input l_0 is determined. We follow the solution of this problem that is given by Holmlund (1997): wage-setting in the public sector is implemented in conjunction with so-called *cash limits*, which are fixed amounts of money available for pay prior to negotiations. The idea is that the government imposes a cash limit which the private agents take as given. This is consistent with our earlier assumption that the government is the Stackelberg leader and the other agents are Stackelberg followers in the economy.

Everyone in trade 0 is subject to the same preferences as the other workers in the economy. Let w_0 be the consumer wage, t_0 the payroll tax, T_0 the employment tax, h_0 the producer wage and q_0 the value of a new job (4.2) for trade 0. If G is the cash limit on the use of labour input l_0, then we obtain the constraint

$$h_0 l_0 \leq G, \quad \text{where} \quad h_0 = (1 + t_0)(w_0 + T_0). \tag{4.19}$$

Since the union takes the limit G as given but increases the wage w_0 for $h_0 l_0 < G$, it ends up with the equilibrium condition $h_0 l_0 = G$ and the labour demand function

$$l_0 = G/h_0 = G/[(1 + t_0)(w_0 + T_0)]. \tag{4.20}$$

The wage elasticity of the employment function (4.20) – when the cash limit G is held constant – is given by

$$E_0 \doteq - (h_0/l_0)\partial l_0/\partial h_0 \equiv 1.$$

Given the profit function (4.15) and the labour demand function (4.20), the unions' objective functions (4.11) become

$$U^0(w_0, t_0, T_0, b, G) = u^k(w_0, l_0, b),$$

$$U^k(w, t, T, l_0, n, b) = u^k(w_k, n_k - \partial\pi(h, l_0)/\partial h_k, b) \quad \text{for } k > 0.$$

4.5.3 General equilibrium

Because each union k maximizes its target U^k by the choice of the wage w_k, we obtain the equilibrium conditions (4.12) for the unions representing trades $k = 1, \ldots, K$ and the condition

$$\partial U^0/\partial w_0 = u_w^0 + u_l^0(\partial l_0/\partial h_0)\partial h_0/\partial w_0$$

$$= u_w^0 + (1 + t_0)u_l^0\partial l_0/\partial h_0 = 0 \quad \text{for } l_0 < L_0 \tag{4.21}$$

for the union representing trade 0. Given (4.15)–(4.21), we obtain the following result (see appendix 4b):

Proposition 4.5: Assume that there is labour input 0 which is employed only in the government sector and for the use of which the government sets a cash limit. Define the marginal product of this input at the level of the whole economy as the producer price of this input. Then such an input should be taxed according to the same principles as the other inputs $k = 1, \ldots, K$.

The generalization to the case of many labour inputs having no private demand is straightforward.

4.5.4 Discriminating unions

Given this theory, it is also possible to extend the results for the case where, in some trade k, the union is able to set different wages for the private and public sectors. Since the union's objective function is additive over the workers, it behaves as if there were two separate unions: one (labelled as $k \neq 0$, for instance) for the private sector and the other (labelled as 0) for the public sector. The former union behaves as union k does in section 4.4 and the latter one behaves as union 0 does in this section. Thus we arrive at the following conclusion:

Proposition 4.6: Assume that some unions are able to discriminate between the private and public sector in their wage-setting. Then, if the government is able to set sector-specific payroll and employment taxes for the members of these unions, propositions 4.1–4.4 hold as they stand.

4.6 Private profits

4.6.1 Capitalists

In the preceding sections, intermediate results were obtained assuming, very unrealistically, that the government is able to tax all private profits away. Now we are going to examine how these results can be generalized so that this assumption is relaxed. Let us denote the profit tax rate by $\tau < 1$.

With profit income, we must introduce households who do not supply labour and who receive all profit in the economy. This immediately raises two problems. The first one is how in the social welfare function the utilities of workers and capitalists should be compared. We take, for convenience, the simplest approach to this problem and assume that the capitalists comprise so small a group relative to the whole population that their weight in the social welfare function is negligible. It follows that we can still use the direct sum of the workers' utilities (4.10) as a measure of social welfare. In the case where the capitalists' social weight is significant, one should introduce some tax instrument to control the distribution of income between the workers and the capitalists.

The second problem is the complication that, with profit income, consumer demands are functions of producer wages. In such a case, it is impossible to separate consumption and production decisions from each other, so that aggregate production efficiency must be abandoned. This problem is solved by the assumption that the workers and capitalists consume different goods. One can imagine, for instance, that the former consume 'necessities' while the latter purchase only 'luxuries'.

In particular, we assume that the capitalists spend their entire income on services that are supplied by trade 0.[5] The workers do not demand these services at all. Let w_0 be the consumer wage, t_0 the payroll tax, T_0 the employment tax, h_0 the producer wage, l_0 employment, L_0 total labour force and q_0 the value of a new job (4.2) in trade 0. The workers in trade 0 are subject to the full-employment constraint $l_0 \leq L_0$ and to the same preferences as the other workers.

The capitalists' budget constraint is given by $h_0 l_0 = (1 - \tau)\pi(h)$, from which we solve the labour demand function

$$h_0 = (1 - \tau)\pi(h)/l_0, \tag{4.22}$$

where $h_0 = (1 + t_0)(w_0 + T_0)$ and $h = (h_1, \ldots, h_n)$. Since the union representing trade 0 takes the producer wages for other trades $h = (h_1, \ldots, h_k)$ as fixed, it assumes that its after-tax profit income $(1 - \tau)\pi(h)$ is held constant. Then the wage elasticity of the labour demand function (4.22) is given by

$$E_0 \doteq -(h_0/l_0)\partial l_0/\partial h_0 \equiv 1.$$

The equilibrium of this union is determined in the same way as that of the other unions. The result can be summarized as follows:

Proposition 4.7: Assume that the capitalists receive only profit income and purchase only labour input 0 and that this input has no other demand. Then such an input should be taxed according to the same principles as the other inputs $k = 1, \ldots, K$.

Note that because the government can fully control the wage w_0 and the level of employment, l_0, by the payroll and employment taxes (t_0, T_0), the profit tax τ plays no role in the outcome and can therefore be eschewed. Proposition 4.7 is easily extended for the case where the profit-earners consume several labour inputs. The only precondition is that the 'wage-goods' and 'profit-goods' can somehow be distinguished from each other. Given this result, one can ignore profit income that is distributed beyond the workers.

4.6.2 Profit-sharing

Now we assume that the unions representing trades $k \in J$ bargain over the basic wage w_k and the workers' profit-sharing ratio while the unions

---

[5] We use here label 0 only for convenience. In subsection 4.5.1, the same label was used for the public good. One can easily introduce both the public good and the services to the capitalists into a single model and still obtain the same results.

representing the rest of the trades, $k \notin J$, bargain over the basic wage only. Since there cannot be profit-sharing in the government sector, we assume, for convenience, that the government sector does not employ labour inputs $k \in J$: $n_k \equiv 0$ and $l_k = m_k$ for $k \in J$.

Assume that each trade $k \in J$ with profit-sharing is employed by one private firm labelled as k. Then, by duality, the profit of firm k, Π_k, is determined by producer wages h as follows:

$$\Pi_k(h), \quad m_k(h) = -\partial \Pi_k / \partial h_k = -\partial \pi / \partial h_k, \quad \partial m_k / \partial h_k < 0.$$

$$(4.23)$$

Now the total pay per employed worker, which we denote by w_k, differs from the base wage, which we denote by φ_k. It is better to define t_k as a value-added tax for firm k rather than as a payroll tax for input k. Then the base wage and a worker's profit share are taxed at the same rate t_k and we obtain simpler tax rules.

Suppose that the only reason that prevents a union from depriving an employer of all profits is the possibility of concealing profits. Then there are administrative costs for the employer in terms of the numeraire good. According to proposition 2.2, the workers' profit share $0 < \beta_k < 1$ for each firm k is fixed, and union k otherwise behaves as if the wage were the only instrument of bargaining. Given the value-added tax t_k, the firm's profit net of taxes is equal to $\Pi_k / (1 + t_k)$. Because the workers' share β_k of net profit $\Pi_k / (1 + t_k)$ is paid over employment l_k, an employed worker's profit income in trade k, r_k, is determined as follows:

$$r_k(h, t_k) \doteq \beta_k \Pi_k / [(1 + t_k) l_k]$$
$$= \beta_k \Pi_k(h) / [(1 + t_k) m_k(h)] \quad \text{for } k \in J. \tag{4.24}$$

4.6.3 General equilibrium

To obtain a common notation for all inputs k, define $\beta_k \equiv 0$ and $r_k \equiv 0$ for trades $k \notin J$ with no profit-sharing. Then by (4.24), we obtain the total pay per employed worker in trade k as

$$w_k = \varphi_k + r_k(h, t_k). \tag{4.25}$$

Given this modification, equations (4.1), (4.2), (4.9), (4.10) and (4.11) remain the same as in the basic model. The producer wages h_k are nevertheless determined by the basic wages φ_k as follows:

$$h_k = (1 + t_k)(\varphi_k + T_k). \tag{4.26}$$

Given that the total pay w_k is determined by (4.25) and the producer wage h_k by (4.26), the union representing trade k maximizes its utility (4.11) by the choice of the base wage φ_k, taking taxes and the other workers' revenues w_j for $j \neq k$ as fixed. Noting (4.4), (4.25) and (4.26), this leads to the following equilibrium conditions for the unions:

$$\partial U^k / \partial \varphi_k = u_w^k \partial w_k / \partial \varphi_k + u_l^k (\partial m_k / \partial h_k) \partial h_k / \partial \varphi_k$$

$$= 0 \text{ for } k \text{ with } l_k < L_k. \tag{4.27}$$

Using (4.24)–(4.26), (4.2), (4.4), (4.6) and (4.27), we obtain the following result (see appendix 4c):

Proposition 4.8: Assume that the unions representing trades $k \in J$ bargain over the wage and the worker's profit share while the unions representing the rest $k \notin J$ bargain only over the wage. Define t_k for $k \in J$ as a value-added tax. Then, provided that the tax rules (4.14) are replaced by the rules

$$-t_k^* \doteq 1 + (1 - \beta_k)\underline{h}/[(r_k - q)E_k] \qquad \text{for } k \text{ with } l_k < L_k,$$

$$-T_k^* \doteq \begin{cases} w_1 - r_k + (r_k - q)E_k/(1 - \beta_k) & \text{for } k \text{ with } l_k < L_k, \\ w_1 - h_k/(1 + t_k) & \text{for } k \text{ with } l_k = L_k, \end{cases}$$

propositions 4.1–4.4 hold as they stand.

It is easy to see that when there is no profit-sharing, $\beta_k = r_k = 0$, this result is equivalent to proposition 4.3. To apply these tax rules, one must know an employed worker's profit income r_k and the workers' profit share β_k for each trade k.

4.7 Conclusions

This chapter examined optimal taxation and government production when some or all trades are organized in monopoly unions. The main findings can be summarized as follows.

First, it may be socially optimal to support some unemployment in the economy. With fixed labour time, jobs cannot be divided and with non-competitive wage-fixing, an equilibrium with unemployment is possible. Then, with decreasing returns to scale in production, it can be optimal to employ only some of the workers.

The minimum set of tax instruments supporting aggregate production efficiency consists of specific employment subsidies to all labour inputs and specific payroll subsidies to trades that are subject to unemployment.

If all workers have the same weight in the social welfare function, they should optimally have the same income. To change the environment for the unions so that these will set the same wages, the employment subsidy should be lower and the payroll subsidy higher, the more elastic is the demand for labour or the higher is the value of a new job in terms of income. Since the subsidies cause a wedge between the consumer and producer wages, production and consumption decisions are independent and aggregate production efficiency is desirable: the private and public sector should use the same producer prices.

In the production of pure public goods, which have no proper markets, the same principles of taxation apply as above in the production of private goods on the condition that the government uses the marginal product of labour at the level of the whole economy as the producer wage for labour. With positive profits, a precondition for the maintenance of aggregate production efficiency is that 'wage-goods' and 'profit-goods' can somehow be distinguished and also taxed separately. Finally, in the case of profit-sharing, the payroll subsidy must be replaced by a value-added subsidy. This ensures that there is a uniform subsidy rate for all of a worker's income. Otherwise, aggregate production efficiency is desirable and labour taxation depends on the elasticity of employment and the value of a new job as in the case of ordinary wages above.

Appendix 4a. *The proof of propositions* **4.1–4.4**

Given the profit function (4.3), the firm's net demands (4.4) and the government production constraint (4.7), we can change the definitions (4.8), the equilibrium condition for the goods market (4.9), the full-employment constraints (4.5) and the equilibrium conditions for the unions (4.12) into the form

$$F(n) + \pi(h) - h\pi_h(h) - \sum_{k=1}^{K}[l_k w_k + (L_k - l_k)b]$$

$$\geq g + y - \sum_{k=1}^{K}[w_k l_k + (L_k - l_k)b] = 0, \quad (4a.1)$$

$$L_k - l_k \geq 0 \quad \text{for } k = 1, \ldots, K, \quad (4a.2)$$

$$n - \partial\pi(h)/\partial h - l = 0, \quad (4a.3)$$

$$(1 + t_k)(w_k + T_k) - h_k = 0 \quad \text{for } k = 1, \ldots, K, \quad (4a.4)$$

$$u_w^k(w_k, l_k, b) - (1 + t_k)u_l^k(w_k, l_k, b)\partial^2\pi(h)/\partial h_k^2 = 0$$

$$\text{for } k \text{ with } l_k < L_k. \quad (4a.5)$$

The government attempts to maximize social welfare (4.10) subject to (4a.1)–(4a.5) using taxes (t, T), public employment n as well as the private-sector endogenous variables h, w and l as control variables. It is easy to see that $2K$ variables t and T enter only in the last $2K$ equations (4a.4) and (4a.5) and not in the objective function (4.10). Therefore, equations (4a.4) and (4a.5) and control variables t and T can be omitted. Thus the government's problem can be equivalently expressed as follows: maximize (4.10) subject to (4a.1)–(4a.3), by the choice of n, h, w and l. The Lagrangean for this latter problem is given by

$$Q = \sum_{k=1}^{K} L_k u^k(w_k, l_k, b) + \sum_{k=1}^{K} \mu_k(L_k - l_k) + \alpha[n - \pi_h(h) - l]$$

$$+ s\left\{ F(n) + \pi(h) - h\pi_h(h) - \sum_{k=1}^{K}[w_k l_k + (L_k - l_k)b] \right\}, \quad (4a.6)$$

where α_k are Lagrangean multipliers, and s and μ_k are multipliers satifying the Kuhn–Tucker conditions

$$s\left\{ F(n) + \pi(h) - h\pi(h) - \sum_{k=1}^{K}[w_k l_k + (L_k - l_k)b] \right\} = 0, \quad s \geq 0,$$

$$(4a.7)$$

$$\mu_k(L_k - l_k) = 0 \text{ and } \mu_k \geq 0 \text{ for all } k. \quad (4a.8)$$

By the choice of the vectors α, n, w, h and l, the Lagrangean (4a.6) must be maximized subject to (4a.7) and (4a.8). This yields the first-order conditions

$$\partial Q/\partial n_k = \alpha_k + sF_k(n) = 0 \qquad \text{for } k \in S, \quad (4a.9)$$

$$\partial Q/\partial h = -(sh + \alpha)\pi_{hh} = 0, \quad (4a.10)$$

$$\partial Q/\partial w_k = L_k u_w^k - sl_k = 0, \quad (4a.11)$$

$$\partial Q/\partial l_k = L_k u_l^k - \mu_k - \alpha_k + (b - w_k)s = 0 \quad \text{for all } k. \quad (4a.12)$$

According to (4a.11) and (4a.7), variable s can never be equal to zero and constraint (4a.1) always takes the form of equality. Since $\pi_{hh} \neq 0$ by the concavity of the profit function π, condition (4a.10) implies $\alpha = -sh$ and

$$\alpha_k = -sh_k \quad \text{for all } k. \tag{4a.13}$$

From equations (4a.9) and (4a.13) result (4.12) follows. So proposition 4.1 is proven.

Given (4.1) and (4a.11), we obtain that variable s is the marginal utility of income for a worker:

$$s = (L_k/l_k)u_w^k = v'(w_k) \quad \text{for } k = 1, \dots, K. \tag{4a.14}$$

This implies that the consumer wage must be the same for all workers: $w_k = w_1$ for $k = 2, \dots, K$. Substituting (4a.13), (4.2) and (4a.14) into (4a.12) and noting (4.1) and (4a.8), we obtain

$$\mu_k = L_k u_l^k - \alpha_k + (b - w_k)s = L_k u_l^k + (h_k + b - w_k)s$$
$$= v(w_k) - V(b) + (h_k + b - w_k)s = (q_k + h_k + b - w_k)s$$

and

$$h_k = w_k - q_k - b + \mu_k/s \begin{cases} = w_k - q_k - b & \text{for } k \text{ with } l_k < L_k, \\ > w_k - q_k - b & \text{for } k \text{ with } l_k = L_k. \end{cases} \tag{4a.15}$$

So proposition 4.2 is proven.

Given the union's first-order condition (4.12) or (4a.5), and (4.2), (4.6) and (4.8), we obtain

$$0 = 1 - (1 + t_k)(u_l^k/u_w^k)\partial^2\pi/\partial h_k^2$$
$$= 1 - (1 + t_k)(q_k/l_k)\partial^2\pi/\partial h_k^2$$
$$= 1 - (1 + t_k)q_k E_k/h_k = 1 - q_k E_k/(w_k + T_k). \tag{4a.16}$$

This and definition (4.8) lead to equations (4.14). This completes the proof of proposition 4.3.

Maximizing the Lagrangean (4a.6) by the choice of the unemployment benefit b and noting (4.1) and (4a.14) leads to the first-order condition

$$\partial Q/\partial b = L_k u_b^k - s \sum_{k=1}^{K}(L_k - l_k) = [V'(b) - s]\sum_{k=1}^{K}(L_k - l_k) = 0$$

and $V'(b) = s = v'(w_k)$. This proves proposition 4.4.

Appendix 4b. *The proof of proposition* **4.5**

Taking the same measures as in appendix 4a, we obtain a Lagrangean that corresponds to the function (4a.6):

$$Q = \sum_{k=0}^{K} L_k u^k(w_k, l_k, b) + \sum_{k=0}^{K} \mu_k(L_k - l_k) + \alpha[n - \pi_h(h, l_0) - l]$$

$$+ s\left\{ F(n) + \pi(h, h_0) - h\pi_h(h, l_0) - \sum_{k=0}^{K}[w_k l_k + (L_k - l_k)b] \right\},$$

(4b.1)

where α_k are Lagrangean multipliers, and s and μ_k are multipliers satifying the Kuhn–Tucker conditions

$$s\left\{ F(n) + \pi(h, l_0) - h\pi(h, l_0) - \sum_{k=0}^{K}[w_k l_k + (L_k - l_k)b] \right\} = 0,$$

$$s \geq 0, \quad (4b.2)$$

$$\mu_k(L_k - l_k) = 0 \text{ and } \mu_k \geq 0 \text{ for all } k. \quad (4b.3)$$

By the choice of the vectors α, n, w, h and l, the Lagrangean (4b.1) must be maximized subject to (4b.2) and (4b.3). This yields the first-order conditions (4a.9)–(4a.12) and

$$\partial Q/\partial l_0 = s(\partial\pi/\partial l_0) - (sh + \alpha)\partial^2\pi/(\partial h\partial l_0)$$

$$+ L_0 u_l^0 - \mu_0 + (b - w_0)s = 0.$$

Substituting (4a.13), (4.2), (4.16) and (4a.14) into this, and noting (4.1) and (4b.3), we obtain

$$\mu_0 = L_0 u_l^0 + (\partial\pi/\partial l_0 + b - w_0)s$$

$$= v(w_0) - V(b) + (h_0 + b - w_0)s = (q_0 + h_0 + b - w_0)s$$

and (4a.15) for $k = 0$. So propositions 4.1–4.4 hold as they stand for $k = 0, 1, \ldots, K$. This proves proposition 4.5.

Appendix 4c. *The proof of proposition* **4.8**

Given (4.23)–(4.26), (4.4) and (4.6), we obtain

$$\partial w_k/\partial \varphi_k = 1 + (\partial r_k/\partial h_k)\partial h_k/\partial \varphi_k = 1 + (1 + t_k)\partial r_k/\partial h_k$$
$$= 1 + \beta_k[(1/m_k)\partial \Pi_k/\partial h_k - (\Pi_k/m_k^2)\partial m_k/\partial h_k]$$
$$= 1 - \beta_k[1 + (\Pi_k/m_k^2)\partial m_k/\partial h_k]$$
$$= 1 - \beta_k[1 - (\Pi_k/m_k)E_k/h_k]$$
$$= 1 - \beta_k + (1 + t_k)r_k E_k/h_k$$
$$= 1 - \beta_k + r_k E_k/(\varphi_k + T_k). \tag{4c.1}$$

Given that the total pay w_k is determined by (4.25) and the producer wage h_k by (4.26), the union representing trade k maximizes its utility (4.11) by the choice of the base wage φ_k, taking taxes (t, T) and the other workers' revenues w_j for $j \neq k$ as fixed. Noting (4.2), (4.6), (4.27) and (4c.1), this leads to the following equilibrium conditions for the unions:

$$\partial U^k/\partial \varphi_k = u_w^k \partial w_k/\partial \varphi_k + u_l^k(\partial m_k/\partial h_k)\partial h_k/\partial \varphi_k$$
$$= u_w^k[1 - \beta_k + r_k E_k/(\varphi_k + T_k)] + (1 + t_k)u_l^k \partial m_k/\partial h_k$$
$$= u_w^k[1 - \beta_k + r_k E_k/(\varphi_k + T_k)$$
$$\quad + (1 + t_k)(q_k/l_k)\partial m_k/\partial h_k]$$
$$= u_w^k[1 - \beta_k + r_k E_k/(\varphi_k + T_k) - (1 + t_k)q_k E_k/h_k]$$
$$= u_w^k[1 - \beta_k + r_k E_k/(\varphi_k + T_k) - q_k E_k/(\varphi_k + T_k)]$$
$$= u_w^k[1 - \beta_k + (r_k - q_k)E_k/(\varphi_k + T_k)] = 0$$
$$= u_w^k[1 - \beta_k + (r_k - q_k)E_k/(w_k - r_k + T_k)] = 0$$

for k with $l_k < L_k$.

Solving T_k from this and noting $w_k = w_1$ from proposition 4.2, we obtain the lower rule in proposition 4.8. Substituting T_k from the lower rule and w_k from (4.25) into (4.26), and noting $h_k = \underline{h}$ from proposition 4.2, yields the corresponding upper rule.

5 Credibility in collective bargaining

5.1 Introduction

Chapters 2–4 examined wage-setting in a static framework with no investment. Also, when the market for investment goods is perfect, the model is basically the same as when there is no investment. If any amount of capital goods can be purchased or sold at the same market price, then at each moment, each firm adjusts its capital stock to the optimal level. This means that capital input behaves in the same way as any other input. To obtain a genuinely dynamic model, there must be some sort of imperfection in the market for investment goods.

Given the assumed imperfection, the purchase and resale prices for capital are different and collective bargaining is complicated by the problem of *credibility*. The union has an incentive to announce its intention of asking for low wages in the future, because this will encourage present investment. Once the machines are installed, the union has an incentive to renege on its announcement and to claim a better deal than it has promised. For this reason, the firm does not consider the union's intentions credible and it accumulates less capital than in the case where the contracts are credible. With a lower level of capital stock, the economy ends up with a lower level of employment, which also harms the union's interests.

The credibility of pay contracts can be maintained by the formation of *reputation*. Then there will be (at least) two equilibria: one is called *reputational*, in which the parties in bargaining trust each other's promises; the other(s) is (are) called *non-reputational*, in which the parties in bargaining expect each other to cheat whenever possible. A reputational equilibrium is stable if both parties know that a shift to any non-reputational equilibrium will decrease the opponent's welfare: in this case, the opponent has every incentive to keep his/her promises.

We assume here, for tractability, that labour contracts and investment decisions are made at discrete intervals and that the firms are subject to sunk costs in investment.[1] Then the problem of credibility can be analysed as follows. First, we examine one-shot games where labour contracts are, for some unspecified reason, either *credible*, so that investment decisions are based on the given levels of the pay parameters, or *non-credible*, so that decisions on the pay parameters are based on the given level of investment. Then comparing the equilibria in the presence and absence of credible contracts and assuming that the game is repeated indefinitely, we see exactly when the maintenance of reputation is of mutual interest.

Comparing credible and non-credible contracts in a one-shot framework, Grout (1984) established the following results.[2] In the absence of credible contracts, profits and inputs are identical to those that would emerge if contracts were credible and the firm faced a cost of capital which is a linear combination of the capital, purchase price and the resale value of capital. A switch from credible to non-credible contracts reduces the owner's income but it decreases or increases labour income depending on whether union power is above or below some critical level. With high union power, both parties are better off in the presence of credible contracts even when there is full employment.

This chapter extends and modifies Grout's (1984) framework in two ways.[3] First, we replace the union that maximizes labour income by the union that maximizes the expected utility for its members. This leads to a two-part wage scheme where the union and the firm bargain about the wage and the profit share simultaneously. Second, we also examine the reputational equilibrium with the assumption that the game is repeated indefinitely. The plan of the study is as follows. Section 5.2 presents the model, while section 5.3 considers and compares bargaining in the presence and in the absence of credible contracts. Section 5.4 examines the formation of reputation when the game is repeated.

5.2 The model

5.2.1 The workers

We assume that a fixed number L of workers are organized in the union and that the firm can employ only members of the union. Then

---

[1] The next chapter considers the case where labour contracts and investment decisions are made continuously in time.

[2] As a matter of fact, Grout termed credible contracts *binding* and non-credible contracts *non-binding*. This is because he assumed contracts to be binding by law, not credible by reputation as in this study.

[3] One minor difference is that this paper assumes CES technology in production, for tractability, but Grout, having an otherwise simpler model, did not need such an assumption.

the full-employment constraint is given by $l \leq L$, where l is the level of employment. For tractability, we specify the union's utility function U in the form

$$U(W,l) = u(W)l, \quad u > 0, \ u' > 0, \ u'' < 0, \tag{5.1}$$

where W is the worker's income when he/she is employed.

5.2.2 Production

For tractability, we specify the firm's technology as follows. First, labour l and capital k form a composite input through the CES production function $F(k,l)$ that satisfies Inada conditions.[4] Second, to obtain positive profits, there are decreasing returns to scale in revenue. Third, either output is produced from some non-traded resource and the composite input $F(k,l)$ according to Cobb–Douglas technology, or the firm faces a constant-elasticity demand curve for its output $F(k,l)$. Then denoting the elasticity of substitution of the function $F(k,l)$ by ε and the returns-to-scale parameter by γ, the firm's sales revenue y is determined according to the function

$$y(k,l) = F(k,l)^{\gamma}, \quad 0 < \gamma < 1, \ 0 < F_k F_l/(F_{kl}F) = \varepsilon \leq 1, \tag{5.2}$$

where subscripts k and l denote the partial derivatives of the functions $y(k,l)$ or $F(k,l)$ with respect to the first and second argument, respectively, Given that the function $F(k,l)$ is of CES form and the function $y(k,l)$ is homogeneous of degree γ, we obtain the following properties:

$$y_k > 0, \ y_l > 0, \ y_{ll} < 0, \ y_{kk} < 0, \ y_{kk}y_{ll} > y_{kl}^2, \ \gamma y = y_l l + y_k k,$$

$$y_{kl}k + y_{ll}l = (\gamma - 1)y_l < 0, \ y_{kk}k + y_{kl}l = (\gamma - 1)y_k < 0,$$

$$0 < [y_k y_l]/[y_{kl}y] = \gamma/(\gamma - 1 + 1/\varepsilon) \leq 1, \ y_{kl} > 0. \tag{5.3}$$

5.2.3 Investment and income

We specify the imperfection in the market for capital goods such that the purchase price of capital is c per unit, but once installed, capital has a smaller resale price q per unit:

$$c > q. \tag{5.4}$$

---

[4] One of the Inada conditions says that if the level of some input (e.g. labour) is zero, then the level of output must be zero as well. Therefore, the elasticity of substitution of the function $F(k,l)$ cannot exceed one.

Income for the owner of the firm is given by

$$\pi \doteq y(k,l) - wl - ck - x, \tag{5.5}$$

where $y(k,l)$ is output, w is the (base) wage, l labour input, k capital input, c unit cost of capital and x the workers' profit share on top of the base wages wl. The union and the firm bargain over both the wage w and the profit share x. Assuming that income x is distributed among the workers in proportion to labour input, the total pay per employed worker is given by

$$W \doteq w + x/l. \tag{5.6}$$

Since the profit share x cannot be negative, we obtain

$$W \geq w. \tag{5.7}$$

Substituting (5.6) into (5.5) yields

$$\pi = y(k,l) - Wl - ck. \tag{5.8}$$

5.3 One-shot bargaining

5.3.1 General

This section assumes, for simplicity, that the game is played only once. Then there are two solutions to bargaining: if, for any unspecified reason, the investor knows that the pay parameters w and x will not be changed, then the contracts on these are called *credible*; but if he/she knows that the union changes the pay parameters whenever it finds it optimal to do so, then the contracts are called *non-credible*. In terms of game theory, this distinction is based on the order in which decisions on the level of investment and the pay parameters are made. In the presence of credible contracts, investors take the announced levels of the bargaining instruments w and x as given, while in their absence, the parties to bargaining have to take the existing levels of capital as given.

5.3.2 Credible contracts

Assume that at stage 1, the parties in bargaining decide on the pay parameters, and then at stage 2, the firm chooses its levels of inputs (k,l). The solution of this subgame perfect is carried out recursively backwards. So first at stage 2, the firm chooses inputs (k,l) to maximize the profit π assuming that the pay parameters (x,w) are held constant. This means that capital and labour are employed efficiently:

$$y_k(k,l) \doteq \partial y(k,l)/\partial k = c, \quad y_l(k,l) \doteq \partial y(k,l)/\partial l = w. \tag{5.9}$$

At stage 1, by the choice of the pay parameters (x, w), the union attempts to maximize its utility (5.1) and the firm attempts to maximize its profit (5.8), given the firm's equilibrium conditions (5.9), inequality (5.7) and the full-employment constraint $l \leq L$. Since the firm receives no profit when the union stops production, and the union obtains zero utility when the firm stops production, there exist the status quo levels $\pi = 0$ and $U = 0$ and the generalized Nash product

$$Q \doteq \pi^{1-\alpha} U^{\alpha} = [y(k, l) - Wl - ck]^{1-\alpha} u(W)^{\alpha} l^{\alpha} \tag{5.10}$$

of the parties' objective functions, where constant α $(0 < \alpha < 1)$ is the union's relative bargaining power. The parties' equilibrium is obtained by the maximization of the product (5.10) by the choice of the bargaining instruments (x, w), given the constraints (5.7), (5.9) and $l \leq L$. This problem leads to the following result:

Proposition 5.1: Assume that labour contracts are credible. There exists $\hat{\alpha} \in (0, 1)$ such that for $\alpha \in (0, \hat{\alpha}]$, there is full employment $l = L$ and no profit-sharing $W = w$. Where there is unemployment $l < L$, the workers' share of profit is equal to $\alpha \in (\hat{\alpha}, 1]$, and labour input l, capital input k, a worker's income W, the owner's income π and the base wage w are given by

$$y_k(k, l) = c, \quad y_l(k, l) = w(W) \doteq W - u(W)/u'(W), \quad w'(W) < 0,$$

$$W = (1 - \alpha)w(W) + \alpha[y(k, l) - ck]/l,$$

$$\pi = (1 - \alpha)[y(k, l) - w(W)l - ck].$$

The formal proof of this proposition is placed in appendix 5a. Exploiting our earlier results on the right-to-manage bargaining (see section 2.5), we give here a less formal proof as follows. After the firm has chosen the profit-maximizing level of capital input k, the average and marginal products of labour are given by $(y - ck)/l$ and $w = y_l$, respectively. Now given proposition 2.4, the equilibrium is chosen on the contract curve $W = y_l + u(W)/u'(W)$ so that the total pay per worker is equal to the weighted sum of the average and marginal products of labour. The respective weights are the union's and the firm's relative bargaining power

$$W = \alpha[y - ck]/l + (1 - \alpha)w.$$

Proposition 5.1 yields a system of three equations, (5.9) and

$$\alpha[y(k, l) - wl - ck] + (w - W)l = 0, \tag{5.11}$$

with three endogenous variables w, l and k, and one exogenous variable α. By the comparative statics of this system, the following corollary is obtained (see appendix 5b):

Proposition 5.2: When contracts are credible, the increase in the relative bargaining power of the union, α, increases investment k, employment l and the total pay per employment W but decreases the base wage w.

The use of two-part tariffs in bargaining explains this paradoxical result. When the union becomes stronger, it can take a larger part of the profit. In such a case, the union finds it optimal to decrease the base wage w in order to get higher employment l. With a lower base wage, capital input k increases as well.[5]

5.3.3 Non-credible contracts

Assume that at stage 1, the firm determines its level of capital input k, at stage 2, the parties to bargaining determine the pay parameters (x, w), and finally, at stage 3, the firm chooses its level of employment l. Again, the subgame perfect must be solved backwards. So at stage 3, given the wage w, the profit share x and capital input k, the firm chooses employment l so that the marginal product equals the wage:

$$y_l(k, l) = w. \tag{5.12}$$

At stage 2, by the choice of the pay parameters (x, w), the union attempts to maximize its utility (5.1) and the firm attempts to maximize its profit (5.8), given the firm's equilibrium condition (5.12), inequality (5.7) and the full-employment constraint $l \leq L$. Since the resale value of capital is q and since the union can prevent production taking place, the firm's status quo level is obtained by selling its entire capital k (which has been purchased at price c), at price q and gaining a (negative) revenue

$$\bar{\pi} \doteq (q - c)k. \tag{5.13}$$

The union's status quo level is $U = 0$, as before. Then the generalized Nash product of the parties' objective functions takes the form

$$\Omega \doteq [\pi - \bar{\pi}]^{1-\alpha} U^{\alpha} = [y(k, l) - Wl - qk]^{1-\alpha} u(W)^{\alpha} l^{\alpha}, \tag{5.14}$$

---

[5] Grout (1984) missed this point by using a model where the union maximizes labour income. In such a case, it is optimal to choose the base wage w equal to the exogenously determined minimum wage, $w = b$, and there is no effect through the decrease in w.

where $0 < \alpha < 1$ is the union's relative bargaining power, as before. The parties' equilibrium is obtained by the maximization of the product (5.10) by the choice of the bargaining instruments (x, w), given the constraints (5.7), (5.12) and $l \leq L$. This problem leads to the following result:

Proposition 5.3: Assume that labour contracts are not credible. There exists $\underline{\alpha} \in (0, 1)$ such that for $\alpha \in (0, \underline{\alpha}]$, there is full employment $l = L$ and no profit-sharing $W = w$. Where there is unemployment $l < L$, the workers' share of profit is equal to $\alpha \in (\underline{\alpha}, 1]$, and employment l, a worker's income W, the owner's income π and the base wage w are given by

$$y_l(k, l) = w(W) \doteq W - u(W)/u'(W), \quad w'(W) < 0,$$

$$W = (1 - \alpha)w(W) + \alpha[y(k, l) - qk]/l,$$

$$\pi = (1 - \alpha)[y(k, l) - w(W)l - \mu k],$$

where $\mu \doteq (c - \alpha q)/(1 - \alpha)$.

The formal proof of proposition 5.3 is placed in appendix 5c. Exploiting our earlier results on right-to-manage bargaining (see section 2.5), we give here a less formal proof as follows. If the firm knows that the union can change the pay parameters at will, then in the worst case the firm has to sell capital. For this reason, the firm's marginal cost of capital is the resale price q. Then total revenue is given by $y - qk$, and the average and marginal products of labour are given by $(y - qk)/l$ and $w = y_l$, respectively. Now, according to proposition 2.4, the equilibrium is chosen on the contract curve $W = y_l + u(W)/u'(W)$ so that the total pay per worker is equal to the weighted sum of the average and marginal products of labour weighted respectively by the union's and the firm's relative bargaining power:

$$W = \alpha[y - qk]/l + (1 - \alpha)w.$$

However, since at the moment of investment the true price of capital was the purchase price c, the owner's income is equal to revenue y minus labour cost Wl and capital cost ck:

$$\pi = y - Wl - ck = (1 - \alpha)[y - wl - \mu k].$$

In appendix 5d, noting the revenue function (5.2), we prove the following corollary to proposition 5.3:

Proposition 5.4: In the absence of credible contracts, the increase in capital input leads to a higher base wage: there exists a function $w = w^o(k, \alpha, q)$ with $\partial w^o / \partial k > 0$.

The interpretation of this result is straightforward: higher capital stock means higher employment at any given level of the wages, which allows the union to press higher wages for its members.

Noting proposition 5.3, the owner's income is given by

$$\pi = \pi^o(k, \mu, q) \doteq (1 - \alpha)[y(k, l^*) - w^o(k, q)l^* - \mu k], \qquad (5.15)$$

where, by duality and by condition $y_l = w$, the value l^* of l can be taken as given. At stage 1, the firm maximizes the owner's income (5.15) by the choice of capital input k. This leads to the first-order condition

$$d\pi^o / dk = (1 - \alpha)[y_k(k, l) - l\,\partial w^o / \partial k - \mu] = 0. \qquad (5.16)$$

From $0 < \alpha < 1$, (5.4), (5.16), proposition 5.4 and the definition of μ in proposition 5.3, we obtain the marginal product of capital η as

$$\eta \doteq y_k(k, l) = l \frac{\partial w^o}{\partial k} + \mu > \mu \doteq \frac{c - \alpha q}{1 - \alpha} > \frac{c - \alpha c}{1 - \alpha} = c > q. \qquad (5.17)$$

This says that in the absence of credible contracts, the marginal product of capital, η, must be greater than the purchase price of capital, c. When it is possible that labour cost may increase after an agreement has been made, the expected rate of return paid to capital is smaller than when such a possibility does not exist. Therefore, the switch from the presence to the absence of credible contracts is equivalent to the imposition of a tax $\eta - c$ on capital in the presence of credible contracts.

5.3.4 The properties of the equilibria

We also obtain the second corollary of proposition 5.3 as follows:

Proposition 5.5: (*a*) In the absence of credible contracts, the base wage w, employment l, capital input k, the owner's income π and a worker's welfare U are given by functions $w(\eta, q)$, $l(\eta, q)$, $k(\eta, q)$, $\pi(\eta, \mu, q)$ and $U(\eta, q)$, with the following properties:

$$l_q = -\alpha k y_{kk}/A < 0,$$

$$l_\eta = [(1 - \alpha - 1/w')ly_{kl} + \alpha(\eta - q)]/A < 0,$$

$$k_q = \alpha k y_{kl}/A < 0, \quad k_\eta = [W - w - (1 - \alpha - 1/w')ly_{ll}]/A < 0,$$

$$w_q = \alpha k[y_{kl}^2 - y_{kk}y_{ll}]/A > 0,$$

$$w_\eta = [(W - w)y_{kl} + \alpha(\eta - q)y_{ll}]/A,$$

$$U_q = \alpha k\{u'(W)l[y_{kl}^2 - y_{kk}y_{ll}]/w' - u(W)y_{kk}\}/A < 0,$$

$$U_\eta = \{(1 - \alpha)u(W)ly_{kl} + \alpha(\eta - q)$$
$$\times [u(W) + u'(W)ly_{ll}/w']\}/A < 0,$$

$$\pi_q = (1 - \alpha)\alpha k[y_{kl} + (y_{kk}y_{ll} - y_{kl}^2)l]/A < 0,$$

$$\pi_\mu = (\alpha - 1)k < 0,$$

$$\pi_\eta = (1 - \alpha)\{(\eta - q)[W - w + (1/w' - 1)ly_{ll}]$$
$$+ (w - W)ly_{kl} + (q - \mu)\alpha ly_{ll}\}/A,$$

where $A < 0$, and subscripts q, η and μ denote partial derivatives with respect to these arguments.

(b) In the presence of credible contracts, given the functions that are constructed in part (a) above, the base wage is obtained by $w(c,c)$, employment by $l(c,c)$, capital input by $k(c,c)$, the owner's income by $\pi(c,c,c)$ and a worker's welfare by $U(c,c)$.

The formal proof of proposition 5.5 is placed in appendix 5e. Here, we explain it as follows. Assume first that the marginal cost of capital, η, is exogenously increased. This leads to a lower level of both investment and employment: $k_\eta < 0$ and $l_\eta < 0$. The decrease in employment at given wages reduces the possibilities for the union to maximize its members' welfare, so that a worker's anticipated welfare U falls, $U_\eta < 0$.

Second, assume the resale price of old capital goods, q, decreases while the price of new capital goods, c, as well as the marginal cost of capital, η, are held constant. With a higher sunk cost in investment (i.e. with higher $c - q$), the union's position is strengthened and its member's welfare U must increase. Surprisingly, employment l, capital input k and the owner's income π will increase but the base wage w will decrease. This result may seem to be counterintuitive, but it is easily explained by the simultaneous use of the base wage and the profit share in collective bargaining.[6] When the base wage w is held constant, the increase in sunk cost $c - q$ increases

---

[6] For the same reason as in note 5, Grout (1984) misses this point as well.

the profit of the firm, the workers' profit share and a single worker's total income W. In such a situation, the union has an incentive to improve employment by reducing the base wage. With a lower base wage, there will be higher capital input and higher profit for the owner.

5.3.5 The comparison of the equilibria

Since proposition 5.5 puts the regimes of credible and non-credible contracts in the same framework, it is now possible to compare the discrete changes of the equilibrium:

> **Proposition 5.6:** A change from credible to non-credible contracts decreases both employment l and capital input k. There exists $\bar{\alpha} \in (0, 1)$ such that if there is unemployment, $l < L$, and the union's relative bargaining power is high enough for $\alpha > \bar{\alpha}$ to hold, then the union's welfare U is higher and the owner's income π is higher in the presence than in the absence of credible contracts. If α is just below $\bar{\alpha}$, then at least one of the parties is better off in the absence of credible contracts.

The proof of proposition 5.6 is complex. Therefore, we place it in appendix 5f and replace it by the following explanation. Propositions 5.1 and 5.3 indicate that in both the presence and absence of credible contracts, profits are divided in fixed proportion to the union's and firm's relative bargaining power. This means that the change from credible to non-credible contracts has effects only through (i) the base wage w and (ii) the firm's capital cost.

By breaking its promises, the union can raise the base wage. Then, however, the firm loses its confidence and faces higher capital cost owing to sunk cost in investment. This reduces investment and consequently the level of employment. The problem for the union is whether the benefit from a higher wage outweighs the loss from a lower level of employment. Because the members of a strong union already receive a high profit share, the increase in the wage benefits them only a little and the employment effect is more important for the union. Correspondingly, because the members of a weak union receive only a low profit share, the increase in the wage benefits them a lot and the wage effect is more important for the union. From this it follows that a strong union prefers credible, and a weak union non-credible contracts.

The possibility of undermining existing contracts increases the firm's capital cost. On the other hand, in the absence of credible contracts, the firm is able to use investment as an instrument to change the union's choice-set and therefore to control the base wage.[7] Because a weak firm (i.e. a firm facing a strong union) receives only a small profit share, the effect of investment on the total pay per worker is insignificant and the effect through capital cost is more important for the firm. This shows why firms, at least when they are weak in bargaining, prefer credible contracts.

5.4 The formation of reputation

5.4.1 Microfoundations

In section 5.3, it was assumed that decisions on investment and the pay parameters were made only once, i.e. once capital goods are installed, they last forever. Now we relax this assumption and assume instead that capital goods have a finite lifetime, so that the decision on investment must be revised after a fixed interval. Inevitably, this leads to a game where the decisions on investment and the pay parameters are repeated alternately.

Concerning the microfoundations of the game, the prospect of a repeated game poses a minor problem. As explained in chapter 1, the stage of collective bargaining – the outcome of which can be established by the maximization of the generalized Nash product – is composed of the union's and the firm's offers which follow each other alternately at fixed intervals, until an agreement on the pay parameters is reached. When capital lasts forever, one can safely assume that in the absence of credible contracts, bargaining on the pay parameters is never started until machines are installed, while in the presence of credible contracts, investment decisions are never carried out until an agreement on the pay parameters is reached. The problem is that when machines are installed at fixed intervals, the periods of investment and bargaining may overlap.

The simplest way of solving this problem is the following. First, assume that although the lifetime of capital goods is finite, it is nevertheless much longer than the periods in which the union and the firm make offers alternately. Second, assume that there is wear and tear in machines only when these are used in production. Then, since there is no production while the parties are only making offers to each other, there is no wear and tear at all as long as negotiations are going. Consequently, the finite lifetime of capital is not the real time that has elapsed from the purchase of capital: it is measured by the time in which there is some negotiated agreement on the pay parameters holding.

---

[7] This latter effect operates through the base wage w. Therefore, for the same reason as in note 5, Grout (1984) misses it and ends up with the result that the owner's income is always higher in the presence of credible contracts.

5.4.2 Repeated game

Now let us assume non-credible contracts and examine what happens if the game is repeated. In the last game, the union has an incentive to renege on its announced strategies. Because the firm will be unable to punish the union, the latter has no reason to attempt to build a reputation. Consequently, the only outcome for the last game is one with non-credible contracts. Since in the penultimate game, given the outcome of the final game, the union has no incentive to demonstrate its intentions of sticking to its announcements, the outcome with non-credible contracts will prevail. It follows from backwards induction that, when the game between the union and the firm is repeated a finite number of times, each game leads to outcomes with non-credible contracts. In other words, a finitely repeated game is no different from the one-shot game which was described in section 5.3.3.

The situation is changed when the game is repeated indefinitely. Then it may be worthwhile for the union to develop a reputation for sticking to its announcements. Let us denote the strategy played by the parties in section 5.3.2 by C and that played by them in section 5.3.3 by N, i.e. C is the strategy when the wage agreements are expected to be credible, and N is that when these are expected to be non-credible. Assume that for some unspecified reason, the firm (or the union) plays C. Now, if the union (the firm) responds by playing N, then the firm (the union) loses its confidence and it has therefore an incentive to play N indefinitely. If the union (the firm) happens to be better off with strategy C, we can say that the firm (the union) actually punishes the union (the firm) for playing N. So in order to have a reputational equilibrium with both playing C, both parties must be better off with C. Given proposition 5.6, there is such a case for $\bar{\alpha} < \alpha \le 1$ and we obtain our final result as follows:

Proposition 5.7: There exists a critical level $\bar{\alpha}$ of the union's relative bargaining power α, such that there is a reputational equilibrium when $\alpha > \bar{\alpha}$ holds, and a non-reputational equilibrium when α is just below $\bar{\alpha}$.

5.4.3 Public policy evaluation

Finally, let us consider the prospects for labour market reforms. It is assumed that the government can affect (for example, by legislation) the relative bargaining power of the union, α. Since the model contains at least two types of consumers, workers and owners, welfare evaluation is impossible without subjective utility comparisons. For this reason, we evaluate the consequences of public policy only in terms of employment and investment.

Given propositions 5.3 and 5.7, there are two critical levels of the relative bargaining power of the union, $\underline{\alpha}$ and $\overline{\alpha}$, which determine the outcome of the bargaining game as follows:[8]

$0 \leq \alpha \leq \underline{\alpha}$ non-reputational equilibrium with full employment;

$\underline{\alpha} < \alpha \leq \overline{\alpha}$ non-reputational equilibrium with unemployment;

$\overline{\alpha} < \alpha < 1$ reputational equilibrium.

To make the problem of credibility relevant, it is implicitly assumed that $\underline{\alpha} < \overline{\alpha}$. If $\underline{\alpha} \geq \overline{\alpha}$, there would be only a reputational equilibrium, which is associated with unemployment for $\hat{\alpha} < \alpha < 1$ and with full employment for $0 \leq \alpha \leq \hat{\alpha}$.

In the regime of credible contracts $\overline{\alpha} < \alpha \leq 1$, given proposition 5.2, employment l and capital input k is an increasing function of the relative bargaining power of the union, α:

$$\partial l / \partial \alpha > 0 \text{ and } \partial k / \partial \alpha > 0 \text{ for } \overline{\alpha} < \alpha \leq 1. \tag{5.18}$$

Given proposition 5.6, employment l and capital input k fall discontinuously when α decreases below the point $\overline{\alpha}$:

$$\lim_{\alpha \to \overline{\alpha}-} l < \lim_{\alpha \to \overline{\alpha}+} l, \quad \lim_{\alpha \to \overline{\alpha}-} k < \lim_{\alpha \to \overline{\alpha}+} k. \tag{5.19}$$

Results (5.18) and (5.19) are presented graphically in figure 5.1. Curve $l(\alpha)$ is horizontal at the level of full employment, i.e. for $0 \leq \alpha \leq \underline{\alpha}$, increasing for $\overline{\alpha} < \alpha < 1$ and it has an unknown shape for $\underline{\alpha} < \alpha \leq \overline{\alpha}$. There is a vertical drop of curve $l(\alpha)$ at the point $\alpha = \underline{\alpha}$ and a vertical jump at the point $\alpha = \overline{\alpha}$. Now this can be explained as follows. Assume that we start from the level of a monopoly union, $\alpha = 1$. Now when the union's relative bargaining power α is decreased, the union is able to claim a smaller share of the profit for its members over and above the base wages wl. Then the union finds it optimal to increase the base wage w and sacrifice some employment to get higher income for its members when these are employed. When α is decreased over the level $\overline{\alpha}$, pay contracts lose their credibility and this leads to a sharp fall in employment. Since investment k

---

[8] Actually, the regime of non-credible contracts is some limit $\overline{\alpha} - \epsilon < \alpha < \overline{\alpha}$, where ϵ is a small number (see appendix 5f). The situation would be even more complex if we allowed a switching from non-credible to credible contracts between $\underline{\alpha}$ and $\overline{\alpha}$. The basic result – a decrease of α over the critical level $\overline{\alpha}$ causes a fall in the levels of investment and employment – would nevertheless be the same as here. Therefore, for the sake of clarity, the case of double switching is omitted.

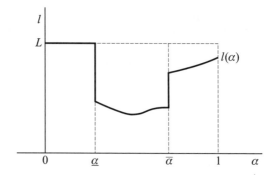

Figure 5.1 Employment and the union's relative bargaining power.

moves in the same direction as employment l, we arrive at the following conclusion:

Proposition 5.8: Starting from the initial position of credible contracts, $\bar{\alpha} < \alpha < 1$, any labour market reform decreasing marginally the relative bargaining power of the union, α, will reduce both employment l and investment k.

Only if the decrease of the union's relative bargaining power is large enough to restore full employment (i.e. to drop α below $\underline{\alpha}$), will employment and investment unambiguously increase, but as long as there remains some unemployment (i.e. α remains above $\underline{\alpha}$), this will not be the case.

5.5 Conclusions

This chapter examined collective bargaining between a firm and a union on the assumption that the firm is subject to sunk cost in investment. It was shown that as long as there is involuntary unemployment, there will also be profit-sharing: the parties in bargaining will not only set the level of the base wage but also share the profit among themselves in fixed proportion to their relative bargaining power. Only in the case of full employment is there no profit-sharing, for the following reason. The union uses two-part tariffs to ensure higher employment given the level of a worker's total income. Since there is no possibility of increasing employment, the union has no need of bargaining instruments other than the base wage.

In the absence of credible contracts, the levels of employment and investment are lower than in the presence of credible contracts. This is because the risk of undermining pay agreements decreases the expected rate of return paid to capital in the same way as a tax on capital in the presence of credible contracts would do. Given such a tax, capital and labour inputs must fall.

It is also shown that if the union is strong and the firm is weak in collective bargaining, then there is a reputational equilibrium where the pay contracts are credible. Since in both the presence and absence of credible contracts, profits are divided in fixed proportion to the union's and firm's relative bargaining power, the change from credible to non-credible contracts has effects through the base wage and the firm's capital cost.

By reneging on its promises, the union can raise the base wage. In such a case, however, the firm loses its confidence and faces higher capital cost owing to sunk cost in investment. This reduces investment and consequently the level of employment. Now the union must judge whether the benefit from a higher wage outweighs the loss from a lower level of employment. Because the members of a strong union already receive a high profit share, the increase in the wage benefits them only a little and the employment effect is more important for the union. Correspondingly, because the members of a weak union receive only a low profit share, the increase in the wage benefits them a lot and the wage effect is more important for the union. We conclude that a strong union prefers credible and a weak union non-credible contracts.

The possibility of undermining existing contracts increases the firm's capital cost. On the other hand, in the absence of credible contracts, the firm is able to use investment as an instrument for changing the union's choice-set and therefore for controlling the base wage. Because a weak firm receives only a small profit share, the effect of investment on the total pay per worker is insignificant and the effect through capital cost is more important for the firm. Consequently, a weak firm prefers credible contracts. Considering a union and a firm together, we find that both parties choose credible contracts if the relative bargaining power of the union is large enough.

Finally, it was shown that if contracts are initially credible, any reform decreasing union power marginally tends to reduce the level of both employment and investment. This can be explained by two effects which both lead in the same direction. First, when the union becomes weaker, it can claim a smaller part of the profits for its members over and above the base wage. Thus the union finds it optimal to increase the base wage and sacrifice some employment to get higher income for its employed members. Second, when the union becomes so weak that contracts are no longer credible, the loss of credibility decreases investment and employment even further. So in general, weaker union power is associated with a lower level of both employment and investment.

Appendix 5a. *The proof of proposition* **5.1**

We maximize the product (5.10) by the choice of the pay parameters (x, w) and the endogenous variables of the firm, (l, k), given (5.7), $l \leq L$ and the equilibrium conditions of the firm (5.9). Noting relations $c = y_k(k, l)$ and (5.3), we establish a positive dependence between capital stock and labour,

$$k(l), \quad k' = -y_{kl}/y_{kk} > 0. \tag{5a.1}$$

Since there is one-to-one correspondence between (W, l) and (x, w) through $w = y_l(k, l)$ and (5.6), and since $\log Q$ is an increasing function of Q, it is equivalent to maximize $\log Q$ by the choice of (W, l), given

$$W \geq y_l(k(l), l), \quad L \geq l. \tag{5a.2}$$

The Lagrangean of this problem is given by

$$\mathcal{L} = (1 - \alpha) \log[y(k, l) - Wl - ck] + \alpha \log u(W) + \alpha \log l$$
$$+ \lambda[W - y_l(k(l), l)] + \nu[L - l],$$

where the multipliers λ and ν must satisfy the Kuhn–Tucker conditions

$$\lambda[W - y_l(k(l), l)] = 0, \quad \lambda \geq 0, \quad \nu[L - l] = 0, \quad \nu \geq 0. \tag{5a.3}$$

The first-order conditions for this problem are (5a.3) and

$$\partial\mathcal{L}/\partial W = \alpha u'(W)/u(W) + (\alpha - 1)l/\pi + \lambda = 0,$$

$$\partial\mathcal{L}/\partial l = (1 - \alpha)[y_l - W]/\pi + \alpha/l + \lambda[y_{kl}^2 - y_{ll}y_{kk}]/y_{kk} - \nu$$
$$= 0. \tag{5a.4}$$

Noting (5.3), (5.9), (5a.3) and (5a.4), and assuming $\alpha \to 0$, we obtain

$$\lambda = l/\pi > 0, \quad W = y_l = w, \quad \nu = \lambda[y_{kl}^2 - y_{ll}y_{kk}]/y_{kk} > 0, \quad L = l.$$

So if the union becomes weak enough, $\alpha \to 0$, there is no profit-sharing, $W = w$, and there is always full employment, $l = L$. Denoting

$$\hat{\alpha} = \sup\{\alpha | l = L\},$$

we obtain $l < L$ for $\alpha > \hat{\alpha}$.

Next consider the case $\hat{a} < \alpha < 1$, where $L > l$ holds. Then the Kuhn–Tucker conditions (5a.3) yield $\nu = 0$, and the first-order conditions (5a.4) imply that $1/\pi$ must be finite and $\pi > 0$. Assume first that $\lambda > 0$. Then given (5.3), (5a.3) and (5a.4), we obtain

$$W = y_l, \quad 0 < \alpha/l = \lambda[y_{ll}y_{kk} - y_{kl}^2]/y_{kk} < 0,$$

which cannot be true. So it must be the case that $\lambda = 0$. Given $\pi > 0$, (5.9) and $\nu = \lambda = 0$, conditions (5a.4) become of the form

$$\alpha u'(W)/u(W) + (\alpha - 1)l/\pi = 0, \quad (1 - \alpha)[w - W]/\pi + \alpha/l = 0.$$
$$(5a.5)$$

Finally, relations (5.8) and (5a.5) imply

$$(W - w)l/\pi = \alpha/(1 - \alpha),$$
$$\pi/(1 - \alpha) = (W - w)l/\alpha = \pi + (W - w)l = y - wl - ck,$$
$$W - w = (\pi/l)\alpha/(1 - \alpha) = u(W)/u'(W),$$
$$w = W - u(W)/u'(W),$$
$$dw/dW = u''(W)u(W)u'(W)^{-2} < 0.$$

Rearranging terms yields proposition 5.1. When $\alpha \to 1$, we obtain the monopoly union which takes the whole surplus of the firm.

Appendix 5b. *The proof of proposition 5.2*

Noting (5.3) and differentiating equations (5.9) totally, we obtain $y_{kl}dl + y_{kk}dk = 0$ and

$$dk = -(y_{kl}/y_{kk})dl,$$
$$dw = y_{kl}dk + y_{ll}dl = (1/y_{kk})[y_{ll}y_{kk} - y_{kl}^2]dl.$$
$$(5b.1)$$

Differentiating equation (5.11) totally and noting $0 < \alpha < 1$, (5.7), (5.9), (5b.1) and $w' < 0$ by proposition 5.1 yields

$$0 = (y - wl - ck)d\alpha + (w - W)dl + (1 - \alpha - dW/dw)l\,dw$$
$$= (y - wl - ck)d\alpha$$
$$\quad + [w - W + (1 - \alpha - 1/w')(l/y_{kk})(y_{ll}y_{kk} - y_{kl}^2)]dl$$

and

$$dl/d\alpha = (y - wl - ck)$$
$$\times [W - w + (\alpha - 1 + 1/w')(l/y_{kk})(y_{ll}y_{kk} - y_{kl}^2)]^{-1}$$
$$> 0.$$

Substituting this into (5b.1) and noting (5.3) implies

$$dk/d\alpha = -(y_{kl}/y_{kk})dl/d\alpha > 0,$$
$$dw/d\alpha = (1/y_{kk})[y_{ll}y_{kk} - y_{kl}^2]dl/d\alpha < 0.$$

Appendix 5c.　*The proof of proposition* 5.3

We maximize the product (5.14) by the choice of (W,l) and the firm's endogenous variable l, given (5.7), $l \le L$ and the firm's equilibrium condition (5.12), and holding capital stock k fixed. Since there is one-to-one correspondence between (W,l) and (x,w) through (5.6) and (5.12), and since $\log Q$ is an increasing function of Q, it is equivalent to maximize $\log Q$ by the choice of (W,l), given

$$W \ge y_l(k,l), \quad L \ge l. \tag{5c.1}$$

The Lagrangean of this problem is given by

$$\mathcal{L} = (1 - \alpha)\log[y(k,l) - Wl - qk] + \alpha \log u(W) + \alpha \log l$$
$$+ \lambda[W - y_l(k,l)] + \nu[L - l],$$

where the multipliers λ and ν satisfy the Kuhn–Tucker conditions

$$\lambda[W - y_l(k,l)] = 0, \quad \lambda \ge 0, \quad \nu[L - l] = 0, \quad \nu \ge 0. \tag{5c.2}$$

The first-order conditions for this problem are (5c.2) and

$$\partial\mathcal{L}/\partial W = \alpha u'(W)/u(W) + (\alpha - 1)l/(\pi - \bar{\pi}) + \lambda = 0,$$
$$\partial\mathcal{L}/\partial l = (1 - \alpha)[y_l - W]/(\pi - \bar{\pi}) + \alpha/l - \nu - \lambda y_{ll} = 0. \tag{5c.3}$$

Assume first that $\alpha \to 0$. Then noting (5.12), (5c.2) and (5c.3), we obtain

$$\lambda = l/(\pi - \bar{\pi}) > 0, \quad W = y_l = w, \quad \nu = -\lambda y_{ll} > 0, \quad L = l.$$

This means that if the union becomes weak enough, $\alpha \to 0$, there is no profit-sharing, $W = w$, and there is full employment, $l = L$. Denoting

$$\underline{\alpha} = \sup\{\alpha | l = L\},$$

we obtain $l < L$ for $\alpha > \underline{\alpha}$.

Now consider the case $\underline{\alpha} < \alpha < 1$, which yields $L > l$ and $\nu = 0$. Since $1/(\pi - \bar{\pi})$ must be finite in (5c.3), there must be $\pi > \bar{\pi}$. Assume first that $\lambda > 0$. Then given (5c.2), (5c.3) and $y_{ll} < 0$, we obtain

$$W = y_l, \quad 0 \le \lambda = \alpha/(l y_{ll}) < 0,$$

which cannot be true. So it must be the case that $\lambda = 0$ as well. Furthermore, given (5c.2), (5c.3), $\pi > \bar{\pi}$ and $\nu = \lambda = 0$, conditions (5c.3) take the form (5a.5), which implies

$$(W - w)l/(\pi - \bar{\pi}) = \alpha/(1 - \alpha),$$

$$(\pi - \bar{\pi})/(1 - \alpha) = (W - w)l/\alpha = y - wl - qk,$$

$$W - w = [\alpha(\pi - \bar{\pi})]/[(1 - \alpha)l] = u(W)/u'(W),$$

$$w = W - u(W)/u'(W),$$

$$dw/dW = u''(W)u(W)u'(W)^{-2} < 0.$$

Rearranging terms and noting (5.13) yields proposition 5.3. When $\alpha \to 1$, we obtain the monopoly union which takes the whole surplus of the firm.

Appendix 5d. *The proof of proposition 5.4*

Relations (5.2), (5.3) and (5.12) yield

$$
\begin{aligned}
(wl &+ qk - y)y_{kl} + (q - y_k)l y_{ll} \\
&= (wl + qk - y)y_{kl} + (q - y_k)[(\gamma - 1)y_l - ky_{kl}] \\
&= (wl + ky_k - y)y_{kl} + (\gamma - 1)(q - y_k)y_l \\
&= (ly_l + ky_k - y)y_{kl} + (\gamma - 1)(q - y_k)y_l \\
&= (1 - \gamma)(y_k y_l - y y_{kl} - q y_l) < (1 - \gamma)(y_k y_l - y y_{kl}) < 0.
\end{aligned}
\tag{5d.1}
$$

According to proposition 5.3, we can define a function

$$W(w), \quad W' = 1/w' < 0, \tag{5d.2}$$

as well as a system of two equations

$$w - y_l(k, l) = 0, \quad [w - W(w)]l + \alpha[y(k, l) - wl - qk] = 0,$$
$$(5d.3)$$

with two endogenous variables w and l. The right-hand equation can also be expressed as follows:

$$W - w = [y - wl - qk]\alpha/l. \qquad (5d.4)$$

By the comparative statics of system (5d.3), and by results (5d.1), (5d.2) and (5d.4), we obtain

$$\begin{pmatrix} 1 & -y_{ll} \\ (1 - \alpha - W')l & w - W \end{pmatrix} \begin{pmatrix} dw \\ dl \end{pmatrix} + \begin{pmatrix} -y_{kl} \\ (y_k - q)\alpha \end{pmatrix} dk = 0$$

and

$$\begin{aligned} \mathcal{A}\, dw/dk &= (W - w)y_{kl} + (y_k - q)\alpha y_{ll} \\ &= \alpha(y - wl - qk)y_{kl}/l + (y_k - q)\alpha y_{ll} \\ &= -\alpha[(wl + qk - y)y_{kl} + (q - y_k)ly_{ll}]/l > 0, \end{aligned}$$

where

$$\mathcal{A} \doteq W - w - [1 - \alpha - W'(w)]\, y_{ll}l > 0.$$

This implies $\partial w/\partial k > 0$ and proposition 5.4.

Appendix 5e. *The proof of proposition 5.5*

Part (a). Given proposition 5.3, we obtain equations

$$W - w = u(W)/u'(W), \quad (W - w)l = \alpha[y(k, l) - wl - qk],$$
$$y_l(k, l) = w, \qquad (5e.1)$$

and $dW/dw = 1/w' < 0$. Differentiating definition $\eta = y_k(k, l)$ as well as the two latter equations in (5e.1) totally, we obtain

$$d\eta = y_{kl}dl + y_{kk}dk, \quad dw = y_{ll}dl + y_{kl}dk,$$
$$(1/w' - 1)l\, dw + (W - w)dl = \alpha[(\eta - q)dk - l\, dw - k\, dq],$$

which in terms of matrices are as follows:

$$
\begin{pmatrix}
y_{kl} & y_{kk} & 0 \\
y_{ll} & y_{kl} & -1 \\
W - w & (q - \eta)\alpha & (1/w' - 1 + \alpha)l
\end{pmatrix}
\begin{pmatrix}
dl \\
dk \\
dw
\end{pmatrix}
$$

$$
+ \begin{pmatrix}
-1 & 0 \\
0 & 0 \\
0 & \alpha k
\end{pmatrix}
\begin{pmatrix}
d\eta \\
dq
\end{pmatrix} = 0. \tag{5e.2}
$$

Noting $0 \leq \alpha \leq 1, \eta \doteq y_k$, (5.2), (5.3), (5.17) and (5e.1), we obtain from the system (5e.2) the Jacobian with reversed sign

$$
\begin{aligned}
A &\doteq (W - w)y_{kk} + \alpha(\eta - q)y_{kl} + (1 - \alpha - 1/w')l[y_{kl}^2 - y_{ll}y_{kk}] \\
&< (W - w)y_{kk} + \alpha(\eta - q)y_{kl} \\
&< (W - w)(-ly_{kl}/k) + \alpha(\eta - q)y_{kl} \\
&= y_{kl}[(\eta - q)\alpha k + (w - W)l]/k \\
&= y_{kl}[(y_k - q)\alpha k + (w - W)l]/k \\
&= y_{kl}[(y_k - q)\alpha k + (qk + wl - y)\alpha]/k = \alpha y_{kl}[wl + y_k k - y]/k \\
&= \alpha y_{kl}[y_l l + y_k k - y]/k = \alpha y_{kl}(\gamma - 1)y/k < 0,
\end{aligned}
$$

as well as the properties of the functions $k(\eta, q)$, $l(\eta, q)$ and $w(\eta, q)$ in proposition 5.5.

Differentiating (5.1) and π from proposition 5.3 totally and noting definition $\eta = y_k$, we obtain

$$
\begin{aligned}
d\pi &= (1 - \alpha)[(\eta - \mu)dk - l\,dw - k\,d\mu], \\
dU &= u'(W)(1/w')l\,dw + u(W)dl.
\end{aligned} \tag{5e.3}
$$

Substituting the partial derivatives in proposition 5.5 into (5e.3), and noting $u' > 0$, (5.3), (5.17) and (5e.1), one obtains the properties of the functions π and U:

$$
\begin{aligned}
A\,\partial\pi/\partial\eta &= (1 - \alpha)[(\eta - \mu)A\,\partial k/\partial\eta - lA\,\partial w/\partial\eta] \\
&= (1 - \alpha)\{(\eta - \mu)[W - w - (1 - \alpha - 1/w')ly_{ll}] \\
&\quad - l[(W - w)y_{kl} + \alpha(\eta - q)y_{ll}]\} \\
&= (1 - \alpha)\{(\eta - q)[W - w + (1/w' - 1)ly_{ll}] \\
&\quad + (w - W)ly_{kl} + (q - \mu)\alpha ly_{ll}\},
\end{aligned}
$$

$$A\, \partial\pi/\partial q = (1 - \alpha)[(\eta - q)A\, \partial k/\partial q - lA\, \partial w/\partial q]$$

$$= (1 - \alpha)\{(\eta - q)\alpha k y_{kl} - l\alpha k[y_{kl}^2 - y_{kk}y_{ll}]\}$$

$$= (1 - \alpha)\alpha k[y_{kl} + l(y_{kk}y_{ll} - y_{kl}^2)] > 0,$$

$$\partial\pi/\partial\mu = (\alpha - 1)k < 0,$$

$$A\, \partial U/\partial\eta = u(W)A\, \partial l/\partial\eta + u'(W)(l/w')A\, \partial w/\partial\eta$$

$$= u(W)[(1 - \alpha - 1/w')ly_{kl} + \alpha(\eta - q)]$$

$$+ u'(W)(l/w')[(W - w)y_{kl} + \alpha(\eta - q)y_{ll}]$$

$$= (l/w')y_{kl}[u'(W)(W - w) - u(W)] + (1 - \alpha)u(W)ly_{kl}$$

$$+ \alpha(\eta - q)[u(W) + u'(W)ly_{ll}/w']$$

$$> \alpha(\eta - q)[u(W) + u'(W)ly_{ll}/w']$$

$$= (1 - \alpha)u(W)ly_{kl} + \alpha(\eta - q)[u(W) + u'(W)ly_{ll}/w']$$

$$> 0,$$

$$A\, \partial U/\partial q = u(W)A\, \partial l/\partial q + u'(W)(l/w')A\, \partial w/\partial q$$

$$= \alpha k\{u(W)y_{kk} + u'(W)(l/w')[y_{kl}^2 - y_{kk}y_{ll}]\} > 0.$$

These yield the partial derivatives in part (a).

Part (b). By comparing propositions 5.1 and 5.3, we see that the outcome in the presence of credible contracts is obtained by the outcome in the absence of credible contracts by choosing $\eta = c$ and $q = c$. This and the functions being derived in part (a) lead directly to part (b).

Appendix 5f. *The proof of proposition* 5.6

Let the operator Δ denote the difference in the value of a variable between the equilibrium without credible contracts and that with credible contracts. Then, given the mean value theorem, there exist $\varphi_\eta \in [c, \eta]$ and $\varphi_q \in [q, c]$ such that

$$\Delta k \doteq k(\eta, q) - k(c, c)$$

$$= k_\eta(\varphi_\eta, \varphi_q)(\eta - c) + k_q(\varphi_\eta, \varphi_q)(q - c), \qquad (5f.1)$$

there exist $\sigma_\eta \in [c, \eta]$ and $\sigma_q \in [q, c]$ such that

$$\Delta l \doteq l(\eta, q) - l(c, c)$$

$$= l_\eta(\sigma_\eta, \sigma_q)(\eta - c) + l_q(\sigma_\eta, \sigma_q)(q - c), \tag{5f.2}$$

there exist $\xi_\eta \in [c, \eta]$, $\xi_q \in [q, c]$ and $\xi_\mu \in [c, \mu]$ such that

$$\Delta\pi \doteq \pi(\eta, \mu, q) - \pi(c, c, c)$$

$$= \pi_\eta(\xi_\eta, \xi_\mu, \xi_q)(\eta - c) + \pi_q(\xi_\eta, \xi_\mu, \xi_q)(q - c)$$

$$+ \pi_\mu(\xi_\eta, \xi_\mu, \xi_q)(\mu - c), \tag{5f.3}$$

and there exist $\delta_\eta \in [c, \eta]$ and $\delta_q \in [q, c]$ such that

$$\Delta U \doteq U(\eta, q) - U(c, c)$$

$$= U_\eta(\delta_\eta, \delta_q)(\eta - c) + U_q(\delta_\eta, \delta_q)(q - c). \tag{5f.4}$$

From (5.17) and $0 \leq \alpha \leq 1$, it follows that

$$q - \mu = q - \frac{c - \alpha q}{1 - \alpha}$$

$$= \frac{q - c}{1 - \alpha} \quad \text{or} \quad (1 - \alpha)(q - \mu) = q - c,$$

$$\eta - c > \frac{c - \alpha q}{1 - \alpha} - c = \frac{\alpha}{1 - \alpha}(c - q) \quad \text{or} \quad q - c > \left(1 - \frac{1}{\alpha}\right)(\eta - c),$$

$$\eta - q > \frac{c - \alpha q}{1 - \alpha} - q = \frac{c - q}{1 - \alpha} \quad \text{or} \quad (1 - \alpha)(\eta - q) > c - q. \tag{5f.5}$$

Given propositions 5.1, 5.3 and 5.5 as well as relations (5.3), (5.17), (5f.1), (5f.2) and (5f.5), the changes in capital input take the form

$$A\,\Delta l = Al_\eta(\eta - c) + Al_q(q - c) > (\eta - c)[Al_\eta + (1 - 1/\alpha)Al_q]$$

$$= (\eta - c)[(1 - \alpha - 1/w')ly_{kl} + \alpha(\eta - q) + (1 - \alpha)ky_{kk}]$$

$$> (\eta - c)[(1 - \alpha)(ly_{kl} + ky_{kk}) + \alpha(\eta - q)]$$

$$= (\eta - c)(\eta - \alpha q) > 0,$$

$$A\,\Delta k = Ak_\eta(\eta - c) + Ak_q(q - c) > (\eta - c)[Ak_\eta + (1 - 1/\alpha)Ak_q]$$

$$= (\eta - c)[W - w + (1/w' + \alpha - 1)ly_{ll} + (\alpha - 1)ky_{kl}]$$

$$> (\eta - c)(\alpha - 1)(ly_{ll} + ky_{kl}) = (\eta - c)(\alpha - 1)(\gamma - 1)y_l > 0.$$

Now since $A < 0$, a change from credible into non-credible contracts will decrease labour and capital inputs, $\Delta l < 0$ and $\Delta k < 0$.

Given propositions 5.1, 5.3 and 5.5 as well as relations (5.3), (5.17), (5f.3) and (5f.5), the change of the owner's income takes the form

$$
\begin{aligned}
A\,\Delta\pi = {} & A\pi_\eta(\eta-c)+A\pi_q(q-c)+A\pi_\mu(\mu-c)\\
> {} & A\pi_\eta(\eta-c)+A\pi_q(q-c)\\
> {} & (\eta-c)[A\pi_\eta+(1-1/\alpha)A\pi_q]\\
= {} & (\eta-c)\{(1-\alpha)(\eta-q)[W-w+(1/w'-1)ly_{ll}]\\
& +(1-\alpha)(q-\mu)\alpha ly_{ll}+(1-\alpha)(w-W)ly_{kl}\\
& -(1-\alpha)^2 k[y_{kl}+(y_{kk}y_{ll}-y_{kl}^2)l]\}\\
> {} & (\eta-c)\{(c-q)[W-w+(1/w'-1)ly_{ll}]\\
& +(q-c)\alpha ly_{ll}+(1-\alpha)(w-W)ly_{kl}\\
& -(1-\alpha)^2 k[y_{kl}+(y_{kk}y_{ll}-y_{kl}^2)l]\}\\
= {} & (\eta-c)\{(c-q)[W-w+(1/w'-1-\alpha)ly_{ll}]\\
& \times(1-\alpha)(w-W)ly_{kl}\\
& -(1-\alpha)^2 k[y_{kl}+(y_{kk}y_{ll}-y_{kl}^2)l]\}\\
= {} & (\eta-c)\{(c-q)[\alpha(y-wl-qk)/l+(1/w'-1-\alpha)ly_{ll}]\\
& -(1-\alpha)\alpha(y-wl-qk)y_{kl}\\
& -(1-\alpha)^2 k[y_{kl}+(y_{kk}y_{ll}-y_{kl}^2)l]\}.
\end{aligned}
$$

Now because $A<0$ and

$$
\lim_{\alpha\to1}A\,\Delta\pi=(\eta-c)(c-q)[(y-wl-qk)/l+(1/w'-2)ly_{ll}]>0,
$$

there must be $\lim_{\alpha\to1}\Delta\pi<0$ and the owner of the firm is better off when α is close to one. Defining

$$
\alpha_p \doteq \sup\{\alpha|A\,\Delta\pi\le0\}=\sup\{\alpha|\Delta\pi\ge0\},
$$

we obtain

$$
\Delta\pi<0 \text{ for } \alpha\in(\alpha_p,1]. \tag{5f.6}
$$

Then for $\alpha\in(\alpha_p,1]$, a change from credible into non-credible contracts will decrease the owner's income π.

Given propositions 5.1, 5.3 and 5.5 as well as relations (5.3), (5.17), (5f.4) and (5f.5), the change of a worker's expected utility takes the form

$$A \, \Delta U = AU_\eta(\eta - c) + AU_q(q - c)$$
$$> (\eta - c)[AU_\eta + (1 - 1/\alpha)U_q]$$
$$= (\eta - c)\{(1 - \alpha)uly_{kl} + \alpha(\eta - q)[u + u'ly_{ll}/w']$$
$$+ (1 - \alpha)uky_{kk} + (\alpha - 1)ku'l[y_{kl}^2 - y_{kk}y_{ll}]/w'\}$$
$$= (\eta - c)\{(1 - \alpha)(\gamma - 1)uy_k + \alpha(\eta - q)[u + u'ly_{ll}/w']$$
$$+ (\alpha - 1)ku'l[y_{kl}^2 - y_{kk}y_{ll}]/w'\}$$
$$= \frac{\eta - c}{1 - \alpha}\{(1 - \alpha)^2(\gamma - 1)uy_k$$
$$+ \alpha(1 - \alpha)(\eta - q)[u + u'ly_{ll}/w']$$
$$- (1 - \alpha)^2ku'l[y_{kl}^2 - y_{kk}y_{ll}]/w'\}$$
$$= (\eta - c)\Phi/(1 - \alpha),$$

where

$$\Phi \doteq (1 - \alpha)^2(\gamma - 1)uy_k + \alpha(c - q)[u + u'ly_{ll}/w']$$
$$- (1 - \alpha)^2ku'l[y_{kl}^2 - y_{kk}y_{ll}]/w'.$$

Now because

$$\lim_{\alpha \to 1} \Phi = (c - q)[u + u'ly_{ll}/w'] > 0,$$

$$\lim_{\alpha \to 0} \Phi = (\gamma - 1)uy_k$$
$$- ku'l[y_{kl}^2 - y_{kk}y_{ll}]/w' < 0,$$

there must be some value of α for which $\Phi = 0$. Defining

$$\alpha_u \doteq \sup\{\alpha | \Phi \leq 0\}$$
$$= \sup\{\alpha | A \, \Delta U \leq 0\} = \sup\{\alpha | \Delta U \geq 0\} > 0,$$

we obtain

$$\Delta U < 0 \text{ for } \alpha \in (\alpha_u, 1], \alpha_u > 0. \tag{5f.7}$$

This means that for $\alpha \in (\alpha_u, 1]$, a change from credible into non-credible contracts will decrease the union's welfare.

Given the results (5f.6) and (5f.7) we conclude that there exists a critical value $\bar{\alpha}$ satisfying

$$0 < \bar{\alpha} \leq \max[\alpha_p, \alpha_u] < 1,$$

so that the following conditions hold. If $\alpha \in (\overline{\alpha}, 1]$, then both the owner's income π and a worker's (and the union's) welfare will decrease when credible contracts are replaced by non-credible contracts. If α is just below $\overline{\alpha}$ – i.e. if $\overline{\alpha} - \epsilon < \alpha < \overline{\alpha}$, where ϵ is a small number – then either the owner of the firm or the union is (or both of them are) better off when credible contracts are replaced by non-credible contracts.

6 Monopoly unions and sluggish investment

6.1 Introduction

Using a model in which the union and the firm make decisions successively at discrete intervals, chapter 5 demonstrated that with strong unions there is a reputational equilibrium, i.e. an equilibrium with credible contracts. Now to confirm this result, we do the same with a different model which is continuous in time and in which, therefore, the decisions cannot be put in a chronological order. Van der Ploeg (1987) and Palokangas (1991a, 1992) have used a more or less similar model but for totally different purposes.

In discrete and static models of collective bargaining, the union and the firm usually maximize the generalized Nash products of their targets. Since in a continuous model such an approach would lead to technical difficulties and problems in the interpretation of the results, we stick to the common special case of a monopoly union which acts as a Stackelberg leader with respect to the firm.

Our purpose is to show that the credibility of contracts is a Pareto improvement and, consequently, there exists a reputational equilibrium. The plan of the study is as follows. Section 6.2 examines the temporary equilibrium of the economy, when the pay parameters and capital stock are given, and section 6.3 specifies collective bargaining in the form of a dynamic game. In section 6.4, we specify how, in the presence of credible contracts, investment and the pay parameters are determined. In 6.5, the same is done in the absence of credible contracts. Section 6.6 examines whether the formation of reputation is possible.

6.2 The model

6.2.1 Adjustment costs for investment

To make the problem of credibility relevant, there must be some imperfection in the market for capital goods. In the discrete-time model of chapter 5, this imperfection was the sunk cost associated with investment: the price for new goods is higher than that for used goods. In the continuous-time model of this chapter, it is commonly assumed that investment in real capital is subject to adjustment costs over and above the base price for capital goods. The common way of justifying this has been the following.[1]

A firm's demand for the particular type of investment goods it needs is a significant proportion of the total demand for these goods. Hence, as the firm's gross investment and demand for new capital goods increases, the price the firm has to pay for these goods increases as well. On the basis of this, the adjustment costs over and above the base price are zero only when the rate of gross investment is zero and they increase at an ever-increasing rate when gross investment increases.

We assume, for convenience, that capital depreciates at some exponential rate μ and that investment is irreversible. Let k be capital stock, t time, b the level of gross investment and q the base price for capital goods that corresponds to zero gross investment. Then the accumulation of capital is determined by

$$\dot{k} \doteq dk/dt = b - \mu k, \quad b \geq 0, \quad \mu > 0, \tag{6.1}$$

where $b \geq 0$ is the irreversibility constraint. The firm's adjustment costs are an increasing and convex function of the level of the firm's gross investment:

$$h(b), \quad h' > 0, \quad h'' > 0, \quad h(0) = 0. \tag{6.2}$$

Since these are paid in addition to base costs qb, the firm's total costs for investment are given by

$$qb + h(b). \tag{6.3}$$

6.2.2 Production and income

The output of the firm is chosen as the numeraire. The firm is subject to a thrice differentiable production function $y = F(k, l)$, where y is output, k the fully employed capital stock and l the level of employment. Denoting

---

[1] See, for example, Nickell (1978), ch. 3.

the labour/capital ratio by z and assuming constant returns to scale, we obtain[2]

$$y = kf(z), \quad f(z) \doteq F(1, z), \quad f' > 0, \quad f'' < 0, \quad z \doteq l/k. \qquad (6.4)$$

We assume that a fixed number n of identical workers are organized in a single union and that the firm can employ only the members of the union. In addition to the base wage w, the union claims some part x of the rate of return paid to capital, which is then delivered to the workers in fixed proportion to employment. Some authors assume that the union's instruments are the base wage and the workers' profit-sharing ratio.[3] This would lead to exactly the same results, but we prefer a simpler model.

The owners' net profit Π is equal to sales income y minus the wages $wl = wzk$, the workers' profit income, xk, and investment cost (6.3): given (6.4), the firm's net profit after investment is

$$\Pi = y - wl - xk - qb - h(b) = [f(z) - wz - x]k - qb - h(b), \qquad (6.5)$$

where the wage w and the workers' profit income per unit of capital, x, are the union's instruments. Since the firm can choose the level of investment, b, and the labour/capital ratio z independently, then to maximize profit (6.5) it sets the marginal product of labour $\partial y/\partial z = f'(z)$ equal to the base wage w:

$$w = f'(z). \qquad (6.6)$$

When setting the pay parameters, the union faces two constraints. The first of these is that the workers' profit income per unit of capital, x, cannot be negative, i.e. that the workers cannot directly subsidize the firm. The second one is that the firm's gross profit before investment, $y - wl - xk$, cannot be negative. Noting (6.2) and (6.4), these constraints are equivalent to the following:

$$0 \le x \le f(z) - wz. \qquad (6.7)$$

We assume that individual labour time is fixed and chosen as unity, so that a worker is either employed or unemployed. The total pay

---

[2] The assumption of decreasing returns to scale in line with Van der Ploeg (1987) would here lead to an excessively complicated model with no increase in our understanding of the problem.
[3] This approach is used, for example, in Hoel and Moene (1988) and Palokangas (1991a, 1992).

per employed worker, v, is equal to the base wage w plus an employed worker's share of capital income, $xk/l = x/z$:

$$v = w + x/z. \tag{6.8}$$

We specify the union's utility function in the form

$$U(v,l) = u(v)l = u(v)zk, \quad u > 0, \quad u' > 0, \quad u'' < 0. \tag{6.9}$$

6.3 The dynamic game

6.3.1 The setting

In our dynamic game, the basic strategic assumption is that the firm is the Stackelberg follower and chooses employment l and the level of gross investment, b, while the union is the Stackelberg leader and sets the base wage w and the workers' profit income per unit of capital, x. This is the case, for example, when there are several firms facing the same union, so that the firm is 'small' when compared to the union.

6.3.2 The players

The firm maximizes the discounted stream of its net profit (6.5). Since the firm has already chosen the labour/capital ratio z optimally according to (6.6), the firm's objective function takes the form

$$P = \int_0^\infty \Pi e^{-rt}dt = \int_0^\infty \{[f(z) - f'(z)z - x]k - qb - h(b)\}e^{-rt}dt, \tag{6.10}$$

where $r > 0$ is the interest rate, subject to the accumulation of capital (6.1), assuming that the union's instruments w and x are held constant. The union maximizes its utility (6.9) over time,

$$\mathcal{U} = \int_0^\infty u(v)zke^{-\rho t}dt, \quad \rho > 0, \tag{6.11}$$

where ρ is the union's rate of time preference, subject to the firm's behaviour as well as inequalities (6.7), by the choice of (w, x).

6.3.3 The two solutions

The solution of this dynamic game depends on the credibility of the labour contracts.[4] If the union can make a credible commitment, then the firm makes its investment decisions according to the sequence of the pay parameters that is announced by the union. In such a case, both agents plan over the whole foreseeable future, and their behaviour can be specified in the form of optimal control theory. Otherwise, if the unions cannot make a credible commitment, the firm chooses its investment programme according to the expected behaviour of the union. In such a case, each agent plans on the assumption that its opponent will make the optimal choices in the future, and the agents' behaviour can be specified in the form of dynamic programming where the game is solved recursively backwards starting from the final period of arbitrary length. These cases are analysed in the next two sections.

6.4 Credible contracts

6.4.1 The setting

In this section, we assume that, for some unspecified reason, labour contracts are credible, so that the union is prevented from reneging on an announced sequence of the pay parameters. Then the formal structure of the interaction between the firm and the union corresponds to an open-loop Stackelberg equilibrium outcome for a non-cooperative, infinite differential game,[5] where the union is the leader and the firm the follower. Technically, the solution of this game will be found as follows. Determine first the unique optimal response of the firm to every strategy of the union. The firm's choices can be made on the basis of the initial or current value of the capital stock without making any difference to the solution. Second, find the union's optimal strategy given the firm's optimal response. Since the union cannot depart from its announced strategy, then, at each moment, the union makes its choices using the information on the initial capital stock.

---

[4] Van der Ploeg (1987) was the first to see the connection between credible contracts and optimal control theory as well as between non-credible contracts and dynamic programming. This chapter extends Van der Ploeg's analysis by introducing profit-sharing, which will have a significant impact on the results.

[5] See, for example Basar and Olsder (1982), sect. 7.2, for the formal solution of the Stackelberg leadership in a differential game.

6.4.2 The firm

The firm maximizes its present value (6.10) subject to the accumulation of capital and the irreversibility constraint in (6.1), by the choice of the level of investment, b. Since the production function (6.4) is subject to constant returns to scale, the firm's optimal accumulation of capital is given by

$$\dot{k} = g(f(z) - zv) - \mu k \quad \text{with}$$

$$g' \begin{cases} > 0 & \text{for } f(z) - zv > (r + \mu)[q + h'(0)], \\ = 0 & \text{for } f(z) - zv \leq (r + \mu)[q + h'(0)], \end{cases} \tag{6.12}$$

where $f(z) - zv$ is the gross rate of return paid to capital. The strict proof of the functions (6.12) is presented in appendix 6a.

6.4.3 The union

Since by the definition (6.8) and the firm's equilibrium condition (6.6), there is one-to-one correspondence from w and x to z and v, we may replace the former by the latter as the union's instruments for optimization. Then inequalities (6.7) can be transformed into following form:

$$v \geq w = f'(z), \quad f(z) \geq zv. \tag{6.13}$$

The union maximizes its utility (6.11) subject to the firm's investment function (6.12) and constraints (6.13), by the choice of the labour/capital ratio z and the total pay per employed worker, v. This maximization yields the following result (see appendix 6b):

> **Proposition 6.1:** In the presence of credible contracts, there is profit-sharing, $v > f'(z) = w$, and the labour/capital ratio z and the total pay per employed worker, v, are given by the system
>
> $$v = f' + u/u', \quad \text{either } u' = g'\gamma/k \text{ or } f = zv, \tag{6.14}$$
>
> where variable γ evolves according to
>
> $$\dot{\gamma} = \rho\gamma - u(v)z, \quad \gamma > 0 \text{ for } f > zv, \quad \lim_{t \to \infty} \gamma k e^{-\rho t} = 0. \tag{6.15}$$

If capital stock k shows stable behaviour, then the adjustment towards equilibrium is unique.

We explain the existence of profit-sharing as follows. Let $\tilde{w}$ be the optimal wage for the union in the absence of profit-sharing, $x = 0$. Now if the wage w is marginally reduced below the level $\tilde{w}$, but so that the total pay per employed worker is the same as before, $v = \tilde{w}$, then the level of employment, l, and the union's utility $U = u(\tilde{w})l$ will increase.

6.4.4 The evolution of the system

Consider what happens to the system when the firm and the union behave in the above-specified manner. If contracts are credible, then given proposition 6.1, adjustment towards a stable equilibrium with positive capital stock is unique. On the other hand, from condition (6.12) it follows that if there is no profit left for the firm, $f(z) = zv$, then capital depreciates, $\dot{k} = -\mu k$. This leads to the following result:

Proposition 6.2: Assume that the pay contracts are credible. Then there are at least two possible development patterns: one which ends up with positive capital stock and which is labelled as I; and (one or more) others which exhaust capital stock and which are labelled as II. If the union prefers to deprive the firm of its profits (i.e. if $f(z) = zv$), then one of the patterns of category II will be the outcome. If capital stock k has a stable positive equilibrium value, then the union prefers pattern I to all patterns of category II.

So if the pay contracts are credible and the firm maintains some positive capital stock, then the monopoly union does not deprive the firm of all its profits although it has the power to do so. The explanation of this is straightforward: if the union leaves too small a profit, the firm loses its incentive to invest, investment b will collapse and future employment and labour income will decrease together with capital stock k.

6.5 Non-credible contracts

6.5.1 The setting

In this section, we assume that contracts are not credible, i.e. that the union can renege on an announced sequence of the pay parameters. This means that the game must be solved backwards, starting from some final period of arbitrary length (t, ∞). At each moment t, both the firm and the union make their choices on the assumption that the opponent will make its choices optimally for the whole period (t, ∞). The crucial property of dynamic programming is that the strategies of both parties are independent of the initial time t.[6]

---

[6] The formal solution of a dynamic programme is given, for example, by Kamien and Schwartz (1985), sect. 21.

6.5.2 The firm

When strategies of the union and the firm are in Stackelberg equilibrium for each point of time from any moment t onwards, then at that moment t, the optimal value of the discounted stream of net profit (6.10) is given by

$$B(k,t) \doteq \max_{\substack{z,b \\ b \geq 0}} \int_t^\infty \{[f(z) - f'(z)z - x]k - qb - h(b)\}e^{-r(\tau-t)}d\tau.$$

$$(6.16)$$

We denote, for convenience, the partial derivatives of B as

$$B_k \doteq \frac{\partial B}{\partial k}, \quad B_t \doteq \frac{\partial B}{\partial t}, \quad B_{kk} \doteq \frac{\partial^2 B}{\partial k^2}, \quad B_{kt} \doteq \frac{\partial^2 B}{\partial k \partial t}, \quad B_{tt} \doteq \frac{\partial^2 B}{\partial t^2}.$$

Since the firm's remaining control variable is the level of investment, b, the Hamilton–Jacobi–Bellman equation for the firm, as applied to (6.16), is given by (see appendix 6c)

$$rB - B_t = \max_{\substack{z,b \\ b \geq 0}} \{[f(z) - f'(z)z - x]k - qb - h(b)$$

$$+ B_k(k,t)[b - \mu k]\}. \tag{6.17}$$

Finding the optimal value of b in (6.17) and noting (6.1), we obtain the firm's behaviour in the following form (see appendix 6d):

$$\dot{k} = b - \mu k \quad \text{with}$$

$$b = \begin{cases} (h')^{-1}(B_k(k,t) - q), & \text{for } B_k > q + h'(0), \\ 0, & \text{for } B_k \leq q + h'(0), \end{cases} \tag{6.18}$$

where $(h')^{-1}$ is the inverse function of $h'(b)$.

6.5.3 The union

The union is the Stackelberg leader and takes the reactions of the firm, i.e. the accumulation of capital (6.18) and the condition $w = f'(z)$, into account when maximizing its utility. Its control instruments are the base wage w and the workers' share of capital income, x. However, because there is the one-to-one correspondence from (w, x) to (z, v) through (6.8) and (6.6), w and x can be replaced by the labour/capital ratio z and the total pay per employed worker, v, in the optimization and the inequalities (6.7) take the form of the constraints (6.13).

At any moment, the optimal value of the discounted stream of the union's objective function (6.11) is given by

$$G(k, t) \doteq \max_{\substack{z,v \\ \text{given } (6.13)}} \int_t^\infty u(v)zke^{-\rho(\tau - t)}d\tau.$$

We denote, for convenience, the partial derivatives of G as

$$G_k \doteq \partial G/\partial k, \quad G_t \doteq \partial G/\partial t, \quad G_{kk} \doteq \partial^2 G/\partial k^2,$$

$$G_{kt} \doteq \partial^2 G/\partial k\partial t, \quad G_{tt} \doteq \partial^2 G/\partial t^2.$$

Since the union's control variables are v and z, the Hamilton–Jacobi–Bellman equation for the union's optimization problem is given by (see appendix 6c)

$$\rho G - G_t = \max_{\substack{z,v \\ \text{given } (6.13)}} \{u(v)zk + G_k[b(B_k - q) - \mu k]\}. \tag{6.19}$$

Finding the optimal values for z and v, we obtain the following result (see appendix 6e):

Proposition 6.3: In the absence of credible contracts, the union deprives the firm of all profits, $x = f - f'z$, and the labour/capital ratio z and the total pay per employed worker v are constants and determined by the system

$$v = f' + u/u', \quad f = zv. \tag{6.20}$$

6.5.4 The evolution of the system

Since the union takes all profit (see proposition 6.3) and since the union's optimal control variables do not depend directly on the capital stock, then by making a proper substitution, the Hamilton–Jacobi–Bellman equations (6.17) and (6.19) as well as the accumulation of capital, (6.18), can be transformed into the form (see appendix 6f)

$$b = 0, \quad \dot{k} = -\mu k < 0, \quad \dot{\gamma} = (\rho + \mu)\gamma - u(v)z. \tag{6.21}$$

The system (6.20) and (6.21) is a special case of the system (6.12), (6.14) and (6.15) with the condition that there is no investment and no profit for the firm, $b = 0$ and $f(z) = zv$: both systems have the same variables v, z, γ and k. Consequently, the system (6.20) and (6.21) produces a development pattern which in the system (6.12), (6.14) and (6.15) corresponds to that of category II, having no growth and no profit. This leads to the following result:

Proposition 6.4: In the absence of credible contracts, the dynamic game produces a steady state which has no profit for the firm, $f(z) = zv$, and which is similar to some steady state of category II in the presence of credible contracts.

Propositions 6.3 and 6.4 can together be explained as follows. If there are no credible contracts, then whatever the union does, the firm expects it in the end to cheat and to take all the benefits of investment. Consequently, the firm loses its incentive to invest. Since the union observes that its behaviour has no effect on investment and future employment, it finds it optimal to maximize current labour income by taking all profits.

6.6 The formation of reputation

In this section, we compare the cases of credible and non-credible contracts, which are presented in sections 6.4 and 6.5, and attempt to find out exactly when the credibility of contracts is a Pareto improvement so that both parties will benefit from it. Then there is a reputational equilibrium. We focus on the case where in the presence of credible contracts, the union leaves some profit for the owners of the firm, i.e. where the union prefers steady state I to any steady state of category II. Otherwise, there would be no investment and the problem of credibility would be trivial.

Since, by proposition 6.3, the firm has some profit in the presence but no profit at all in the absence of credible contracts, it is happy with credible contracts. On the other hand, if capital stock behaves in a stable manner, then by proposition 6.2, the union prefers steady state I to any steady state of category II. Because, by proposition 6.4, the steady state without credible contracts is similar to some steady state of category II with credible contracts, then it is obvious that the union is also happy with credible contracts. So our final result is obtained as follows:

Proposition 6.5: If capital stock shows stable behaviour, then there must be a stable reputational equilibrium.

6.7 Conclusions

This chapter examined an economy with the following properties. First, because of adjustment costs in investment, decisions concerning investment and labour cost are interrelated. Second, the union is the Stackelberg leader setting the pay parameters alone, while the firm is the follower setting unilaterally the levels of employment and investment. It was shown that when the union's control instruments are not restricted just to the base wage, the pay contracts are credible for an economy with a stable capital stock. This result can be intuitively explained as follows.

A monopoly union able to use two-part pay schemes has the power of taking all the profit of the firm whenever it has the incentive to do so. On the other hand, if the firm is left with too small a profit, then it loses all incentives to invest. In this environment, the union has two alternative strategies.

The first strategy for the union is to renege on promises on the pay parameters. In such a case, the firm assumes that the union will always renege. Consequently, the firm dare not invest and the union cannot boost investment by leaving some profit for the firm. The second strategy is to keep the promises. In such a case, the firm makes its investment plans on the basis of the promised pay parameters and converges to some positive capital stock. Consequently, the union observes that a higher profit leads to higher investment and so by leaving some profit for the firm, it ensures higher employment and higher income for its members in future. Since the union is better off with the latter strategy, it has an incentive to maintain its reputation and the contracts are credible.

The outcome of bargaining turns out to be very sensitive to institutional specification. In particular, the credibility of contracts depends critically on the union's possibility of taking all the profits. Assume that the authorities could fix the workers' profit share equal to zero. Then the union could not punish the firm that does not invest enough to maintain the credibility of the pay contracts. In such a case, the parties to bargaining may well end up with non-credible contracts. It is, however, impossible for the authorities to abolish two-part wage schemes altogether, for these can also take some other form than open profit-sharing. For instance, it would be equivalent to profit-sharing to bargain on both the wage and the level of employment and to employ labour over and above the level at which the marginal product of labour is equal to the total pay per employed worker.[7] It follows that at least the monopoly unions are able

---

[7] For this, see, for example, section 2.5 above.

to punish the firm for too little investment and the contracts made with them tend to be credible.

Finally, the results in this and the preceding chapter suggest that it can be a mistake to assume *a priori* that only the base wage is used as an instrument of bargaining. Although much caution must be exercised when a highly stylized mathematical model is used to explain wage-setting, the following conclusion seems nevertheless to be justified. In a model of collective bargaining, a two-wage scheme should be the starting point. Then the possible absence of profit-sharing should be explained by institutional features that are incorporated into the model itself, i.e. one should present the microfoundations of such behaviour.

Appendix 6a. *The proof of results* (6.12)

The firm maximizes (6.10) subject to (6.1), by the choice of (z, b). The Hamiltonian and Lagrangean of this problem are

$$H = [f(z) - wz - x]k - qb - h(b) + \lambda[b - \mu k], \quad L = H + \delta b,$$

$$(6a.1)$$

where λ is the co-state variable evolving according to[8]

$$\dot{\lambda} \doteq d\lambda/dt = r\lambda - \partial H/\partial k$$

$$= (r + \mu)\lambda + x + wz - f(z), \lim_{t \to \infty} \lambda k e^{-rt} = 0, \quad (6a.2)$$

and the multiplier δ satisfies the Kuhn–Tucker conditions

$$\delta b = 0, \quad \delta \geq 0. \quad (6a.3)$$

The maximization of the Lagrangean L in (6a.1) at each moment of time by the choice of b leads to the first-order condition

$$\partial L/\partial b = \lambda - q - h'(b) + \delta = 0. \quad (6a.4)$$

Given (6.2), (6a.3) and (6a.4), it must be the case that

$$h'(0) + q < h'(b) + q = \lambda \text{ for } b > 0 \text{ and}$$

$$h'(0) + q - \lambda = \delta \geq 0 \text{ and } h'(0) + q \geq \lambda \text{ for } b = 0.$$

From this, (6.2) and the differentiation of the relation $h'(b) + q = \lambda$ with respect to b and λ, we obtain

---

[8] The irreversibility constraint $b \geq 0$ is independent of k.

$$b = \begin{cases} \tilde{b}(\lambda - q), & \tilde{b}' = 1/h'' > 0, & \text{for } \lambda > q + h'(0), \\ 0, & & \text{for } \lambda \leq q + h'(0). \end{cases} \tag{6a.5}$$

Given the strict concavity of the production function $f(z)$ and the strict convexity of the adjustment cost function $h(b)$, the Hamiltonian H is concave in z and b. This means that the necessary conditions (6a.2) and (6a.4) are at the same time sufficient conditions. The solution of λ satisfying these conditions is the following: the initial value $\lambda(0)$ is chosen so that at the given wage w, $\dot{\lambda} = 0$, and λ is constant over the planning period $[0, \infty)$. Given the conditions $\dot{\lambda} = 0$, (6.8) and (6a.2), we see that the co-state variable λ is the unit value of capital:

$$\lambda = [f(z) - wz - x]/(r + \mu) = [f(z) - zv]/(r + \mu). \tag{6a.6}$$

Finally, substituting (6a.6) into the function $\tilde{b}$ in (6a.5), we can define the function g as follows:

$$b = g(f(z) - zv) \doteq \begin{cases} \tilde{b}([f(z) - zv]/(r + \mu) - q) > 0 \\ \qquad \text{for } f(z) - zv > (r + \mu)[q + h'(0)], \\ 0 \qquad \text{for } f(z) - zv \leq (r + \mu)[q + h'(0)]. \end{cases} \tag{6a.7}$$

This function has the property

$$\begin{aligned} g' &\doteq dg/d(f - zv) \\ &= \begin{cases} b'/(r + \mu) > 0 & \text{for } f(z) - zv > (r + \mu)[q + h'(0)], \\ 0 & \text{for } f(z) - zv \leq (r + \mu)[q + h'(0)]. \end{cases} \end{aligned} \tag{6a.8}$$

Substituting relations (6a.7) and (6a.8) into equation (6.1) yields (6.12).

Appendix 6b. *The proof of proposition 6.1*

The Hamiltonian H^U and Lagrangean Φ for the union's problem are given by

$$H^U = u(v)zk + \gamma[g(f(z) - zv) - \mu k], \tag{6b.1}$$

$$\Phi = H^U + \theta[v - f'(z)] + \xi[f(z) - zv],$$

where γ is the co-state variable that evolves according to

$$\dot{\gamma} = \rho\gamma - \partial\Phi/\partial k = (\rho + \mu)\gamma - u(v)z, \quad \lim_{t\to\infty} \gamma k e^{-\rho t} = 0, \quad (6b.2)$$

and the multipliers θ and ξ satisfy the Kuhn–Tucker conditions

$$\theta[v - f'(z)] = 0, \quad \theta \geq 0, \quad \xi[f(z) - zv] = 0, \quad \xi \geq 0. \quad (6b.3)$$

Noting (6.12), the maximization of the Lagrangean Φ at each moment of time leads to the first-order conditions

$$\partial\Phi/\partial v = u'zk + \theta - \gamma g'z - \xi z = 0, \quad (6b.4)$$

$$\partial\Phi/\partial z = (f' - v)(\gamma g' + \xi) - \theta f'' + uk = 0. \quad (6b.5)$$

Given the strict concavity of both the utility function u and the production function f, the Hamiltonian H^U in (6b.1) is strictly concave in (v, z) and the necessary conditions (6.12) and (6b.3)–(6b.5) are at the same time sufficient conditions.

Assume $\theta > 0$. Then conditions $f'' < 0$, (6b.3) and (6b.5) yield $v = f'(z)$, $\xi = 0$ and

$$0 = \partial\Phi/\partial z = uk - \theta f'' > 0,$$

which is impossible. So it must be the case that $\theta = 0$, and conditions (6b.4) and (6b.5) take the form

$$u'k - \gamma g' = \xi \geq 0, \quad uk = (v - f')(\gamma g' + \xi) = (v - f')u'k. \quad (6b.6)$$

Given (6b.3) and the left-hand equation in (6b.6), we obtain $\xi = 0$ and $u'k = \gamma g'$ for $f > zv$. This proves the right-hand condition in (6.14). The right-hand equation in (6b.6) implies $u = (v - f')u'$ and the left-hand equation in (6.14). Finally, from (6.9), (6.12), (6b.3) and the left-hand equation in (6b.6) it follows that

$$\gamma = (ku' + \xi)/g' \geq ku'/g' > 0 \quad \text{for} \quad f > zv. \quad (6b.7)$$

From (6b.2) and (6b.7) we obtain conditions (6.15).

Now assume that the control variables z and v are chosen optimally. Then $\dot{k}$ and $\dot{\gamma}$ are functions of k and γ only and we can solve the roots of the system a_1 and a_2 (i.e. the two values of a) from the characteristic equation[9]

$$\begin{vmatrix} \partial\dot{k}/\partial k - a & \partial\dot{k}/\partial\gamma \\ \partial\dot{\gamma}/\partial k & \partial\dot{\gamma}/\partial\gamma - a \end{vmatrix} = 0.$$

By (6b.1) and (6b.2), we obtain $\partial\Phi/\partial\gamma = b = \dot{k}$, and

---

[9] See, for example, Kamien and Schwartz (1985), pp. 306–11.

$$\partial^2 \Phi / (\partial \gamma \partial k) = \partial \dot{k} / \partial k, \quad \partial \dot{\gamma} / \partial \gamma = \rho - \partial^2 \Phi / (\partial \gamma \partial k) = \rho - \partial \dot{k} / \partial k.$$

Now since

$$\partial \dot{\gamma} / \partial \gamma + \partial \dot{k} / \partial k = \rho,$$

the sum of the two roots is positive and there are two possibilities. First, there can be

$$(\partial \dot{k} / \partial k) \partial \dot{\gamma} / \partial \gamma < (\partial \dot{k} / \partial \gamma) \partial \dot{\gamma} / \partial k, \tag{6b.8}$$

in which case there exists one stable and one unstable root and a saddle-point solution. Then, according to the solution from control theory, the co-state variable γ jumps onto the saddle path that leads to the equilibrium and capital stock k shows a stable adjustment towards its equilibrium value. Otherwise, when (6b.8) does not hold, there are two unstable roots and the system is globally unstable. Then capital stock k shows unstable behaviour, moving away indefinitely from its equilibrium.

Appendix 6c. *Optimization with autonomous systems*

An infinite-horizon autonomous problem is given by

$$\max_{u(t)} \int_0^\infty e^{-rt} f(x(t), u(t)) dt, \quad \text{subject to } \dot{x}(t) = g(x(t), u(t)),$$

$$\tag{6c.1}$$

where x is the vector of state variables and u the vector of control variables. Now we define the value function

$$J(t, x(t)) \doteq \max_{u(\tau)} \int_t^\infty e^{-r\tau} f(x(\tau), u(\tau)) d\tau$$

$$= e^{-rt} \max_{u(\tau)} \int_t^\infty e^{-r(\tau - t)} f(x(\tau), u(\tau)) d\tau.$$

Furthermore, defining

$$V(t, x(t)) \doteq \max_{u(\tau)} \int_t^\infty e^{-r(\tau - t)} f(x(\tau), u(\tau)) d\tau,$$

we obtain

$$J(t, x(t)) = e^{-rt} V(t, x(t)),$$

$$\partial J / \partial t = e^{-rt} \partial V / \partial t - r e^{-rt} V, \quad \partial J / \partial x = e^{-rt} \partial V / \partial x. \tag{6c.2}$$

The normal form of the Hamilton–Jacobi–Bellman equation is the following (see, for example, Kamien and Schwartz (1985), part II, sect. 20):

$$\partial J/\partial t + \max_u [e^{-rt}f + g\,\partial J/\partial x] = 0. \tag{6c.3}$$

Substituting (6c.2) into (6c.3), the Hamilton–Jacobi–Bellman equation for the autonomous problem (6c.1) becomes

$$rV(t,x) - \frac{\partial V}{\partial t}(t,x) = \max_{u(t)}\left[f(x(t),u(t)) + \frac{\partial V}{\partial x}(t,x)g(x(t),u(t))\right].$$

Appendix 6d.   *The proof of results* (6.18)

The equilibrium value of b is obtained by the maximization of the term between braces in (6.17) subject to constraint $b \geq 0$. This leads to the Lagrangean

$$\Psi = [f(z) - f'(z)z - x]k - qb - h(b) + B_k(k,t)[b - \mu k] + \chi b,$$

where the multiplier χ satisfies the Kuhn–Tucker conditions

$$\chi b = 0, \quad \chi \geq 0. \tag{6d.1}$$

This yields the first-order condition

$$\chi + B_k = q + h'(b). \tag{6d.2}$$

Assume first that $b > 0$. Now given $h'' > 0$ in (6.2), (6d.1) and (6d.2), we obtain $\chi = 0$ and

$$B_k = q + h'(b) > q + h'(0), \quad b = (h')^{-1}(B_k - q),$$

where $(h')^{-1}$ is the inverse function of h'. Now assume $b = 0$. Then, given (6d.1) and (6d.2), we obtain

$$B_k = q + h'(b) - \chi \leq q + h'(b) = q + h'(0).$$

These results lead to (6.18).

Appendix 6e.   *The proof of proposition* 6.3

The equilibrium values for z and v are obtained by the maximization of the terms between braces in (6.19) subject to (6.13). The Lagrangean for this maximization is given by

$$\mathcal{L} = u(v)zk + G_k(k,t)[b(B_k(k,t) - q) - \mu k]$$
$$+ \eta[v - f'(z)] + \varepsilon[f(z) - zv],$$

where the multipliers η and ε satisfy the Kuhn–Tucker conditions

$$\eta[v - f'(z)] = 0, \quad \eta \geq 0, \quad \varepsilon[f(z) - zv] = 0, \quad \varepsilon \geq 0. \tag{6e.1}$$

This maximization yields the first-order conditions (6e.1) and

$$\partial\mathcal{L}/\partial z = u(v)k - \eta f''(z) + \varepsilon[f'(z) - v] = 0,$$
$$\partial\mathcal{L}/\partial v = u'(v)zk + \eta - z\varepsilon = 0. \tag{6e.2}$$

Given $f > f'(z)$, (6e.1) and (6e.2), we obtain

$$\varepsilon = \eta/z + u'k > 0, \quad f = zv, \quad v = f/z > f', \quad \eta = 0,$$
$$u = u'[v - f'], \quad v = f' + u/u'. \tag{6e.3}$$

These relations lead to result (6.20). Finally, from (6e.3), (6.6) and (6.8) it follows that the union deprives the firm of all profit:

$$x = (v - w)z = f(z) - wz = f(z) - zf'(z).$$

Appendix 6f. *The derivation of equations* (6.21)

Given $x = f - zf'$ in proposition (6.20), the firm's Hamilton–Jacobi–Bellman equation (6.17) takes the form

$$rB - B_t = \max_{b \geq 0}[B_k(k,t)[b - \mu k] - qb - h(b)], \tag{6f.1}$$

where, by duality, the instrument for optimization, b, can be taken as being held constant. Differentiating equation (6f.1) with respect to k yields

$$rB_k(k,t) - B_{kt}(k,t) = B_{kk}(k,t)[b - \mu k] - \mu B_k(k,t). \tag{6f.2}$$

Trying solution $\lambda(t) \doteq B_k(k,t)$ for equation (6f.2), we obtain

$$B_{kk}(k,t) \equiv 0, \quad \dot{\lambda} = B_{kt}(k,t) = (r + \mu)\lambda.$$

This means that the equilibrium value of λ is $B_k(k,t) = \lambda \equiv 0$. Then given (6.18), we obtain the left-hand equation in (6.21):

$$B_k = 0 < q + h', \quad b = 0, \quad \dot{k} = -\mu k. \tag{6f.3}$$

Given (6f.3), the union's Hamilton–Jacobi–Bellman equation (6.19) takes the form

$$\rho G - G_t = \max_{z,v} \ \{u(v)zk - \mu k G_k\}, \tag{6f.4}$$
$$\text{given (6.13)}$$

where, by duality, the instruments for optimization, z and v, can be taken as being held constant. Differentiating equation (6f.4) with respect to k, we obtain

$$\rho G_k(k,t) - G_{kt}(k,t) = u(v)z - \mu[kG_{kk}(k,t) + G_k]. \tag{6f.5}$$

Trying solution $\gamma(t) \doteq G_k(k,t)$ for equation (6f.5), we obtain $G_{kk}(k,t) = 0$ and the right-hand equation in (6.21):

$$\dot{\gamma} = G_{kt}(k,t) = (\rho + \mu)\gamma - u(v)z.$$

7 Ordinary wages versus profit-sharing

7.1 Introduction

The results in the two preceding chapters suggest that if output prices are given for the union, then profit-sharing is always superior to ordinary wages. Now, relaxing the assumption that the union is a price-taker, this chapter tries to find out the reason why agreements on ordinary wages are still common in reality. Since efficient bargaining over both the wage and the level of employment is shown to be equivalent to profit-sharing,[1] we obtain simultaneously the explanation of why efficient bargaining is not so frequently used in the economy.

Hoel and Moene (1988) claimed that ordinary wages are dominant for the reason that the introduction of profit-sharing harms the interests of both parties by reducing investment. Their model was, however, based on the assumption that the decisions on investment are made strategically before those on the pay parameters, that is, they assume that the pay contracts are non-credible. Because the analysis in chapters 5 and 6 suggests that there is a stable reputational equilibrium, we dismiss Hoel and Moene's outcome and take credible contracts as the starting point.

Dobson (1997) claimed that in oligopolistic competition where each oligopolist faces a different union, the use of ordinary wages may be a likely outcome.[2] A strategic commitment by the parties in bargaining to avoid profit-sharing may benefit both of them: this entails higher wages which, by dampening competition in the product market, may increase the amount of surplus generated by the parties. Dobson's explanation is interesting but holds only for bargaining at the level of a single firm. This

---

[1] See subsection 2.5.3.
[2] As a matter of fact, Dobson (1997) compared efficient bargaining with right-to-manage bargaining on the base wage. Since, given the analysis in section 2.5, efficient bargaining is equivalent to right-to-manage bargaining with two instruments, we can say that Dobson compared profit-sharing with the use of ordinary wages.

chapter shows that product differentiation is a common cause of the use of ordinary wages even when collective bargaining is not firm-specific.

Using a model that was in many respects similar to that in chapter 6, Palokangas (1991a, 1992) showed that 'large' unions prefer profit-sharing while 'small' unions are satisfied with ordinary wages. A union controlling only a small section of the economy can ignore all macroeconomic effects of its wage policy. Consequently, this union has an incentive to raise its members' base wage relative to that for the others and to drop the workers' profit share down to zero to ensure future employment. On the other hand, a union operating at the level of the whole economy observes that its wage policy has a big impact on the price level, and that there is only a slim possibility of raising its real base wage relative to the others. Therefore, such a union prefers to claim a high profit share and to ensure future employment by setting a low basic wage. In this chapter, we extend the model of Palokangas (1991a, 1992) so that product differentiation also exists for intermediate products, and so that, in the differentiation of final goods, the Cobb–Douglas function is replaced by a CES function.

The plan of the study is as follows. We incorporate product differentiation, much in the same way as in section 2.6, into the continuous-time model with real investment that was presented in chapter 6. Section 7.2 constructs the basic model as well as the temporary equilibrium of the economy when the pay parameters and capital stock are given. In section 7.3, we specify how investment and the pay parameters are determined in collective bargaining. In 7.4, the roles of profit-sharing and the degree of centralization are considered more closely.

7.2 The model

7.2.1 The industries

Let there be a fixed number m of industries, which are subject to the same technology. Each of these industries produces a single commodity and faces a single union. The products $i = 1, \ldots, m$ of these industries form a composite product through the CES function

$$y = m \left[\frac{1}{m} \sum_{i=1}^{m} y_i^{1-1/\varepsilon} \right]^{\varepsilon/(\varepsilon-1)} \quad \text{for } \varepsilon > 0 \text{ and } \varepsilon \neq 1, \tag{7.1}$$

where ε is the elasticity of substitution, y the output of the composite good and y_i is the output of industry i. This composite good is used in both consumption and investment and its price p is chosen as the numeraire:

$p = 1$. Given the production function (7.1), the price p_i for product i must be equal to the marginal product of y_i being used as an input:

$$p_i(y_1, \ldots, y_m) = \partial y / \partial y_i = y^{1/\varepsilon}(my_i)^{-1/\varepsilon},$$

$$(y_i/p_i)\partial p_i/\partial y_i = (1/\varepsilon)[p_i y_i/y - 1]. \tag{7.2}$$

7.2.2 The intermediate goods

Let the firms buy intermediate products from each other. We specify that labour l_i and the composite product of all goods form an intermediate input Z_i according to the CES unit cost function

$$s(w_i) \doteq [(1/m)w_i^{1-\phi} + (1 - 1/m)\delta p^{1-\phi}]^{1/(1-\phi)}$$

$$= [(1/m)w_i^{1-\phi} + (1 - 1/m)\delta]^{1/(1-\phi)}, \quad \phi > 0, \quad \phi \neq 1, \tag{7.3}$$

where w_i is the wage for industry i, $p = 1$ the price for the composite product and ϕ is the elasticity of substitution between labour and the composite product. The unit cost function (7.3) has the following useful properties:

$$0 < \eta(w_i) \doteq s'(w_i)w_i/s(w_i) = 1/[1 + (m-1)\delta w_i^{\phi-1}] \leq 1,$$

$$w_i s''(w_i)/s'(w_i) = \phi[w_i s'(w_i)/s(w_i) - 1] = \phi[\eta(w_i) - 1], \tag{7.4}$$

where $\eta(w_i)$ is the expenditure share falling on labour.

7.2.3 Production

The production function is given by

$$y_i = F(k_i, Z_i), \quad \partial F/\partial Z_i > 0, \quad \partial^2 F/\partial Z_i^2 < 0,$$

where y_i is output, k_i the fully employed and non-depreciating capital stock, and Z_i is the composite input of labour and intermediate goods defined above. On the assumption that the function F is concave and thrice differentiable, and that it is subject to constant returns to scale, we obtain

$$y_i = f(z_i)k_i, \quad f(z_i) \doteq F(1, z_i), \quad f' > 0, \quad f'' < 0, \quad z_i \doteq Z_i/k_i. \tag{7.5}$$

With this technology, the elasticity of substitution between capital and other inputs, σ, is given by

$$\sigma(z_i) = \frac{F_1(1, z_i)F_2(1, z_i)}{F_{12}(1, z_i)F(1, z_i)} = \frac{[z_i f'(z_i) - f(z_i)]f'(z_i)}{z_i f''(z_i)f(z_i)}, \tag{7.6}$$

where the subscripts 1 and 2 denote the partial derivatives of F with respect to the first and second arguments. Relation (7.6) can be transformed into a more convenient form as follows:

$$f''(z_i) = [f'(z_i)/f(z_i) - 1/z_i]f'(z_i)/\sigma(z_i). \tag{7.7}$$

Noting the unit cost function (7.3) for the composite input Z_i as well as the definition of z_i in (7.5), labour input is given by

$$l_i = s'(w_i)Z_i = s'(w_i)z_i k_i \text{ for } i = 1, \ldots, m. \tag{7.8}$$

The total pay per employed worker v_i is the sum of the base wage w_i and the workers' profit share per employee, $x_i k_i / l_i$. Thus, given (7.8), we obtain

$$v_i = w_i + x_i k_i / l_i = w_i + x_i / [s'(w_i)z_i]. \tag{7.9}$$

7.2.4 Investment[3]

If t is time and b_i the level of investment in industry i, then the accumulation of capital in industry i is given by

$$\dot{k}_i \doteq dk/dt = b_i. \tag{7.10}$$

It is assumed, for simplicity, that capital does not depreciate.[4] Furthermore, we assume that $q + h(b_i)/b_i$ units of the numeraire good can be converted into one unit of investment, where q is the constant unit cost that corresponds to zero investment, and h is the convex and increasing adjustment cost function:

$$h(b_i), \quad h' > 0, \quad h'' > 0, \quad h(0) = 0. \tag{7.11}$$

In such a case, total investment costs in industry i are given by

$$qb_i + h(b_i). \tag{7.12}$$

7.3 Collective bargaining

7.3.1 The firms

We assume that in each industry i, the owner of a single firm takes the output price p_i and the pay parameters (w_i, x_i) as fixed. Noting the unit cost function (7.3) as well as the production function (7.5), the representative owner's income in industry i is determined by

---

[3] This subsection is constructed in much the same way as subsection 6.2.1.
[4] The extension to the case of exponential depreciation is possible but it would make the analysis of the steady state much more complicated.

$$\pi_i = p_i y_i - s(w_i)Z_i - x_i k_i - q b_i - h(b_i)$$
$$= [p_i f(z_i) - s(w_i)z_i - x_i]k_i - q b_i - h(b_i), \qquad (7.13)$$

where $p_i y_i$ is sales revenue, sZ_i the cost of labour and the intermediate inputs, $x_i k_i$ the worker's share of profit and $q b_i + h$ investment expenditure (7.12).

In the model of chapter 6, it was assumed that a union takes the interest rate as fixed. This assumption would be problematic here, because we are now considering the economy as a whole. If the number of unions is small (possibly just one), then each union is so large that it will internalize the determination of the interest rate rather than take the interest rate as being held constant. To avoid this problem, we assume here that in each industry i, the owners of the firms have the same intertemporal utility function

$$\Pi(\pi_i) = \int_0^\infty \pi_i e^{-rt} dt, \quad r > 0, \qquad (7.14)$$

where π_i is the owner's income and r is the constant rate of time preference. In this specification, the rate of time preference r acts as the interest rate in the model of chapter 6.

The owner of a firm in industry i maximizes his/her utility (7.14) by the choice of the labour/capital ratio z and the level of investment, b, taking into account that his/her revenue is determined by (7.13) and that capital is accumulated by (7.10). In appendix 7a, we obtain the following result:

Proposition 7.1: In each industry i, the owners' optimal behaviour is characterized by

$$p_i f' = s(w_i), \quad x_i = p_i[f - z_i f'] - r\lambda_i, \qquad (7.15)$$

$$\dot{k}_i = b_i = b(\lambda_i - q) \quad \text{with} \quad b' = 1/h'' > 0, \qquad (7.16)$$

$$w_i(z_1, \ldots, z_n, k_1, \ldots, k_n) \quad \text{with}$$

$$\partial w_i / \partial k_i = (p_i y_i / y - 1) w_i / [\varepsilon k_i \eta(w_i)] < 0,$$

$$\partial w_i / \partial z_i = \{(p_i y_i / y - 1) f'(z_i) / [\varepsilon f(z_i)]$$
$$+ [f'(z_i) / f(z_i) - 1/z_i] / \sigma(z_i)\} w_i / \eta(w_i) < 0, \qquad (7.17)$$

$$v_i(\lambda_i, z_1, \ldots, z_m, k_1, \ldots, k_m) \quad \text{with}$$

$$\partial v_i / \partial \lambda_i = -r / [s'(w_i) z_i] < 0,$$

$$\partial v_i / \partial k_i |_{v_i = w_i} = [f / (z_i f')] \partial w_i / \partial k_i,$$

$$\partial v_i / \partial z_i |_{v_i = w_i} = (p_i y_i / y - 1) w_i / [z_i \varepsilon \eta(w_i)], \qquad (7.18)$$

where λ_i is the value of a unit of capital in industry i, and f, f', f'' and σ are functions of z_i. If the condition $y_i = y/m$ holds, then functions w_i, v_i, $[k_i(\partial w_i/\partial k_i)]$, $[\partial w_i/\partial z_i]$, $[k_i(\partial v_i/\partial k_i)]$ and $[\partial v_i/\partial z_i]$ depend only on the input ratios $z_1, \ldots, z_n$.

7.3.2 The unions

In each industry i, the union sets the base wage w_i and the worker's profit income per unit of capital, x_i. The pay contracts are assumed to be credible. To obtain a differential game, we must somehow specify the strategic dependence of the unions. The simplest way to do this is to introduce a modification of Bertrand behaviour as follows: when the union in industry i is setting its pay parameters (w_i, x_i), it takes the real levels of the unit costs in the other industries,

$$s(w_j)/p_j \text{ for } j \neq i, \tag{7.19}$$

as being held constant. Any other specification for a union's strategy would lead to complications that are difficult to cope with.

Let all workers have the same preferences. Then, given (7.8), we obtain the utility for union i, U^i, as follows:

$$U^i = u(v_i)l_i = u(v_i)s'(w_i)z_ik_i, \quad u' > 0, \tag{7.20}$$

where $u(v_i)$ is a member's utility from being employed and v_i an employed worker's income in industry i. Because $u'(v_i)$ is a worker's marginal utility of income, the value of a new job in terms of income is given by the ratio u/u', and relative to a worker's income by the ratio

$$\beta(v_i) = u(v_i)/[u'(v_i)v_i]. \tag{7.21}$$

The higher $\beta(v_i)$, the more the union i prefers employment to total income. We assume that the workers cannot directly subsidize the firms. Noting (7.9), this constraint takes the form

$$v_i \geq w_i. \tag{7.22}$$

7.3.3 The solution of the dynamic game

The union in industry i maximizes its instantaneous utility (7.20) over time,

$$\int_0^\infty U^i e^{-\rho t} dt = \int_0^\infty u(v_i)s'(w_i)z_ik_ie^{-\rho t} dt, \tag{7.23}$$

where ρ is the union's rate of time preference, by the choice of the wage w_i and the workers' profit income per unit of capital, x_i. When doing this, it takes the price function (7.2), the accumulation of capital in the industry (7.10), the firm's behaviour and the inequality (7.22) as constraints, and the real unit costs of the other industries, (7.19), as fixed. Given this behaviour of the unions, we obtain a differential m-person game. Because there is perfect symmetry over the unions $i = 1, \ldots, m$ as well as over the products $i = 1, \ldots, m$, capital input k_i, the input ratio z_i, the level of output, y_i, the wage w_i, the total pay per employed worker, v_i, the level of investment, b_i, and the output price p_i must be the same for $i = 1, \ldots, m$:

$$k_i = k, \quad z_i = z, \quad y_i = y/m, \quad w_i = w, \quad v_i = v, \quad b_i = b, \quad p_i = p = 1.$$

Using this property, the differential game can be solved and in appendix 7b, we obtain the following result:

$$\Lambda\xi\theta = 1 + (1/\eta - 1)\phi[(1 - 1/m)f'z/f + (1/\sigma)(1 - f'z/f)]$$
$$+ (1/m - 1)/(\varepsilon\eta\beta) \quad \text{for } v = w, \tag{7.24}$$

$$(v - w)\theta = 0, \quad \theta \geq 0, \quad v \geq w, \tag{7.25}$$

where $\Lambda < 0, 0 < \eta \leq 1, f > f'z$ and

$$\xi \doteq (1/m - 1)/\varepsilon + 1/\sigma. \tag{7.26}$$

7.4 The choice of the regime

7.4.1 The setting

The inverse of the number of industries, $1/m$, can be used as a measure of the degree of centralization in collective bargaining. At one extreme, $m = 1$ and $1/m = 1$, collective bargaining is fully centralized, and at the other, $m \to \infty$ and $1/m \to 0$, it is fully decentralized. If $1/m$ is somewhere in the middle between zero and one, then one can say that collective bargaining is at a medium level of centralization. If relation (7.24) produces $\theta < 0$ for $v = w$, then given (7.25), profit-sharing, $v > w$, is the only possible outcome. In other words, to find the limits of the profit-sharing regime it is enough to show exactly when $\theta < 0$ holds, i.e. when the multiplier (7.26) and the right-hand side of equation (7.24) have the same sign.

7.4.2 Homogeneous final goods

Assume first that all final goods $i = 1, \ldots, m$ are perfect substitutes, i.e. that the elasticity of substitution in (7.1) is arbitrarily large: $\varepsilon \to \infty$ and $1/\varepsilon \to 0$. Now since $\xi = 1/\sigma > 0$ by (7.26) and

$$\Lambda \xi \theta = 1 + (1/\eta - 1)\phi[(1 - 1/m)f'/f + (1/\sigma)(1/z - f'/f)] > 0$$

by (7.24), we obtain $\theta < 0$ and our first result as follows:

Proposition 7.2: If there is no variation among the final goods, $\varepsilon \to \infty$, then there will be profit-sharing at all levels of centralization of collective bargaining.

Now we explain why variation among the final goods is necessary for the existence of the ordinary-wage regime. Assume first that for some unspecified reason, a union has refrained from using profit-sharing but has chosen the base wage optimally. Where all final goods are homogeneous, this union is a price-taker. In such a case, by marginally decreasing the wage w but by still holding the total pay per employed worker v constant, the union can increase the level of employment and the workers' welfare.

7.4.3 Heterogeneous final goods

Next, we relax the assumption that the outputs of the firms are perfect substitutes but assume for the moment that either $\phi = 0$ or $\eta = 1$ holds.[5] Now if either the degree of centralization in collective bargaining, $1/m$, is high enough for

$$1/m > 1 - \varepsilon \min [\eta\beta, 1/\sigma]$$

to hold, or if $1/m$ is low enough for

$$1/m < 1 - \varepsilon \max [\eta\beta, 1/\sigma]$$

to hold, then $\theta < 0$ and there is profit-sharing. This result can also be written in the following form:

Proposition 7.3: Assume that either there is no substitution between labour and the intermediate inputs, $\phi = 0$, or that there are no intermediate inputs, $\eta = 1$. Then the unions prefer ordinary wages within the regime

$$1 - \varepsilon \max [\eta\beta, 1/\sigma] < 1/m < 1 - \varepsilon \min [\eta\beta, 1/\sigma],$$

and switch to profit-sharing outside this regime.

[5] The case $\eta = 1$ is obtained if $\delta = 0$ in the cost function (7.3).

A precondition for a 'small' union with

$$0 < 1/m < 1 - \varepsilon \max [\eta\beta, 1/\sigma]$$

to prefer profit-sharing is that capital and the other inputs are close enough substitutes (i.e. σ is large enough) or that there is sufficiently small variation among the final goods (i.e. ε is small enough) for $\sigma > \varepsilon$ to hold. Then by decreasing the basic wage w and by holding the total pay per employed worker v constant, the union can increase employment and the workers' welfare. However, since the elasticity of substitution between capital and other inputs, σ, is commonly less than one, and the elasticity of substitution between final goods, ε, is commonly greater than one, it is very likely that $\sigma \leq \varepsilon$ holds and there is profit-sharing. Thus we have obtained the following corollary to proposition 7.3:

Proposition 7.4: Assume that either there is no substitution between labour and the intermediate inputs, $\phi = 0$, or that there are no intermediate inputs at all, $\eta = 1$. Furthermore, assume that the elasticity of substitution between capital and other inputs, σ, is smaller than or equal to the elasticity of substitution between the final goods, ε. Then the ordinary-wage regime is given by the condition that the share of the economy controlled by one union, $1/m$, plus the value of a job as a share of a worker's income, β, times the cost share of labour in production costs, η, times the elasticity of substitution between the final goods, ε, is less than one: $1/m + \beta\eta\varepsilon < 1$.

These results can be explained as follows. A union can increase its members' income in two ways: by *real wage rivalry*, in which case the union attempts to raise its members' basic real wage relative to the other workers; and by *rent extraction*, in which case the union attempts to take part of capital rent by profit-sharing. A small union $(1/m < 1 - \beta\eta\varepsilon)$ has an incentive to real wage rivalry, because it can ignore the effect of its wage policy on the price level of the economy. It raises the basic wage w_i and ensures high future capital stock and employment by dropping the workers' profit share ratio down to zero. If a union is large $(1/m > 1 - \beta\eta\varepsilon)$, its basic wage has a considerable effect on the price level and there is only a slight possibility of raising the basic real wage relative to the others. In such a case, the union prefers rent extraction: it raises the workers' profit share above zero and ensures high future employment by temporarily reducing the basic wage.

If the value of a new job relative to a worker's income, β, is high, then the union attempts to maintain high current employment by shifting the structure of labour cost from basic wages to profit shares. On the other hand, if the share of base wages in the unit cost of production, η, is high, or if the elasticity of substitution between the final goods, ε, is high, then the wage elasticity of employment is high and an increase in the base wage leads to a bigger fall in employment. For these reasons, high values for β, η and ε make profit-sharing more likely.

Note that in the analysis above, sluggish investment plays a crucial role. If there are no adjustment costs, firms can make arbitrarily large changes in capital stock at constant unit cost q. Then (with constant returns to scale, as assumed) the output price is driven down to the unit cost of output, which is calculated at the basic wage w. This means that in equilibrium there is no surplus to bargain over. If for some unspecified reason the price were above such a unit cost, then the surplus available to the firm and the union would be infinite. The introduction of adjustment costs means that although the output price is above the unit cost, the surplus being divided by the parties is finite and the equilibrium with profit-sharing is possible. Note also that *temporary* changes in the pay parameters can cause *permanent* changes in capital stock. This is because investment models with adjustment cost are generally (but not always) subject to hysteretic adjustment: initial values affect the steady state of the system.

7.4.4 The role of the intermediate products

In contrast to the preceding subsection, assume now that both $\phi > 0$ and $\eta < 1$ hold. We note first that the lower limit of the ordinary-wage regime in proposition 7.3, $1 - \varepsilon \max [\eta\beta, 1/\sigma]$, is the same. When the right-hand side of equation (7.24) with $\phi = 0$ or $\eta = 1$ is reduced from that with $\phi > 0$ and $\eta < 1$, we obtain the amount

$$\Delta \doteq (1/\eta - 1)\phi[(1 - 1/m)f'/f + (1/\sigma)(1/z - f'/f)] > 0.$$

This means that if $\sigma < 1/(\eta\beta)$ holds, the upper limit of the ordinary-wage regime in proposition 7.3, $1 - \varepsilon \min [\eta\beta, 1/\sigma]$, is now decreased to the level

$$1 - \varepsilon \min [(1 + \Delta)\eta\beta, 1/\sigma],$$

but if $\sigma \geq 1/(\eta\beta)$ holds, there is no change in the upper limit. The earlier results remain the same if the unions are small, $1/m \to 0$, or large, $1/m \to 1$. Thus we obtain our final finding as follows:

Proposition 7.5: The substitution between labour and intermediate inputs increases the likelihood of profit-sharing among the unions of medium size, but it has no effect on the behaviour of large or small unions.

As was explained above, the existence of real wage rivalry among the unions is the precondition for the existence of the ordinary-wage regime. Since the substitution between labour and intermediate inputs increases the wage elasticity of employment, it tends to reduce real wage rivalry. However, if the union is small enough so that it faces a low enough wage elasticity of employment, then the motive of real wage rivalry is so strong that it cannot be offset by any effect. On the other hand, if the union is large, then real wage rivalry is already offset by rent extraction. So only at the medium level of centralization of collective bargaining, where real wage rivalry just outweighs rent extraction, does even a small increase in the wage elasticity of employment cause a change to profit-sharing.

7.5 Conclusions

When ordinary wages prevail, there must be some economic reason why the labour market organizations choose the workers' profit share to be equal to zero. This chapter examined an economy where the final products are not perfect substitutes, and where the unions determine the pay parameters for their members. It was shown that profit-sharing agreements are possible and even likely for larger unions, but where collective bargaining is carried out at the level of small industries, then on the fairly general condition that capital and labour are not very close substitutes, a union prefers ordinary wages. This result can be explained as follows.

If there are no adjustment costs in investment – that is, if firms can make arbitrarily large changes in capital stock at constant unit cost – then (with constant returns to scale) output prices are driven down to the unit cost of output which is calculated at the base wage and there is no surplus to bargain over. In the case where there are adjustment costs in investment and some product differentiation among final goods, a union can increase its members' income in two ways: by raising its members' real basic wage relative to the other workers; and by extracting part of capital rent by profit-sharing.

When the union is small, the effect of its wage policy on the price level is insignificant. Therefore, it attempts to benefit at the expense of the other unions by raising the basic wage and it ensures high capital stock and high employment in future by reducing the sharing ratio down to zero. On the other hand, when the degree of centralization is high so that a union's basic wage considerably increases the price level, there is no incentive to rivalry with the other unions and rent extraction is chosen.

The existence of variation among the final goods is necessary for real wage rivalry where each union tries to increase its members' real wage relative to the others. When the final goods are more or less similar, a union takes the output prices as given and there is no economic reason why it should choose the workers' profit share to be equal to zero. To show this, assume that for some unspecified reason, a union has abstained from profit-sharing but chooses the base wage optimally. In such a case, by a small decrease in the base wage while holding the total pay per worker constant, the union can increase employment and its members' welfare.

Finally, it was shown that substitution between labour and intermediate products increases the likelihood of profit-sharing only among unions of medium size. Because substitution between labour and intermediate inputs increases the wage elasticity of employment, it tends to reduce the incentives of real wage rivalry among the unions and therefore to increase the likelihood of profit-sharing. At high levels of centralization, each union is big and rent extraction dominates, while at low levels of centralization, the unions are small and real wage rivalry dominates. Therefore only at the medium level of centralization, where the effect of real wage rivalry just offsets that of rent extraction, a small increase in the elasticity of substitution between labour and intermediate inputs is enough to produce a change from ordinary wages into profit-sharing.

Appendix 7a.   *The proof of proposition* 7.1

The Hamiltonian of the firm's problem is given by

$$H_i = [p_i f(z_i) - s(w_i)z_i - x_i]k_i - qb_i - h(b_i) + \lambda_i b_i,$$

where λ is the co-state variable evolving according to

$$\dot{\lambda}_i = r\lambda_i - \partial H_i/\partial k_i = r\lambda_i + x_i + s(w_i)z_i - p_i f(z_i),$$

$$\lim_{t\to\infty} \lambda_i k_i e^{-rt} = 0. \qquad (7a.1)$$

Given the other control variable z_i, the Hamiltonian H_i must be maximized at each moment of time by the choice of investment b_i and the input ratio z_i. This leads to the first-order conditions

$$\partial H_i/\partial b_i = \lambda_i - q - h'(b_i) = 0, \quad p_i f'(z_i) = s(w_i). \qquad (7a.2)$$

This gives the left-hand equation in (7.15). Taking the inverse function s^{-1} of s and noting the price function (7.2), we obtain, by solving the right-hand condition in (7a.2), the base wage w_i:

$$w_i(z_1,\ldots,z_m,k_1,\ldots,k_m) \doteq s^{-1}(p_i(f(z_1)k_1,\ldots,f(z_m)k_m)f'(z_i)). \qquad (7a.3)$$

With the Hamiltonian H_i being concave with respect to the firm's control variables z_i and b_i, the firm's equilibrium is unique.

The solution of λ_i satisfying the necessary (and sufficient) conditions (7a.1) and (7a.2) is the following: the initial value $\lambda_i(0)$ is chosen so that at given price p_i and wage w_i, λ_i is constant over the planning period $[0, \infty)$. Substituting $\dot{\lambda} = 0$ into (7a.1) yields the right-hand function in (7.15):

$$x_i = p_i[f(z_i) - z_i f'(z_i)] - r\lambda_i.$$

Furthermore, substituting this into (7.9), we obtain the total pay per worker v_i as follows:

$$v_i(z_1, \ldots, z_n, k_1, \ldots, k_n) = w_i + \frac{1}{s'(w_i)z_i}$$
$$\times \{p_i[f(z_i) - z_i f'(z_i)] - r\lambda_i\}. \quad (7a.4)$$

Now we derive the properties of the functions (7a.3) and (7a.4). Differentiating the left-hand equation (7a.2) and noting (7.11), we obtain the investment function (7.16). From (7.4) it follows that

$$s'(w_i) = \eta(w_i)s(w_i)/w_i. \quad (7a.5)$$

Using results (7.7) and (7a.5) as well as the properties of the price function (7.2) and production function (7.5), we obtain the partial derivatives of the wage function (7a.3) or (7.17):

$$\partial w_i/\partial k_i = (f'/s')(\partial p_i/\partial y_i)\partial y_i/\partial k_i = [sy_i/(p_i s' k_i)]\partial p_i/\partial y_i$$
$$= [w_i y_i/(\eta p_i k_i)]\partial p_i/\partial y_i = (p_i y_i/y - 1)w_i/(\varepsilon k_i \eta), \quad (7a.6)$$
$$\partial w_i/\partial z_i = [f'(\partial p_i/\partial y_i)\partial y_i/\partial z_i + p_i f'']/s'$$
$$= [(f')^2 k_i \partial p_i/\partial y_i + p_i f'']/s'$$
$$= [f'(f'/f)(y_i/p_i)\partial p_i/\partial y_i + f'']p_i/s'$$
$$= [(p_i y_i/y - 1)(f')^2/(\varepsilon f) + f'']p_i/s'$$
$$= [(p_i y_i/y - 1)f'/(\varepsilon f) + f''/f']p_i f'/s'$$
$$= [(p_i y_i/y - 1)f'/(\varepsilon f) + f''/f']s/s'$$
$$= [(p_i y_i/y - 1)f'/(\varepsilon f) + (f'/f - 1/z_i)/\sigma]s/s'$$
$$= [(p_i y_i/y - 1)f'/(\varepsilon f) + (f'/f - 1/z_i)/\sigma]w_i/\eta, \quad (7a.7)$$

where f, f', f'' and σ are functions of z_i, and s, s' and η functions of w_i. Using results (7.2), (7a.1), (7a.2), (7a.5), (7a.6) and (7a.7), we obtain the properties of the function (7a.4):

$$\partial v_i/\partial \lambda_i = -r/(s'z_i) < 0, \tag{7a.8}$$

$$
\begin{aligned}
\partial v_i/\partial k_i &= \partial w_i/\partial k_i - [s''(s')^{-2}/z_i][(f - z_i f')p_i - r\lambda_i]\partial w_i/\partial k_i \\
&\quad + [(f - z_i f')/(s'z_i)](\partial p_i/\partial y_i)\partial y_i/\partial k_i \\
&= \partial w_i/\partial k_i - (s''/s')(v_i - w_i)\partial w_i/\partial k_i \\
&\quad + [(f - z_i f')/(s'z_i)](\partial p_i/\partial y_i)\partial y_i/\partial k_i \\
&= \partial w_i/\partial k_i - (s''/s')(v_i - w_i)\partial w_i/\partial k_i \\
&\quad + [(f - z_i f')/(z_i f')]\partial w_i/\partial k_i \\
&= [(w_i - v_i)s''/s' + f/(z_i f')]\partial w_i/\partial k_i, \tag{7a.9}
\end{aligned}
$$

$$
\begin{aligned}
\partial v_i/\partial z_i &= \partial w_i/\partial z_i - [s''(s')^{-2}/z_i][(f - z_i f')p_i - r\lambda_i]\partial w_i/\partial z_i \\
&\quad + [(f - z_i f')/(s'z_i)](\partial p_i/\partial y_i)\partial y_i/\partial z_i \\
&\quad - [(f - z_i f')p_i - r\lambda_i]/(s'z_i^2) - p_i f''/s' \\
&= \partial w_i/\partial z_i - [s''/(s'z_i)](v_i - w_i)\partial w_i/\partial z_i \\
&\quad + [(f - z_i f')/(s'z_i)](\partial p_i/\partial y_i)\partial y_i/\partial z_i \\
&\quad - (v_i - w_i)/z_i - p_i f''/s' \\
&= \partial w_i/\partial z_i - [s''/(s'z_i)](v_i - w_i)\partial w_i/\partial z_i \\
&\quad + [(f - z_i f')/(z_i f')][\partial w_i/\partial z_i - p_i f''/s'] \\
&\quad - (v_i - w_i)/z_i - p_i f''/s' \\
&= [s''(s'z_i)](w_i - v_i)\partial w_i/\partial z_i \\
&\quad + [f/(z_i f')][\partial w_i/\partial z_i - p_i f''/s'] + (w_i - v_i)/z_i, \tag{7a.10}
\end{aligned}
$$

where f, f', f'' and σ are functions of z_i, and s, s', s'' and η functions of w_i. Setting $v_i = w_i$ for (7a.9) and (7a.10) and noting (7.7) and (7a.7), we obtain properties of the function (7.18):

$$\partial v_i/\partial k_i|_{v_i=w_i} = [f/(z_i f')]\partial w_i/\partial k_i,$$

$$
\begin{aligned}
\partial v_i/\partial z_i|_{v_i=w_i} &= [f/(z_i f')][\partial w_i/\partial z_i - p_i f''/s'] \\
&= [f/(z_i f')](p_i y_i/y - 1)(f')^2 p_i/(\varepsilon f s') \\
&= (p_i y_i/y - 1)f' p_i/(z_i \varepsilon s') = (p_i y_i/y - 1)s/(z_i \varepsilon s') \\
&= (p_i y_i/y - 1)w_i/(z_i \varepsilon \eta).
\end{aligned}
$$

Therefore, noting relations (7.2), (7a.4), (7a.6), (7a.7), (7a.9) and (7a.10), we obtain properties

$$p_i|_{y_i=y/m} = 1, \quad \partial p_i/\partial y_i|_{y_i=y/m} = (1/m - 1)/\varepsilon,$$

$$w_i|_{y_i=y/m} = s^{-1}(f'),$$

$$v_i|_{y_i=y/m} = w_i + [f - z_i f' - r\lambda_i]/[s'(w_i)z_i],$$

$$[k_i \partial w_i/\partial k_i]_{y_i=y/m} = (1/m - 1)w_i/[\varepsilon\eta(w_i)],$$

$$[\partial w_i/\partial z_i]_{y_i=y/m} = [(1/m - 1)f'/(\varepsilon f) + (f'/f - 1/z_i)/\sigma]$$
$$\times [w_i/\eta(w_i)],$$

$$[k_i \partial v_i/\partial k_i]_{y_i=y/m} = [(w_i - v_i)s''(w_i)/s'(w_i) + f/(z_i f')]$$
$$\times [k_i \partial w_i/\partial k_i]_{y_i=y/m},$$

$$[\partial v_i/\partial z_i]_{y_i=y/m} = \{s''(w_i)/[s'(w_i)z_i]\}\{w_i - v_i + f/(z_i f')\}$$
$$\times [\partial w_i/\partial z_i]_{y_i=y/m}$$
$$- ff''/[z_i f's'(w_i)] + (w_i - v_i)/z_i,$$

where f, f' and f'' and σ are functions of z_i only. We see that when $y_i = y/m$, the functions w_i, v_i, $[k_i(\partial w_i/\partial k_i)]$, $[\partial w_i/\partial z_i]$, $[k_i(\partial v_i/\partial k_i)]$ and $[\partial w_i/\partial z_i]$ are all independent of the capital stocks of the industries, $k_1, \ldots, k_n$.

Appendix 7b. *The proof of results (7.24) and (7.25)*

Since, given (7.9), (7.17) and (7.18), there is one-to-one correspondence from (w_i, x_i) to (z_i, λ_i), we may substitute, in the optimization, the latter for the former as the instrument for union i. Furthermore, $s(w_j)/p_j = f'(z_j)$ from (7.15), so that since union i takes (7.19) as fixed, it takes the labour/capital ratios z_j $(j \neq i)$ as fixed as well. We conclude that the union's problem is to maximize (7.23) subject to the price function (7.2), the accumulation of capital in the industry (7.10), the firm's investment function (7.16) and the constraints (7.22), by the choice of the input ratio z_i and the unit value of capital, λ_i, taking the input ratios in the other industries, z_j for $j \neq i$, as fixed.

The Hamiltonian of the problem of union i is given by

$$H_i^U = u(v_i)s'(w_i)z_i k_i + \gamma_i b(\lambda_i - q), \tag{7b.1}$$

and the Lagrangean by

$$\Phi^i = H_i^U + \theta_i[v_i - w_i], \tag{7b.2}$$

where the functions v_i and w_i are defined by (7.17) and (7.18), γ_i is a co-state variable evolving according to

$$
\begin{aligned}
\dot{\gamma}_i &= \rho\gamma_i - \partial\Phi^i/\partial k_i = \rho\gamma_i - \partial H_i^U/\partial k_i + \theta_i[\partial w_i/\partial k_i - \partial v_i/\partial k_i] \\
&= \rho\gamma_i - u'(v_i)s'(w_i)z_ik_i\partial v_i/\partial k_i \\
&\quad - u(v_i)[s'(w_i) + k_is''(w_i)\partial w_i/\partial k_i]z_i \\
&\quad + \theta_i[\partial w_i/\partial k_i - \partial v_i/\partial k_i], \quad \lim_{t\to 0}\gamma_ik_ie^{-\rho t} = 0,
\end{aligned}
\tag{7b.3}
$$

and where θ_i is a multiplier satisfying the Kuhn–Tucker conditions

$$\theta_i[v_i - w_i] = 0, \quad \theta_i \geq 0. \tag{7b.4}$$

At each moment, the Lagrangean (7b.2) is maximized by the choice of the union's control variables (z_i, λ_i) and the multiplier θ_i. Given (7.4) and $\partial v_i/\partial\lambda_i$ in (7.18), this leads to the first-order conditions (7b.4) and

$$
\begin{aligned}
(1/k_i)\partial\Phi^i/\partial\lambda_i &= (1/k_i)\partial H_i^U/\partial\lambda_i + (\theta_i/k_i)\partial v_i/\partial\lambda_i \\
&= [u'(v_i)s'z_i + \theta_i/k_i]\partial v_i/\partial\lambda_i + b'(\lambda_i - q)\gamma_i/k_i \\
&= b'(\lambda_i - q)\gamma_i/k_i - r[u'(v_i) + \theta_i/(k_is'z_i)] \\
&= 0,
\end{aligned}
\tag{7b.5}
$$

$$
\begin{aligned}
(1/k_i)\partial\Phi^i/\partial z_i &= (1/k_i)\partial H_i^U/\partial z_i + (\theta_i/k_i)[\partial v_i/\partial z_i - \partial w_i/\partial z_i] \\
&= u(v_i)[s' + z_is''\partial w_i/\partial z_i] + u'(v_i)s'z_i\partial v_i/\partial z_i \\
&\quad + (\theta_i/k_i)[\partial v_i/\partial z_i - \partial w_i/\partial z_i] \\
&= u(v_i)s'[1 + (s''/s')z_i\partial w_i/\partial z_i] + u'(v_i)s'z_i\partial v_i/\partial z_i \\
&\quad + (\theta_i/k_i)[\partial v_i/\partial z_i - \partial w_i/\partial z_i] \\
&= s'u(v_i)\{1 + \phi(z_i)[(\eta - 1)/w_i]\partial w_i/\partial z_i\} \\
&\quad + u'(v_i)s'z_i\partial v_i/\partial z_i + (\theta_i/k_i)[\partial v_i/\partial z_i - \partial w_i/\partial z_i] \\
&= 0,
\end{aligned}
\tag{7b.6}
$$

where s, s', s'' and η are functions of w_i. If H_i^U is concave in (λ_i, z_i) for all $i = 1, \ldots, m$, the necessary conditions (7.10), (7.22) and (7b.3)–(7b.6) are at the same time sufficient conditions for all $i = 1, \ldots, m$. Then there exists a unique equilibrium where (7.10), (7.22) and (7b.3)–(7b.6) hold for all $i = 1, \ldots, m$.

From (7b.1)–(7b.6) and (7.16) it follows that

$$\partial \Phi^i / \partial \gamma_i |_{(z_i, \lambda_i, \theta_i) = (z_i^*, \lambda_i^*, \theta_i^*)} = b_i = \dot{k}_i,$$

and

$$\partial \dot{\gamma}_i / \partial \gamma_i |_{(z_i, \lambda_i, \theta_i) = (z_i^*, \lambda_i^*, \theta_i^*)} = \rho - \partial^2 \Phi^i / \partial \gamma_i \partial k_i |_{(z_i, \lambda_i, \theta_i) = (z_i^*, \lambda_i^*, \theta_i^*)}$$

$$= \rho - \frac{\partial \dot{k}_i}{\partial k_i} |_{(z_i, \lambda_i, \theta_i) = (z_i^*, \lambda_i^*, \theta_i^*)}, \tag{7b.7}$$

where $(z_i^*, \lambda_i^*, \theta_i^*)$ is the value of $(z_i, \lambda_i, \theta_i)$ that satisfies conditions (7b.4), (7b.5) and (7b.6). It is assumed that initially capital stock is equal for all industries, i.e. that $k_i(0) = k(0)$ for all $i = 1, \ldots, m$. Since the structure of the model is otherwise such that there exists perfect symmetry over $i = 1, \ldots, m$, given (7.1), (7.2), we obtain

$$k_i = k, \quad z_i = z, \quad y_i = y/m, \quad w_i = w, \quad v_i = v,$$

$$b_i = b, \quad \lambda_i = \lambda, \quad \theta_i = \theta, \quad \gamma_i = \gamma, \quad p_i = 1. \tag{7b.8}$$

Now we reduce the original system of $2m$ differential equations into a system of only two differential equations: substituting (7b.8) into (7.16), (7b.3), (7b.4), (7b.5), (7b.6) and (7b.7), we obtain

$$\dot{k} = b(\lambda - q), \tag{7b.9}$$

$$\dot{\gamma} = \rho \gamma - u'(v) s' z [k_i \partial v_i / \partial k_i] - zu(v) \{ s' + s'' [k_i \partial v_i / \partial k_i] \} + (\theta/k)$$

$$\times \{ [k_i \partial w_i / \partial k_i] - [k_i \partial v_i / \partial k_i] \}, \quad \lim_{t \to \infty} \gamma k e^{-\rho t} = 0, \tag{7b.10}$$

$$b' \gamma / k - r[\theta / (ks'z) + u'(v)] = 0, \tag{7b.11}$$

$$s' u(v)[1 + (\eta - 1)(\phi z / w) \partial w_i / \partial z_i]$$

$$+ u'(v) s' z \partial v_i / \partial z_i + (\theta/k)[\partial v_i / \partial z_i - \partial w_i / \partial z_i] = 0, \tag{7b.12}$$

$$(v - w)\theta / k = 0, \quad \theta/k \geq 0, \tag{7b.13}$$

for which

$$\partial \dot{k} / \partial k + \partial \dot{\gamma} / \partial \gamma = \rho > 0. \tag{7b.14}$$

In the system (7b.9)–(7b.13), there exists one state variable k, one co-state variable γ and three endogenous variables λ, z and θ/k. Given proposition 7.1, the functions v, w, b, η, σ, s, s', s'', $\partial w_i / \partial z_i$, $\partial v_i / \partial z_i$, $[k_i(\partial w_i / \partial z_i)]$ and $[k_i(\partial v_i / \partial z_i)]$ are all dependent on λ, z, θ/k and γ/k but independent of k or γ directly. This means that after the endogenous variables λ, z and θ/k are solved from equations (7b.11)–(7b.13) and substituted into the differential equations (7b.9) and (7b.10), we obtain $\dot{k}$ and $\dot{\gamma}$ as functions of k and γ. Given this and (7b.14), there are two possibilities: if

$$(\partial\dot{k}/\partial k)\partial\dot{\gamma}/\partial\gamma < (\partial\dot{k}/\partial\gamma)\partial\dot{\gamma}/\partial k$$

holds, then there exists a saddle-point solution, but otherwise the system is globally unstable. This means that if the system has a stable equilibrium, then the adjustment towards this equilibrium is unique.

Substituting the partial derivatives $\partial w_i/\partial z_i$ and $\partial v_i/\partial z_i$ from proposition 7.1 into condition (7b.12), requiring symmetry $w_i = w = v = v_i$, $y_i = y/m$ and $p_i = 1$, and dividing by $s'u$ yield

$$0 = 1 + (\eta - 1)(z/w)\phi\partial w_i/\partial z_i + (u'/u)z\partial v_i/\partial z_i$$

$$+ (s'uk)^{-1}\theta[\partial v_i/\partial z_i - \partial w_i/\partial z_i]$$

$$= 1 + (\eta - 1)(z/\eta)\phi[(1/m - 1)f'/(\varepsilon f) + (f'/f - 1/z)/\sigma]$$

$$+ (1/m - 1)(\varepsilon\eta u)^{-1}wu'$$

$$+ (s'uk)^{-1}\theta\{(1/m - 1)(\varepsilon\eta z)^{-1}w$$

$$- (w/\eta)[(1/m - 1)f'/(\varepsilon f) + (f'/f - 1/z)/\sigma]\}.$$

From this and the definition (7.21) it follows $u'w/u = 1/\beta$ and

$$0 = 1 + (1 - 1/\eta)\phi[(1/m - 1)f'z/(\varepsilon f) + (f'z/f - 1)/\sigma]$$

$$+ (1/m - 1)(\varepsilon\eta\beta)^{-1}$$

$$+ \theta[(1/m - 1)/\varepsilon + 1/\sigma](1/z - f'/f)w/(s'u\eta k).$$

Now noting (7.3), (7.4) and (7.5) and defining

$$\Lambda \doteq (f'/f - 1/z)(s'u\eta k)^{-1}w < 0,$$

where $f > f'z$ and $0 < \eta \leq 1$, we obtain (7.24). Condition (7.22) and result (7b.13) yield (7.25).

8 Unions and economic growth

8.1 Introduction

In models where labour is homogeneous, one readily obtains the result that in the long run unions reduce capital stock, employment and income.[1] The reason for this is the following. When a labour union raises the wage above the level corresponding to full employment, profits and the level of investment fall. In the long run, this decrease in investment results in smaller capital stock, lower employment and lower income. To challenge this result, we consider here an economy where labour is heterogeneous. In such a case, unionism also affects the level of investment through the allocation of labour among different sectors of production.

In order to examine how the allocation of resources affects the growth of consumption, we distinguish two categories of labour and term these 'skilled' and 'unskilled' labour, for convenience. The supply of these labour inputs is endogenous: the households can, before entering the labour market, change their occupation at some cost.[2] Furthermore, we assume that technological knowledge arises from intentional investment decisions made by profit-maximizing agents. Technology is assumed to be a non-rival input: its use by one firm in no way limits its use by another. Then, since the introduction of a rival good leads to increasing returns to scale, the equilibrium must be supported by monopolistic competition.[3]

---

[1] See, for example, Kemp, van Long and Shimomura (1991), ch. 5. In order to obtain a stable equilibrium with unemployment, these authors had to make the controversial assumption that labour income is a decreasing function of employment.

[2] This specification is reminiscent of a Harris–Todaro model where a worker must decide first in which sector he/she is going to work. See, for example, Calvo (1978).

[3] With this specification, our model resembles Romer (1990) in many respects. The major difference is the introduction of collective bargaining into the labour market. In Romer's model, intermediate inputs are differentiated and the firm is subject to Cobb–Douglas technology. In the model of this chapter, consumer goods are differentiated and the household's preferences are of Cobb–Douglas type. From the technical point of view, these two specifications are equivalent.

With technology being a non-rival input, research and development (R&D) yields externality for the economy as a whole. It is commonly suggested that in order to eliminate this externality, the government should directly subsidize R&D.[4] In reality, however, R&D is mostly carried out by research departments of companies that are also producing other goods, so that neither the government nor the unions can completely distinguish between inputs being used in research and those being used somewhere else. Then direct subsidy to R&D is commonly non-feasible and the unions cannot set different wages for research and ordinary production.

So far, only Palokangas (1996) has examined the relationship of union power and balanced growth and he has obtained the following results. Both parties in collective bargaining find it optimal to have all skilled labour employed, because this increases technological change and future labour income. When the union increases the wage for unskilled labour above the level corresponding to full employment, the employment of both skilled and unskilled labour in ordinary production decreases. This fall in the demand for skilled labour reduces the wage for skilled labour and the unit cost of a new design. With a lower unit cost, the production of new designs expands, speeding up economic growth.

Palokangas (1996) made, however, the restrictive assumptions that the supply of both skilled and unskilled labour is exogenous, and that collective bargaining is carried out at the level of the whole economy and concerns only the base wages. In contrast, this study makes the labour supply endogenous through the change of occupation, considers bargaining at different levels of centralization of collective bargaining, and also examines the case of profit-sharing. In order to motivate collective bargaining, there must be some profits. In Palokangas (1996), profits were due to decreasing-returns-to-scale technology. This study introduces, more plausibly, monopoly profits for the same purpose. In other respects, this study follows Palokangas (1996).

We consider here the effect of union power on growth and the welfare evaluation of union power for a growing economy. This is done as follows. Sections 8.2 and 8.3 indicate briefly the institutional background and the overall structure of the model. Sections 8.4 and 8.5 specify the fine details of the individual agents' behaviour and the equilibrium of the system. Section 8.6 examines the consequences of collective bargaining. Section 8.7 generalizes the results for the case of

---

[4] See, for example, Romer (1990).

non-unionized workers and section 8.8 does this for profit-sharing. Finally, section 8.9 examines the desirability of union power from the welfare point of view.

8.2 The setting

8.2.1 Unions and firms

We consider a closed economy where there is a fixed number m of labour unions. In such a model, it is possible to examine collective bargaining at different levels of centralization: bargaining is centralized for $m = 1$ and decentralized for large m. This chapter focuses in particular on a fully unionized economy. The case of a partly unionized economy will be considered in chapter 9.

The basic inputs to production are skilled labour, unskilled labour and an index of the level of technology. Each union controls a sector which produces one primary good and a variety of refined goods so that the index of the level of technology in the sector determines the size of this variety. In each sector, the primary and refined goods form a final good according to Cobb–Douglas technology. Since coexistence of several final goods would excessively complicate the analysis, we assume that all sectors produce identical final goods.[5] Then the price of this uniform final good can be chosen as unity, for convenience.

It is assumed that an oligopolist cannot alone finish a refined product. Then in each sector that is controlled by one union, there exists one oligopolist that employs skilled and unskilled labour, produces the primary good and constructs new designs for refined goods by research, and a number of monopolists that assemble refined goods and use only the final good as an input. After the oligopolist has designed such a product, it sells that design to a monopolist that will complete the product and sell it back to the oligopolist. All producers, oligopolists and mono-polists alike, behave in a Cournot manner: when making production decisions, each of them takes output levels of the others as fixed.

This specification of the behaviour of the firms has two advantages. The first one is that since the monopolists do not employ labour, each union has the oligopolist as the only opponent in collective bargaining. Second,

---

[5] This concerns the proof of the main result in appendix 8c. If perfect substitutability is assumed, the strategic dependence of the unions and oligopolists can be expressed in the form that research input g_j for oligopolist j depends on the primary output by the same oligopolist, z_j, and the research inputs for the other oligopolists, g_h with $h \neq j$. In the case of imperfect substitutability, there would be no strategic equilibrium.

the free entry of monopolists supports the equilibrium with technology as a non-rival input.

8.2.2 Production

In the model, the substitution of skilled and unskilled labour plays a crucial role. We assume, for tractability, that the production of the primary good is subject to CES technology that satisfies Inada conditions. One of these conditions says that when the level of some input is zero, the level of output will be zero as well. This means that the elasticity of substitution between the two labour inputs cannot exceed one.

The production function is specified so that a new refined good is a closer substitute for any old one than two old ones are for each other. This assumption is somewhat problematic here since it ignores (for example) obsolescence, but, following Romer (1990), it is made for tractability. Aggregate knowledge is an input to research and it can be proxied by the variety of refined goods in the economy. To obtain continuous growth, we assume that the productivity of research is in fixed proportion to aggregate knowledge. Otherwise, economic growth would end some time in the future. It would be a plausible assertion that research used certain inputs (e.g. skilled labour) relatively more than ordinary production. Since this assertion as it stands would lead to technical complications, then, following Romer (1990), we translate it to the extreme specification in which research employs only skilled labour.

8.2.3 Input markets

A union and an oligopolist bargain over the pay parameters for the union members given the oligopolist's demand for skilled and unskilled labour. The stronger is the union's relative bargaining power, the more concessions the oligopolist must make in bargaining. In the case of no bargaining, wages are competitively determined so that there will be full employment. Only when the union expects to get from bargaining at least as good an outcome as it gets in full employment, will it decide to start bargaining over the pay parameters. This assumption is realistic and it simplifies the analysis by eliminating a number of irrelevant outcomes. We assume, for the moment, that labour contracts consider only wages. Later, in section 8.8, we consider the case where the parties bargain simultaneously over wages and the workers' profit share.

Since there are several union–oligopolist pairs bargaining simultaneously over wages, we must specify their strategic dependence. In any static model, it would be obvious to assume that each pair behaves in a Bertrand manner, taking the wages being set by the other pairs as given. In a balanced growth model, however, wages must grow at the same rate as the real variables of the economy. This means that if some wages are chosen to maximize some objective function assuming that the other wages are held constant in real terms, then these wages must be constants in real terms as well and persistent growth cannot be maintained. For this reason, we assume that each pair of a union and an oligopolist behaves in a Cournot manner, taking the quantities (i.e. the levels of employment) for the other pairs as given.

8.2.4 The households

There are similar preferences for all households. To make the parties to collective bargaining independent, we assume that a household does not own any part of its employer. The support of those having no job is arranged very simply: since all workers are identical, they support themselves in periods of unemployment by evening out their consumption over periods of employment and unemployment. We assume that a single worker's labour time is fixed and that spare time yields no utility. Otherwise, the substitution of consumption and spare time would excessively complicate the analysis.

The households supply skilled and unskilled labour, and they can change the relative supply of these at some cost. If relative wages change, the workers will change their occupations accordingly. The costs associated with this change are specified as follows. There is a convex transformation function so that when the supply of skilled labour increases, the more unskilled labour must be transformed to get one more unit of skilled labour (and vice versa). A household must determine which labour it is going to supply *before* entering the labour market. Therefore, it has to make this decision by the expected income (=the wage times the expected rate of employment) in each occupation.

8.2.5 Steady-state analysis

Since we are interested in finding out how the balanced growth rate of the economy depends on collective bargaining, we can focus entirely on the steady state of the model. The problem of how bargaining affects growth during the transitional period (i.e. before the steady state is reached) is technically too complicated to be analysed here: there is no solution for such a complex differential game. When the model is examined in the steady state, the conditions for the alternating-offers game hold and – in contrast to the models that were used in chapters 6 and 7 – there is no need to be restricted to the special case of the monopoly union. The outcome of bargaining is given by the generalized Nash product, where the weight of the union's objective function can be used as a measure of the union's relative bargaining power.

On a balanced growth path, the agents of the model – the households, oligopolists, monopolists, unions and the government (or nature) – act as players in an extensive game. The strategic order of their decisions is as follows:

Stage 1 The government (or nature) sets the environment for the labour market. This determines the relative power of a union and an oligopolist in collective bargaining.

Stage 2 Each union–oligopolist pair sets its wages (and possibly its workers' profit share) in an alternating-offers game, taking the levels of employment for the other pairs as given.

Stage 3 The oligopolists and monopolists decide on production and the use of inputs.

Stage 4 The households choose their consumption as well as their supplies of skilled and unskilled labour.

The alternating-offers game between a union and an oligopolist forms a single stage for the whole extensive game. The firms make production decisions after the parties in collective bargaining have reached an agreement. Although all agents in the model have perfect foresight, this extensive game can produce involuntary unemployment so that a single household is willing to work more for given wages. A player acting at a specific stage takes the instruments of those acting at the earlier stage as given and the optimal responses of those acting at the later stages as constraints.

8.3 The overall structure of the model

8.3.1 Consumption and the labour supply

All households in the economy have the same Ramsey-type preferences and there is no substitution of consumption and spare time. Then the representative household maximizes the utility function[6]

$$\int_0^\infty U(C)e^{-\rho t}dt \text{ with } U(C) = (C^{1-\sigma} - 1)/(1 - \sigma)$$

$$\text{for } \sigma \in (0,1) \cup (1,\infty) \text{ and } \rho > 0, \tag{8.1}$$

---

[6] This yields a logarithmic utility $U(C) = \log C$ as a limit case for $\sigma \to 1$.

where t is time, C economy-wide consumption, ρ the subjective discount rate and σ the inverse of the intertemporal elasticity of substitution. In each sector j of the unionized economy, there is one union and one oligopolist and these are labelled j. This union–oligopolist pair faces the employment constraints

$$L_j \geq l_j \geq g_j \geq 0, \quad N_j \geq n_j \geq 0, \tag{8.2}$$

where L_j (N_j) is the supply of skilled (unskilled) labour by the members of union j, l_j (n_j) the input of skilled (unskilled) labour by oligopolist j, and g_j is skilled labour that oligopolist j devotes to research.

The representative member of union j can change its supply of labour through the convex transformation function as follows:

$$N_j = R(L_j), \quad R' < 0, \quad R'' < 0. \tag{8.3}$$

Because the marginal rate of transformation, $-R'$, increases with the supply L_j of skilled labour, more and more unskilled labour N_j must be transformed in order to create one more unit of skilled labour. Given this, there exists an equilibrium composition of the labour supply for the representative household.

8.3.2 The goods

Sector j assembles the final good from the output of the primary good, z_j, and the output of refined goods, $x_j(i)$ with $i \in D_j$, according to the Cobb–Douglas function

$$y_j = z_j^{\beta} \int_{D_j} x_j(i)^{1-\beta} di \text{ with } 0 < \beta < 1, \tag{8.4}$$

where y_j is output, D_j the variety of refined goods and β is the expenditure share of the primary good. Let $p_j(i)$ be the price oligopolist j faces for input i. For the case where oligopolist j does not use input i at all, $x_j(i) = 0$, we define $p_j(i) = \infty$. The output of the primary good, z_j, is produced by CES technology satisfying Inada conditions[7]

$$z_j = f(l_j - g_j, n_j) \doteq [\gamma(l_j - g_j)^{1-1/\theta} + (1-\gamma)n_j^{1-1/\theta}]^{\theta/(\theta-1)}$$

with $0 < \theta < 1$ and $0 < \gamma < 1$, \tag{8.5}

where g_j is skilled labour devoted to research, $l_j - g_j$ skilled labour being used in ordinary production, θ the elasticity of substitution between

---

[7] We obtain the Cobb–Douglas production function $z_j = l_j^{\gamma} n_j^{1-\gamma}$ as a special case for $\theta \to 1$.

skilled and unskilled labour, and γ the weight parameter of skilled labour in the CES production function.

Since at any moment the number of refined products must be finite, there exist the equilibrium values A_j, A and $\bar{x}_j$ such that

$$A_j \doteq \int_{D_j} di, \quad A \doteq \sum_{j=1}^{m} A_j, \quad x_j(i) = \begin{cases} \bar{x}_j & \text{for } i \in D_j, \\ 0 & \text{for } i \notin D_j. \end{cases} \quad (8.6)$$

Now substituting (8.6) into the production function (8.4), we see that the final output y_j of sector j is determined by

$$y_j = z_j^{\beta} \bar{x}_j^{1-\beta} A_j. \quad (8.7)$$

We assume that η units of final output are converted into one unit of refined good $i \in D_j$ for all j, where η is a constant. The rest of the final-good output $\sum_j y_j$ is consumed. Given this and equation (8.6), we obtain aggregate consumption

$$C = \sum_{j=1}^{m} y_j - \eta \sum_{j=1}^{m} \int_{D_j} x_j(i) di = \sum_{j=1}^{m} [y_j - \eta \bar{x}_j A_j]. \quad (8.8)$$

8.3.3 Research

Oligopolist j produces new designs Y_j from skilled labour g_j only, with constant returns to scale. The productivity of skilled labour is assumed to be in fixed proportion δ to the aggregate stock of designs A, so that the production of new designs by oligopolist j is given by $Y_j = \delta A g_j$. We choose, for convenience, the unit of skilled labour so that $\delta = 1$. The aggregate production of new designs, $\sum_j Y_j$, must increase the stock of designs, A: $\dot{A} \doteq dA/dt = \sum_j Y_j$. From all this it follows that the exponential growth rate of the stock of designs, $\dot{A}/A$, is given by

$$\dot{A}/A = (Y_1 + \cdots + Y_m)/A = \delta g = g, \quad \text{where } g \doteq g_1 + \cdots + g_m. \quad (8.9)$$

8.4 The behaviour of the individual agents

8.4.1 The solution of the game

The extensive game that was presented in subsection 8.2.5 must be solved backwards. Therefore, we explain first how consumption and labour supply are determined at given prices and wages (stage 4). Second, we show how an oligopolist and a monopolist decide on their use of inputs (stage 3). The determination of the pay parameters is given by sections 8.6 and 8.8 (stage 2) and optimal public policy by section 8.9 (stage 1).

8.4.2 The households

Let w_j (W_j) be the wage and E_j ($\mathcal{E}_j$) the expected wage income for skilled (unskilled) labour in sector j. A household must, before entering the labour market, decide on which combination of skilled and unskilled labour it will supply. Given the transformation function (8.3), the representative worker in sector j maximizes the expected labour income

$$E_j L_j + \mathcal{E}_j N_j = E_j L_j + \mathcal{E}_j R(L_j)$$

by the choice of the supply of skilled labour, L_j. Given this maximization, the relative expected wage income must be equal to the relative marginal rate of transformation for the labour inputs:[8]

$$w_j \frac{l_j}{L_j} \Big/ \left(W_j \frac{n_j}{N_j} \right) = E_j/\mathcal{E}_j = -R'(L_j). \tag{8.10}$$

The representative household of the economy maximizes its welfare (8.1) by the choice of consumption C subject to the accumulation of wealth, assuming that the flow of income and the interest rate r are held constant. Then consumption C is determined by the optimization condition (see appendix 8a)

$$\dot{C}/C = (r - \rho)/\sigma. \tag{8.11}$$

8.4.3 The demand for goods

By duality, the price for primary input z_j, q_j, and that for refined input $x_j(i)$, $p_j(i)$, must be equal to the marginal product of the same input. Since the price for the final good is chosen as unity, then given the production function (8.4), these equilibrium conditions take the form

$$q_j = \partial y_j/\partial z_j = \beta y_j/z_j = \beta z_j^{\beta-1} \int_{D_j} x_j(i)^{1-\beta} di,$$

$$p_j(i) = \partial y_j/\partial x_j(i) = (1 - \beta) z_j^{\beta} x_j(i)^{-\beta}. \tag{8.12}$$

---

[8] Since the unemployed workers do not earn any labour income, the expected wage income for skilled (unskilled) labour, E_j ($\mathcal{E}_j$), is equal to the wage w_j (W_j) times the probability of being employed, l_j/L_j (n_j/N_j).

8.4.4 The monopolists

The opportunity cost of producing one unit of input i is given by η: monopolist $i \in D_j$ converts η units of final output into one unit of refined good $i \in D_j$. Since the monopolist knows the true demand function (8.12), its net revenue is given by

$$\pi_j(i) = p_j(i)x_j(i) - \eta x_j(i) = (1 - \beta)z_j^\beta x_j(i)^{1-\beta} - \eta x_j(i), \qquad (8.13)$$

where $p_j x_j$ is sales revenue and ηx_j total cost. A monopolist uses the interest rate r as the discount rate in evaluating its stream of profit. It decides to produce refined good i only if the discounted value of profit, $\pi_j(i)/r$, covers the price P_j it has to pay for a design for that good. In the steady state, given (8.13), this incentive constraint takes the form

$$P_j \leq \pi_j(i)/r = [(1 - \beta)z_j^\beta x_j(i)^{1-\beta} - \eta x_j(i)]/r \text{ for } i \in D_j. \qquad (8.14)$$

The maximization of profit (8.13) by the choice of output $x_j(i)$, holding constant the output levels of the other producers, z_j and $x_j(h)$ for $h \neq i$, leads to mark-up pricing

$$p_j(i) = \bar{p} = \eta/(1 - \beta) \text{ for } i \in D_j. \qquad (8.15)$$

Substituting this into (8.12) and noting (8.6), we obtain the equilibrium values for quantities and profits as follows:

$$x_j(i) = \bar{x}_j = \phi z_j \text{ and } \pi_j(i) = \bar{\pi}_j \doteq [\phi \eta \beta/(1 - \beta)]z_j$$

$$\text{for } i \in D_j, \text{ where } \phi \doteq (1 - \beta)^{2/\beta}\eta^{-1/\beta}. \qquad (8.16)$$

8.4.5 The oligopolists

Consider oligopolist j. Since one unit of skilled labour g_j produces A units of new designs, the revenue for the construction of new designs is given by $Ag_j P_j$. The oligopolist's sales income is given by $q_j z_j$ and labour cost by $w_j l_j + W_j n_j$. Thus we obtain profit

$$\Pi_j = Ag_j P_j + q_j z_j - w_j l_j - W_j n_j.$$

Substituting the inverse demand function (8.12) into this yields

$$\Pi_j = Ag_j P_j + \beta y_j - w_j l_j - W_j n_j. \qquad (8.17)$$

Oligopolist j behaves in a Cournot manner taking the monopolists' output levels $x_j(i) = \bar{x}_j$ as given. The wages (w_j, W_j) are determined in collective bargaining and are therefore given for oligopolist j. Within the limits of the production functions (8.5) and (8.7), the oligopolist's inverse demand function (8.12) as well as the monopolists' incentive constraints (8.14), the oligopolist maximizes its profit (8.17) by the choice of the price for a design, P_j, and labour inputs (l_j, g_j, n_j). In appendix 8b, this optimization leads to the equilibrium conditions where the price for a design is equal to the discounted value of a monopolist's profit and the wages are equal to the marginal products of labour:

$$P_j = [(1 - \beta)z_j^\beta \bar{x}_j^{1-\beta} - \eta\bar{x}_j]/r,$$

$$W_j = (1 - \gamma)\beta[\beta + (1 - \beta)(A/A_j)g_j/r]y_j z_j^{1/\theta - 1} n_j^{-1/\theta},$$

$$AP_j = w_j = \beta\gamma[\beta + (1 - \beta)(A/A_j)g_j/r]y_j z_j^{1/\theta - 1}(l_j - g_j)^{-1/\theta}$$

(8.18)

for $g_j > 0$.

8.4.6 The demand for skilled labour

Given (8.7), (8.16) and (8.18), we obtain the equilibrium final output and the equilibrium price for a design as follows:

$$y_j = z_j^\beta \bar{x}_j^{1-\beta} A_j = \phi^{1-\beta} z_j A_j,$$

$$P_j = [(1 - \beta)\phi^{-\beta} - \eta]\phi z_j/r = (1 - \beta)^{-1}\phi\eta\beta z_j/r.$$

(8.19)

Substituting P_j from (8.19) and ϕ and $\bar{x}_j$ from (8.16) into the last equation in (8.18), we obtain the employment of skilled labour as follows (see appendix 8b):

$$l_j = g_j + \gamma^\theta[(1 - \beta)^{-1}\beta r A_j/A + g_j]^\theta z_j^{1-\theta} \text{ for } g_j > 0.$$ (8.20)

8.5 Steady state with given labour inputs

8.5.1 Steady-state conditions

If the economy is stable, it converges to some balanced growth path on which labour inputs (l_j, n_j, g_j) and the ratios of the stocks of designs, A_j/A, are held constant. Then by (8.5), (8.16) and (8.19), primary output z_j and refined output $\bar{x}_j$ are constants and output y_j grows at the same rate as A_j and A. Given (8.8), this implies that consumption C must grow at the same rate as y_j and A_j. Finally, from (8.18) it follows that the wages w_j and W_j must grow at the same rate as output y_j. We conclude that the stocks of designs, A and A_j, output y, wages w_j and W_j and consumption C all grow at the same exponential rate. Given this, (8.9) and the household's optimization condition (8.11), we obtain the balanced growth rate of the economy as follows:

$$\sum_{j=1}^{m} g_j = g = \frac{\dot{A}}{A} = \frac{\dot{A}_j}{A_j} = \frac{\dot{y}_j}{y_j} = \frac{\dot{w}_j}{w_j} = \frac{\dot{W}_j}{W_j} = \frac{\dot{C}}{C} = \frac{r-\rho}{\sigma}. \tag{8.21}$$

Given the steady-state conditions (8.21), we obtain

$$r = \rho + \sigma g > 0. \tag{8.22}$$

For the integral in the household's preferences (8.1) to be finite, the growth rate of current utility $(1-\sigma)g$ must be less than the discount rate ρ:

$$\rho + (\sigma - 1)g > 0. \tag{8.23}$$

Thus for $\sigma \in (0,1)$, some kind of overtaking criterion must be used to describe the behaviour of the household.[9] Finally, because on the balanced growth path the interest rate r and the growth rate g are held constant, then, given (8.21) and (8.22), we obtain

$$\int_{0}^{\infty} A_j e^{-rt} dt = A_j(0)/(r-g) = A_j(0)/[\rho + (\sigma - 1)g]. \tag{8.24}$$

8.5.2 *The labour market*

In appendix 8c, it is shown that by the definition (8.9), the equilibrium conditions (8.20), (8.10 and (8.18), the balanced growth condition (8.22), the production function (8.5) and the transformation function (8.3), labour demands (l_j, n_j) and labour supplies (L_j, N_j) can be transformed into functions of inputs z_j, g_j and $g_{-j} = g - g_j$:

$$l_j(z_j, g_j, g_{-j}), \quad \partial l_j/\partial z_j > 0, \quad \partial l_j/\partial g_j > 0, \quad \partial l_j/\partial g_{-j} > 0;$$

$$n_j(z_j, g_j, g_{-j}), \quad \partial n_j/\partial z_j > 0, \quad \partial n_j/\partial g_j < 0, \quad \partial n_j/\partial g_{-j} < 0;$$

$$L_j(z_j, g_j, g_{-j}), \quad [\partial L_j/\partial g_j]_{l_j=L_j} < 0, \quad [\partial L_j/\partial g_{-j}]_{l_j=L_j} < 0;$$

$$N_j(z_j, g_j, g_{-j}), \quad [\partial N_j/\partial g_j]_{l_j=L_j} > 0, \quad [\partial N_j/\partial g_{-j}]_{l_j=L_j} > 0,$$

where $g_{-j} \doteq g - g_j$. \hfill (8.25)

---

[9] For this, see Romer (1990), p. S93.

Furthermore, it can be shown (appendix 8c) that

$$\lim_{\theta \to 1} \partial l_j / \partial z_j = \lim_{\theta \to 1} \partial L_j / \partial z_j = \lim_{\theta \to 1} \partial N_j / \partial z_j = 0. \tag{8.26}$$

Since functions (8.25) are continuous and constraints (8.2) form a compact set from which a pair (z_j, g_j) of inputs is chosen, then given $\sum_{h \neq j} g_j$, there exists a pair $(\bar{z}_j, \bar{g}_j)$ of inputs that corresponds to full employment for the members of union j:

$$l_j(\bar{z}_j, \bar{g}_j, g_{-j}) = L_j(\bar{z}_j, \bar{g}_j, g_{-j}), \quad n_j(\bar{z}_j, \bar{g}_j, g_{-j}) = N_j(\bar{z}_j, \bar{g}_j, g_{-j}). \tag{8.27}$$

We assume that the pair $(\bar{z}_j, \bar{g}_j)$ is unique and that there is some research in full employment, $\bar{g}_j > 0$. Given this assumption, the steady state will be unique.

8.6 Collective bargaining

8.6.1 The players' targets

Consider now union j and oligopolist j. From (8.5), (8.17) and (8.18) it follows that in the production of the primary good, labour income is given by

$$(l_j - g_j)w_j + n_j W_j = \beta[\beta + (1 - \beta)(A/A_j)g_j/r]y_j,$$

and the oligopolist's profit by

$$\Pi_j = \beta y_j - (l_j - g_j)w_j - n_j W_j = (1 - \beta)\beta y_j$$
$$= (1 - \beta)\beta[1 - (A/A_j)g_j/r]y_j. \tag{8.28}$$

Because new designs are produced only by skilled labour, subject to constant returns to scale, the revenue in the research sector, $P_j A g_j$, is paid wholly to skilled labour. From the assumption that spare time yields no utility it follows that at each moment, union j is interested in the maximization of its members' labour income

$$I_j = (l_j - g_j)w_j + n_j W_j + AP_j g_j$$
$$= \beta[\beta + (1 - \beta)(A/A_j)g_j/r]y_j + AP_j g_j. \tag{8.29}$$

Union j and oligopolist j use the interest rate r as the discount rate in evaluating income streams. We choose $t = 0$ as the present time, for convenience. Oligopolist j maximizes the discounted value of profits,

$$P_j \doteq \int_0^\infty \Pi_j e^{-rt} dt,$$

while union j maximizes the discounted value of labour income,

$$W_j \doteq \int_0^\infty I_j e^{-rt} dt.$$

Substituting ϕ, y_j, P_j, r, Π_j and I_j from (8.16), (8.19), (8.22), (8.24), (8.28) and (8.29), these objective functions take the form (see appendix 8d)

$$P_j(z_j, g_j, g_{-j}) = \int_0^\infty \Pi_j e^{-rt} dt$$

$$= (1 - \beta)\beta\phi^{1-\beta}[1 - (\rho + \sigma g)^{-1} g_j A(0)/A_j(0)]$$

$$\times [\rho + (\sigma - 1)g]^{-1} z_j A_j(0), \tag{8.30}$$

$$W_j(z_j, g_j, g_{-j}) = \int_0^\infty I_j e^{-rt} dt$$

$$= \beta^2 \phi^{1-\beta}(\rho + \sigma g)^{-1}[\rho + (\sigma - 1)g]^{-1}$$

$$\times [\rho + \sigma g + 2(1/\beta - 1)g_j A(0)/A_j(0)] z_j A_j(0). \tag{8.31}$$

8.6.2 Wage-setting

In collective bargaining where the wages (w_j, W_j) are determined, oligopolist j attempts to maximize the discounted value of profits, P_j, while union j attempts to maximize that of labour income, W_j. It is assumed that the relative bargaining power is the same constant α for all unions. Now the outcome of collective bargaining is obtained through the maximization of the generalized Nash product of the union's and oligopolist's objective functions (8.30) and (8.31),

$$\Omega_j = W_j(z_j, g_j, g_{-j})^\alpha P_j(z_j, g_j, g_{-j})^{1-\alpha}, \quad 0 < \alpha < 1. \tag{8.32}$$

We assume that each union–oligopolist pair j takes the labour being input to research in the other sectors, g_{-j}, as given.

Since there is one-to-one correspondence from wages (w_j, W_j) to inputs (z_j, g_j) through the production function (8.5), the profit-maximization conditions (8.18) and the balanced growth conditions (8.25), inputs (z_j, g_j) can replace wages (w_j, W_j) as the instruments of optimization. The set of feasible outcomes consists of those pairs (z_j, g_j) for which the union's utility (i.e. the discounted value of labour income) W_j is at least as good as in the case of full employment. This incentive constraint for the union can be written as follows:

$$W_j(z_j, g_j, g_{-j}) \geq W(\bar{z}_j, \bar{g}_j, g_{-j}). \tag{8.33}$$

The generalized Nash product (8.32) must be maximized by the choice of inputs (z_j, g_j), given the functions (8.25), the employment constraints (8.2) and the union's incentive constraint (8.33), holding g_{-j} constant. In appendix 8e, we show that this m-player Cournot game leads to:

Proposition 8.1: The higher is the unions' relative bargaining power α, the more likely that there is some growth in the economy. In such a case, the balanced growth path satisfies the following properties:
(a) skilled labour is always fully employed;
(b) the composite input of skilled and unskilled labour in the production of final goods, $z_j = z$, is a decreasing function of the balanced growth rate g;
(c) the balanced growth rate corresponding to full employment, $\bar{g}$, forms a lower limit for economic growth, $g \geq \bar{g}$;
(d) in the Cobb–Douglas case, $\theta \to 1$, there is always full employment for both labour inputs; and
(e) if there is unemployment, the increase in the unions' relative bargaining power α increases the balanced growth rate g.

Proposition 8.1 can be interpreted as follows. Both labour income and profits can be increased by producing more final goods, until either skilled or unskilled labour is fully employed. This means that a union and an oligopolist do not make an agreement such as causes unemployment for both labour inputs. On the other hand, if there were unemployment for skilled labour and full employment for unskilled labour, then the increase in the use of skilled labour in research increases labour income. Given this, a union prefers full employment to a contract generating unemployment for skilled labour and does not start bargaining at all. We conclude that if there is some research (and growth), then skilled labour is fully employed, and if there is no research (and no growth), then unskilled labour is fully employed.

Consider now the case where there is no research and consequently where there is full employment for unskilled labour. These two conditions determine uniquely the wages for the two labour inputs so that union power has no effect on the outcome of bargaining. As soon as there is some skilled labour being allocated in research, the union can use its bargaining power to improve its position – and the more so, the stronger it is. This means that if the union is strong enough, its outcome with research is so good that it has no incentive to drive research down to zero. Consequently, there will be growth. The increase in union power increases the wage for unskilled labour and the unit cost for the primary good, so ordinary production will fall and employ less skilled labour. This fall in the demand decreases the wage for skilled labour and the unit cost of a new design. With a lower unit cost, the production of new designs expands, speeding up economic growth.

Finally, consider the case with growth, unemployment and Cobb–Douglas technology, $\theta \to 1$. Because (by the results above) this unemployment is for unskilled labour only, by employing more unskilled labour in ordinary production, one can increase labour income. This means that the union prefers full employment to this case and does not start bargaining at all. So only when skilled and unskilled labour are complements in ordinary production, $0 < \theta < 1$, does the use of skilled labour in research restrict the production of the final good so much that unemployment of unskilled labour will occur.

8.7 Non-unionized workers

The results above show that the unions decrease the wages for skilled labour from the level corresponding to full employment. As long as the workers are identical, having equal opportunities to change their occupation, all workers will benefit from the union: the decrease in the wage for skilled labour will be outweighed by the increase in the wage for unskilled labour and a single worker's welfare will nevertheless increase. The situation is, however, changed when the workers are not identical: in such a case, the workers possessing relatively greater skilled labour will lose, while those possessing relatively greater unskilled labour will benefit. This means that the workers having greater skilled labour may have an incentive to leave the union. Therefore, this section considers the case where unskilled workers are unionized but skilled workers are non-unionized.

To examine this problem, we modify the basic model as follows. First, assume that occupation cannot be changed, i.e. that $R' \to 0$ holds for the transformation function (8.3). This means that in each sector j, the supply of skilled labour, L_j, as well as that of unskilled labour, N_j, is fixed. Second, assume that each worker supplies either skilled or unskilled labour but not both. Third, since all skilled workers are non-unionized, we assume that the wages for skilled labour, w_j for all j, adjust to maintain full employment for skilled labour. Then, given (8.18), the employment constraints (8.2), the members' labour income for union j and the discounted value of this (=the objective function for union j), change from (8.29) and (8.31) into the form

$$L_j = l_j \geq g_j \geq 0, \quad N_j \geq n_j \geq 0,$$

$$I_j = (l_j - g_j)w_j + n_j W_j + AP_j g_j - w_j L_j$$

$$= \beta[\beta + (1 - \beta)(A/A_j)g_j/r]y_j + (g_j - L_j)AP_j,$$

$$\mathcal{W}_j(z_j, g_j, g_{-j}) = \int_0^\infty I_j e^{-rt} dt \tag{8.34}$$

$$= \beta^2 \phi^{1-\beta}(\rho + \sigma g)^{-1}[\rho + (\sigma - 1)g]^{-1}$$

$$\times [\rho + \sigma g + (1/\beta - 1)(2g_j - L_j)A(0)/A_j(0)]$$

$$\times z_j A_j(0).$$

In other respects, the model is the same as before. In appendix 8f, we prove the following result:

Proposition 8.2: If there is no change of occupation, all workers supply only one labour input and skilled labour is non-unionized, then proposition 8.1 holds as it stands.

Since, by proposition 8.1, it is in the unions' interests to keep skilled labour fully employed, the unionization of skilled workers makes no qualitative difference to these results.

8.8 Profit-sharing

So far, this study has assumed that only the base wages w_j and W_j are set in collective bargaining. Now we try to extend the results to the case where for all j, union j and oligopolist j agree on both the wages and the worker's profit share s_j. Since the profit share must be non-negative for both parties, we obtain

$$0 \leq s_j \leq 1. \tag{8.35}$$

Because only pure profits (8.28) are to be shared, there will be no changes in the demand and supply functions of labour, (8.25). However, the objective functions of the parties change as follows. Since oligopolist j pays a fixed share s_j of its profit Π_j to the members of union j, the total labour income is now equal to the sum of the wage income I_j and the profit share $s_j \Pi_j$ while the remaining profit for the oligopolist is equal to $(1 - s_j)\Pi_j$. The parties' new targets $\mathcal{P}_j^*$ and $\mathcal{W}_j^*$ are obtained as the present values of these incomes. Given (8.30) and (8.31), these objective functions take the form

$$\mathcal{P}_j^*(z_j, g_j, g_{-j}, s_j) = (1 - s_j) \int_0^\infty \Pi_j e^{-rt} dt$$

$$= (1 - s_j)\mathcal{P}_j(z_j, g_j, g_{-j}),$$

$$\mathcal{W}_j^*(z_j, g_j, g_{-j}, s_j) = \int_0^\infty [I_j + s_j\Pi_j]e^{-rt} dt \qquad (8.36)$$

$$= \int_0^\infty I_j e^{-rt} dt + s_j \int_0^\infty \Pi_j e^{-rt} dt$$

$$= \mathcal{W}_j(z_j, g_j, g_{-j}) + s_j\mathcal{P}_j(z_j, g_j, g_{-j}).$$

Without union j there would be no profit-sharing by oligopolist j, $s_j = 0$, and the oligopolist's wages would be adjusted to maintain full employment, $l_j = L_j$ and $n_j = N_j$. The union must achieve a better outcome for its members than what they would obtain without the union: given the definitions (8.27) and (8.36), we obtain the incentive constraints

$$\mathcal{W}_j^*(z_j, g_j, g_{-j}, s_j) \geq \mathcal{W}_j^*(\bar{z}_j, \bar{g}_j, g_{-j}, 0) = \mathcal{W}_j(\bar{z}_j, \bar{g}_j, g_{-j}). \qquad (8.37)$$

In bargaining, union j and oligopolist j take research input for the rest of the economy, g_{-j}, as constant. Then inputs (z_j, g_j) can represent (w_j, W_j) as the bargaining instruments. We denote a union's relative bargaining power by α, as before. The outcome of collective bargaining is obtained by maximizing the generalized Nash product of the parties' objective functions (8.36)

$$\Omega_j^* = \mathcal{W}_j^*(z_j, g_j, g_{-j}, s_j)^\alpha \mathcal{P}_j^*(z_j, g_j, g_{-j}, s_j)^{1-\alpha}, \quad 0 < \alpha < 1, \quad (8.38)$$

by the choice of (z_j, g_j, s_j), subject to the employment constraints (8.2), the limits of profit-sharing (8.35) and the union's incentive constraint (8.37). In appendix 8g, this maximization problem leads to the following result:

Proposition 8.3: When profit-sharing is feasible, there exists a critical level $0 < \bar{\alpha} < 1$ of the unions' relative bargaining power α so that for weak unions with $\alpha < \bar{\alpha}$, proposition 8.1 holds as it stands, but for strong unions with $\alpha \geq \bar{\alpha}$, union power α has no effect on the balanced growth rate of the economy, $dg/d\alpha \equiv 0$.

We explain this result as follows. If the union is strong enough, $\bar{\alpha} \leq \alpha < 1$, it can claim a share of profits on top of the base wages. In such a case, the union and the oligopolist share the profits in fixed proportions to their relative bargaining power and maximize the discounted value of total income, $\mathcal{P}_j + \mathcal{W}_j$, by the choice of wages. This means that the union's relative bargaining power α has no effect on the choice of wages and, ultimately, on economic growth.[10] On the other hand, if the union is not very strong, $0 < \alpha < \bar{\alpha}$, it has no incentive to claim a share of profits and the choice of wages depends on the unions' relative bargaining power α.

8.9 Welfare evaluation

In this section, we assume that all households are in all respects identical: they possess equal amounts of resources and the profits in the economy are evenly distributed among them. The purpose of this admittedly strong assumption is to allow us to make welfare comparisons, which would be extremely problematic with heterogeneous households. With these comparisons, we are able to show that collective bargaining can improve efficiency even when the distributional aspects of bargaining are ignored.

We assume that initially there is some growth and some unemployment, since otherwise union power has no significance. Then proposition 8.1 and the steady-state condition (8.21) imply

$$z_j = z(g), \quad z' = dz/dg < 0, \quad \dot{A}/A = g \geq \bar{g}, \tag{8.39}$$

where $\bar{g}$ is the balanced growth rate corresponding to full employment. Furthermore, provided that union power has some effect on growth, then, given propositions 8.1 and 8.3, it will increase the balanced growth rate $dg/d\alpha > 0$. Determining the environment for collective bargaining, the government can control the relative bargaining power α and thereby the balanced growth rate g.

Because of perfect symmetry over $j = 1, \ldots, m$, it must be the case that $A_j = A/m$ and $\bar{x}_j = \bar{x}$. Once the design for refined good i has been made, the fixed amount η of final output can be converted into one unit of this input i. Then by (8.6), we construct the following measure for the value of refined goods:

$$K = \eta \sum_{j=1}^{m} \int_{D_j} x_j(i)\,di = \eta \sum_{j=1}^{m} \bar{x}_j A_j = \eta \bar{x} \sum_{j=1}^{m} A_j = \eta \bar{x} A. \tag{8.40}$$

This equation can also be written as $\bar{x}_j = \bar{x} = K/(\eta A)$. Given this, (8.16), (8.19) and (8.39), we obtain aggregate output

---

[10] Total income $\mathcal{P}_j + \mathcal{W}_j$ is maximized by the choice of (w_j, W_j) subject to (8.2) and (8.33) in the same way as Λ_j is maximized by the choice of (w_j, W_j) subject to (8.2) and (8.33) in appendix 8g. One can show that (a) there can be unemployment, but that (b) skilled labour is always fully employed when there is some growth in the economy. The only qualitative difference is that now α has no effect on g.

$$y \doteq \sum_{j=1}^{m} y_j = \sum_{j=1}^{m} z_j^{\beta} \bar{x}_j^{1-\beta} A_j = z(g)^{\beta} \bar{x}^{1-\beta} A = \eta^{\beta-1} z(g)^{\beta} A^{\beta} K^{1-\beta}.$$

(8.41)

In the steady state, the value of refined goods (8.40) accumulates as a result of the difference of aggregate final output y and consumption C:

$$\dot{K} = y - C = \eta^{\beta-1} z(g)^{\beta} A^{\beta} K^{1-\beta} - C.$$ (8.42)

The elasticity of output (8.41) with respect to the growth rate g, when assets A and K are held constant, can be defined as

$$\varphi(g) \doteq \left| \frac{g}{y} \frac{\partial y}{\partial z} \frac{dz}{dg} \right| = - \frac{g}{y} \beta \frac{y}{z} \frac{dz}{dg} = - \beta \frac{g}{z} \frac{dz}{dg} > 0.$$ (8.43)

Now the household's welfare (8.1) should be maximized subject to constraints (8.42) and (8.39), by the choice of input g. In appendix 8h, noting (8.43), the solution of this problem yields the following proposition:

Proposition 8.4: If the growth rate g^* that is determined by

$$[\beta/\varphi(g^*) + 1 - \sigma]g^* = \rho$$ (8.44)

is above the growth rate $\bar{g}$ corresponding to full employment, then unemployment is socially optimal and the increase (decrease) of both the union's relative bargaining power, α, and the growth rate g increases welfare for the balanced growth rates lower than (higher than) g^*.

This result can be explained as follows. If the socially optimal growth rate is high, the maintenance of it requires so much skilled labour in research that with the remaining skilled labour, all unskilled labour cannot be employed in ordinary production. Then starting from the initial position of full employment, the increase in union power promotes research, economic growth and welfare.

8.10 Conclusions

This chapter examined an economy where growth is generated by research that produces new designs for intermediate inputs and where the existence of monopoly profits is the reason for collective bargaining. There are two labour inputs: unskilled labour, which is always unionized and which is used in the production of goods, and skilled labour, which can be unionized or non-unionized and which can be used both in research and in the production of goods. Collective bargaining is either fully centralized or carried out simultaneously in different parts of the economy. If a union does not accept the competitive wages corresponding to full employment, it starts bargaining over the wages (and possibly the profit share) for its members with the corresponding employer. The union attempts to maximize the discounted value of labour income while the employer attempts to maximize the discounted value of profit. The main findings can be summarized as follows.

The first finding is that in a growing economy, skilled labour is always fully employed. With unemployment for both skilled and unskilled labour, both labour income and profits could be increased by producing more final goods until either of these labour inputs is fully employed. With unemployment of skilled labour, the increased use of this in research would raise the level of labour income. Consequently, a union is better off with full employment and so it has no incentive to start bargaining when the expected outcome of bargaining would generate full employment for unskilled but unemployment for skilled labour.

Let the elasticity of substitution between skilled and unskilled labour be unity (=Cobb–Douglas technology) and let there be unemployment for unskilled labour. Then the increased use of unskilled labour in ordinary production would raise the level of labour income. This means that the union is happy with full employment and does not start bargaining. Only when the elasticity of substitution is less than one does the enlarged use of skilled labour in research restrict ordinary production so much that final output will fall and excess supply of unskilled labour will appear.

The second finding is that the increase in the unions' relative bargaining power augments the balanced growth rate. If the union increases the wage for unskilled labour, then the final-goods sector employs less skilled labour. This fall in the demand decreases the wage for skilled labour and the unit cost of a new design. With a lower unit cost, the production of new designs expands, speeding up economic growth.

Third, it is shown that there will be growth with strong unions and no growth with weak unions. Assume that there is no growth. Then there is no research, no production of new designs, and consequently there is unemployment for skilled labour but full employment of unskilled labour. Now when there is no skilled labour in research and full employment for unskilled labour, these two conditions fix the two wages so that union power will have no effect on the outcome of bargaining. When there is some growth and some research, a union can use its power to improve its position – the more so, the stronger it is. If the union is strong enough, its outcome is so good with research that it has no incentive to drive research down to zero.

Provided that the relative bargaining power of the union is not very high, the results above also hold when profit-sharing is introduced into the economy. If a union is already very powerful in bargaining, then, for the following reason, a change in its power has no macroeconomic effects. A strong union is interested in sharing the value-added directly rather than reducing profits by high base wages. In such a case, it is in the interests of both parties to bargain to maximize aggregate income, so that the choice of wages, and consequently the allocation of resources, will be independent of the union's relative bargaining power.

Finally, it is shown that union power can be welfare-enhancing even though it increases unemployment. If the socially optimal growth rate is high, the maintenance of it requires so much skilled labour in research that with the remaining skilled labour, all unskilled labour cannot be employed in the production of final goods. Then, starting from the initial position of full employment, the increase in union power promotes research, economic growth and welfare.

Appendix 8a. *The proof of equation* (8.11)

The household assumes that income J and the interest rate r are held fixed. The accumulation of wealth Q is given by

$$\dot{Q} = rQ + J - C, \tag{8a.1}$$

where C is consumption. The maximization of utility (8.1) subject to (8a.1) yields the Hamiltonian

$$H = U(C) + v[rQ + J - C]$$
$$= [C^{1-\sigma} - 1]/(1 - \sigma) + v[rQ + J - C],$$

where the shadow price for wealth, v, evolves according to

$$\dot{v} = \rho v - \partial H/\partial Q = (\rho - r)v, \quad \lim_{t \to \infty} vQe^{-\rho t} = 0. \tag{8a.2}$$

The maximization of the Hamiltonian by the choice of consumption C yields the first-order condition

$$v = U'(C) = C^{-\sigma} \text{ or } C^{\sigma} = 1/v.$$

With logarithmic transformation, this takes the form

$$\sigma \log C = - \log v.$$

Differentiating this with respect to time and substituting (8a.2), we obtain

$$\sigma \dot{C}/C = -\dot{v}/v = r - \rho \quad \text{and} \quad \dot{C}/C = (r - \rho)/\sigma.$$

Appendix 8b. *The proof of conditions* (8.18)

We prove first that oligopolist j employs both labour inputs in the production of the primary product, $n_j > 0$ and $l_j > g_j$. Assume on the contrary that either $n_j = 0$ or $g_j = l_j$ holds. Then, in accordance with the production functions (8.4) and (8.5), it must be the case that $z_j = y_j = 0$. Because there is perfect symmetry over oligopolists and unions, labelled as $h = 1,\ldots,m$, then, in the steady state of the economy, $y_h = 0$ for all $h = 1,\ldots,m$. This means that there is no output of the final good and consequently no consumption. Since this is impossible, the assumption is not true and $n_j > 0$ and $l_j > g_j$ for all j.

Now we consider the case where oligopolist j undertakes some research, $g_j > 0$. Substituting output y_j from (8.7) and q_j from (8.12) into the profits (8.17) yields

$$\Pi_j = Ag_jP_j + \beta y_j - w_jl_j - W_jn_j$$
$$= Ag_jP_j + \beta z_j^\beta \bar{x}_j^{1-\beta}A_j - w_jl_j - W_jn_j, \tag{8b.1}$$

where z_j is given by (8.5). Oligopolist j maximizes this by the choice of labour inputs (l_j, g_j, n_j) and the price for a design P_j within the limits of the monopolist's incentive constraint (8.14) or

$$(1 - \beta)z_j^\beta \bar{x}_j^{1-\beta} - \eta\bar{x}_j - rP_j \geq 0,$$

taking the wages (w_j, W_j), the interest rate r and the monopolists' equilibrium output $\bar{x}_j$ as fixed. The Lagrangean for this problem is given by

$$\Gamma_j = \Pi_j + \varepsilon[(1 - \beta)z_j^\beta \bar{x}_j^{1-\beta} - \eta\bar{x}_j - rP_j], \tag{8b.2}$$

where the multiplier ε satisfies the Kuhn–Tucker conditions

$$\varepsilon[(1 - \beta)z_j^\beta \bar{x}_j^{1-\beta} - \eta\bar{x}_j - rP_j] = 0, \quad \varepsilon \geq 0. \tag{8b.3}$$

Given (8b.1), the maximization of the Lagrangean (8b.2) with respect to P_j and (l_j, g_j, n_j) yields the first-order conditions

$$\partial \Gamma_j / \partial P_j = Ag_j - r\varepsilon = 0, \tag{8b.4}$$

$$\partial \Gamma_j / \partial l_j = [\beta A_j + (1 - \beta)\varepsilon]$$
$$\times \beta z_j^{\beta-1} \bar{x}_j^{1-\beta} f_1(l_j - g_j, n_j) - w_j = 0, \tag{8b.5}$$

$$\partial \Gamma_j / \partial g_j = AP_j - [\beta A_j + (1 - \beta)\varepsilon]$$
$$\times \beta z_j^{\beta-1} \bar{x}_j^{1-\beta} f_1(l_j - g_j, n_j) = 0, \tag{8b.6}$$

$$\partial \Gamma_j / \partial n_j = [\beta A_j + (1 - \beta)\varepsilon]$$
$$\times \beta z_j^{\beta-1} \bar{x}_j^{1-\beta} f_2(l_j - g_j, n_j) - W_j = 0, \tag{8b.7}$$

where $f_1 \doteq \partial f / \partial(l_j - g_j) > 0$ and $f_2 \doteq \partial f / \partial n_j > 0$. Given (8b.3) and (8b.4), we obtain

$$\varepsilon = Ag_j / r > 0, \quad P_j = [(1 - \beta)z_j^\beta \bar{x}_j^{1-\beta} - \eta \bar{x}_j] / r, \tag{8b.8}$$

and given (8b.5) and (8b.6), we obtain

$$w_j = AP_j \text{ for } g_j > 0. \tag{8b.9}$$

The right-hand equation in (8b.8) proves the first equation in (8.18). Noting the production functions (8.5) and (8.7) as well as the result $g_j < l_j$, and substituting w_j from (8b.9) and ε from (8b.8) into (8b.5) and (8b.7) imply the two latter equations in (8.18):

$$W_j = [\beta A_j + (1 - \beta)\varepsilon]\beta z_j^{\beta-1} \bar{x}_j^{1-\beta} f_2(l_j - g_j, n_j)$$
$$= (1 - \gamma)[\beta A_j + (1 - \beta)\varepsilon]\beta z_j^{1/\theta+\beta-1} \bar{x}_j^{1-\beta} n_j^{-1/\theta}$$
$$= (1 - \gamma)\beta[\beta + (1 - \beta)\varepsilon / A_j]z_j^{1/\theta+\beta-1} \bar{x}_j^{1-\beta} A_j n_j^{-1/\theta}$$
$$= (1 - \gamma)\beta[\beta + (1 - \beta)\varepsilon / A_j]z_j^{1/\theta-1} y_j n_j^{-1/\theta}$$
$$= (1 - \gamma)\beta[\beta + (1 - \beta)(A / A_j)g_j / r]y_j z_j^{1/\theta-1} n_j^{-1/\theta},$$

$$AP_j = [\beta A_j + (1 - \beta)\varepsilon]\beta z_j^{\beta-1} \bar{x}_j^{1-\beta} f_1(l_j - g_j, n_j)$$
$$= \gamma\beta[\beta + (1 - \beta)(A / A_j)g_j / r]y_j z_j^{1/\theta-1}(l_j - g_j)^{-1/\theta}.$$

Finally, substituting P_j from (8b.8) into this last equation and multiplying by rA_j / A, we obtain

$$A_j[(1-\beta)z_j^\beta \bar{x}_j^{1-\beta} - \eta \bar{x}_j] = rA_j P_j$$
$$= \gamma\beta[\beta rA_j/A + (1-\beta)g_j]$$
$$\times y_j z_j^{1/\theta-1}(l_j - g_j)^{-1/\theta}.$$

Substituting $\bar{x}_j = \phi z_j$ from (8.16) and y_j from (8.19) yields

$$A_j[(1-\beta)\phi^{1-\beta}z_j - \eta\phi z_j]$$
$$= \gamma\beta\phi^{1-\beta}[\beta rA_j/A + (1-\beta)g_j]z_j^{1/\theta}(l_j - g_j)^{-1/\theta}A_j.$$

Dividing this by $(1-\beta)\phi^{1-\beta}z_j A_j$, we obtain

$$1 - \eta\phi^\beta/(1-\beta) = \gamma\beta[(1-\beta)^{-1}\beta rA_j/A + g_j]z_j^{1/\theta-1}(l_j - g_j)^{-1/\theta}.$$

Substituting ϕ from (8.16) into this implies

$$\beta = 1 - (1-\beta) = \gamma\beta[(1-\beta)^{-1}\beta rA_j/A + g_j]z_j^{1/\theta-1}(l_j - g_j)^{-1/\theta}$$

and

$$(l_j - g_j)^{1/\theta} = \gamma[(1-\beta)^{-1}\beta rA_j/A + g_j]z_j^{1/\theta-1}.$$

It is easy to see that this leads to (8.20).

Appendix 8c. *The proof of functions* (8.25)

We consider the case $g_j > 0$. Substituting (8.22) into (8.20) and noting $g = g_j + g_{-j}$, we obtain the function

$$l_j(z_j, g_j, g_{-j}) = g_j + \gamma^\theta[(1-\beta)^{-1}\beta(\rho + \sigma g)A_j/A + g_j]^\theta z_j^{1-\theta}$$
$$= g_j + \gamma^\theta\{(1-\beta)^{-1}\beta[\rho + \sigma(g_j + g_{-j})]A_j/A + g_j\}^\theta z_j^{1-\theta},$$

for which

$$\partial l_j/\partial g_j > 1, \quad \partial l_j/\partial g_{-j} > 0, \quad \partial l_j/\partial z_j = (1-\theta)(l_j - g_j)/z_j > 0.$$
$$\tag{8c.1}$$

In the steady state given by (8.21), the ratio $A_j/A = A_j(0)/A(0)$ is fixed. From the linear homogeneous production function f in (8.5) it follows that

$$1 = f_1[\partial l_j/\partial z_j] + f_2[\partial n_j/\partial z_j], \quad 0 = f_1[\partial l_j/\partial g_j - 1] + f_2[\partial n_j/\partial g_j],$$
$$0 = f_1[\partial l_j/\partial g_{-j}] + f_2[\partial n_j/\partial g_{-j}],$$
$$z_j = (l_j - g_j)f_1 + n_j f_2 > (l_j - g_j)f_1, \quad (l_j - g_j)f_1/z_j < 1,$$

where $f_1 \doteq \partial f / \partial (l_j - g_j) > 0$ and $f_2 \doteq \partial f / \partial n_j > 0$. This and $\theta < 1$ imply the function $n_j(z_j, g_j, g_{-j})$ with

$$\partial n_j / \partial z_j = \{1 - f_1[\partial l_j / \partial z_j]\} / f_2$$
$$= [1 - (1 - \theta)(l_j - g_j)f_1 / z_j] / f_2 > [1 - (1 - \theta)] / f_2$$
$$= \theta / f_2 > 0, \tag{8c.2}$$
$$\partial n_j / \partial g_j = (f_1 / f_2)[1 - \partial l_j / \partial g_j] < 0,$$
$$\partial n_j / \partial g_{-j} = -(f_1 / f_2)\partial l_j / \partial g_{-j} < 0.$$

Given (8.18), we obtain

$$w_j / W_j = (1 - \gamma)^{-1} \gamma n_j^{1/\theta} (l_j - g_j)^{-1/\theta}.$$

Substituting this and the function (8.3) into the equilibrium condition (8.10) yields

$$L_j[-R'(L_j)] / R(L_j) = -L_j R'(L_j) / N_j = (w_j / W_j) l_j / n_j$$
$$= (1 - \gamma)^{-1} \gamma n_j^{1/\theta - 1} (l_j - g_j)^{-1/\theta} l_j, \tag{8c.3}$$

where $R' < 0$ and $R > 0$. From (8.3), (8.20), (8.21) and (8c.3) it follows that the supply of labour is given by the functions $L_j(z_j, g_j, g_{-j})$ and $N_j(z_j, g_j, g_{-j})$.

Unfortunately, the effect of g_j and g_{-j} on the labour supplies L_j and N_j is ambiguous. For this reason, we consider the properties of the supply functions only in the vicinity of $l_j = L_j$. Substituting $l_j = L_j$ into (8c.3), we obtain

$$-R'(L_j) / R(L_j) = (1 - \gamma)^{-1} \gamma n_j^{1/\theta - 1} (l_j - g_j)^{-1/\theta}.$$

Then, taking a logarithmic transformation and differentiating with respect to L_j, g_j and g_{-j} implies

$$\left[\frac{R''}{R'} - \frac{R'}{R} \right] dL_j = \left[\frac{1}{\theta} \frac{1}{l_j - g_j} \left(1 - \frac{\partial l_j}{\partial g_j} \right) + \left(\frac{1}{\theta} - 1 \right) \frac{\partial n_j}{\partial g_j} \right] dg_j$$
$$+ \left[\frac{1}{\theta} \frac{1}{g_j - l_j} \frac{\partial l_j}{\partial g_{-j}} + \left(\frac{1}{\theta} - 1 \right) \frac{\partial n_j}{\partial g_{-j}} \right] dg_{-j}. \tag{8c.4}$$

Given (8c.1), (8c.2), (8c.4) and the transformation function (8.3), we obtain

$$[\partial L_j / \partial g_j]_{l_j = L_j} < 0, \quad [\partial L_j / \partial g_{-j}]_{l_j = L_j} < 0,$$
$$[\partial N_j / \partial g_j]_{l_j = L_j} > 0, \quad [\partial N_j / \partial g_{-j}]_{l_j = L_j} > 0. \tag{8c.5}$$

The properties (8.25) are given by (8c.1)–(8c.5). Finally, given (8c.1), (8c.3) and (8.3), we see that

$$\lim_{\theta \to 1} \partial l_j / \partial z_j = \lim_{\theta \to 1} \partial L_j / \partial z_j = \lim_{\theta \to 1} \partial N_j / \partial z_j = 0.$$

Appendix 8d. *The proof of functions* **(8.30)** *and* **(8.31)**

In the steady state (8.21), given (8.19) and (8.22), variables r, P_j, g_j, A/A_j and y_j/A_j are all constants. Then, substituting ϕ, y_j, P_j, r, Π_j and I_j from (8.16), (8.19), (8.22), (8.24), (8.28) and (8.29), respectively, the objective functions for oligopolist j and union j take the form

$$
\begin{aligned}
\mathcal{P}_j(z_j, g_j, g_{-j}) &= \int_0^\infty \Pi_j e^{-rt} dt \\
&= (1 - \beta)\beta[1 - (A/A_j)g_j/r]\frac{y_j}{A_j}\int_0^\infty A_j e^{-rt} dt \\
&= (1 - \beta)\beta\phi^{1-\beta}[1 - g_j(\rho + \sigma g)^{-1}A(0)/A_j(0)] \\
&\quad \times [\rho + (\sigma - 1)g]^{-1} z_j A_j(0),
\end{aligned}
$$

$$
\begin{aligned}
\mathcal{W}_j(z_j, g_j, g_{-j}) &= \int_0^\infty I_j e^{-rt} dt \\
&= \{\beta[\beta + (1 - \beta)(A/A_j)g_j/r]y_j/A_j + P_j g_j A/A_j\} \\
&\quad \times \int_0^\infty A_j e^{-rt} dt \\
&= \{\beta\phi^{1-\beta}[\beta + (1 - \beta)(A/A_j)g_j/r]z_j \\
&\quad + (1 - \beta)^{-1}\phi\eta\beta z_j(g_j/r)A/A_j\}\int_0^\infty A_j e^{-rt} dt \\
&= \beta\phi^{1-\beta}\{\beta r + (1 - \beta)g_j A/A_j \\
&\quad + (1 - \beta)^{-1}\eta\phi^\beta g_j A/A_j\}(z_j/r)\int_0^\infty A_j e^{-rt} dt \\
&= \beta\phi^{1-\beta}[\beta r + 2(1 - \beta)g_j A/A_j](z_j/r)\int_0^\infty A_j e^{-rt} dt \\
&= \beta^2\phi^{1-\beta}[r + 2(1/\beta - 1)g_j A/A_j](z_j/r)\int_0^\infty A_j e^{-rt} dt \\
&= \beta^2\phi^{1-\beta}(\rho + \sigma g)^{-1}[\rho + (\sigma - 1)g]^{-1} \\
&\quad \times [\rho + \sigma g + 2(1/\beta - 1)g_j A(0)/A_j(0)]z_j A_j(0).
\end{aligned}
$$

Appendix 8e. *The proof of proposition* 8.1

This is an extension of the proof of proposition 1 in Palokangas (1996) such that profits result from monopoly power, the supply of the labour inputs is endogenous through the change of occupation, and collective bargaining can be at any level of the economy. We try to find such a steady state of the model that would maximize the generalized Nash product (8.32). For this, we summarize the relevant properties of the model as follows. The logarithmic transformations of the functions (8.30) and (8.31) are

$$\log \mathcal{P}_j = \log z_j - \log[\rho + (\sigma - 1)g] + \log A_j(0)$$

$$+ \log[1 - (\rho + \sigma g)^{-1} g_j A(0)/A_j(0)] + \text{constants},$$

$$\log \mathcal{W}_j = \log z_j - \log(\rho + \sigma g) - \log[\rho + (\sigma - 1)g] \qquad (8e.1)$$

$$+ \log[\rho + \sigma g + 2(1/\beta - 1)g_j A(0)/A_j(0)]$$

$$+ \log A_j(0) + \text{constants},$$

where

$$(\rho + \sigma g)^{-1} g_j A(0)/A_j(0) < 1. \qquad (8e.2)$$

Now given (8e.1), the maximization of the product (8.32) is equivalent to the maximization of the function

$$\Lambda_j(z_j, g_j, g_{-j}, \alpha) \doteq \log \Omega_j = \alpha \log \mathcal{W}_j + (1 - \alpha) \log \mathcal{P}_j$$

$$= \log z_j - \alpha \log(\rho + \sigma g) - \log[\rho + (\sigma - 1)g]$$

$$+ \alpha \log[\rho + \sigma g + 2(1/\beta - 1)g_j A(0)/A_j(0)]$$

$$+ (1 - \alpha) \log[1 - (\rho + \sigma g)^{-1} g_j A(0)/A_j(0)]$$

$$+ \log A_j(0) + \text{constants}. \qquad (8e.3)$$

In this appendix, for convenience, we denote

$$\Lambda_{jz} \doteq \frac{\partial \Lambda_j}{\partial z_j}, \quad \Lambda_{jg} \doteq \frac{\partial \Lambda_j}{\partial g_j}, \quad \mathcal{W}_{jz} \doteq \frac{\partial \mathcal{W}_j}{\partial z_j}, \quad \mathcal{W}_{jg} \doteq \frac{\partial \mathcal{W}_j}{\partial g_j},$$

$$l_{jz} \doteq \frac{\partial l_j}{\partial z_j}, \quad L_{jg} \doteq \frac{\partial L_j}{\partial g_j}, \quad n_{jz} \doteq \frac{\partial n_j}{\partial z_j}, \quad N_{jg} \doteq \frac{\partial N_j}{\partial g_j}.$$

Given this, (8.1), (8.4), (8.5), (8.21), (8.23), (8.25) and (8.32), we obtain

$$\sigma > 0, \quad \sigma \neq 1, \quad \rho > 0, \quad 0 < \beta < 1, \quad 0 < \alpha < 1, \quad \bar{g}_j > 0,$$

$$\rho + (\sigma - 1)g > 0, \quad g = \sum_{h=1}^{m} g_h = g_j + g_{-j}, \quad l_{jz} > 0, \quad l_{jg} > 0,$$

$$n_{jz} > 0, \quad n_{jg} < 0, \quad L_{jg}|_{l_j = L_j} < 0, \quad N_{jg}|_{l_j = L_j} > 0. \tag{8e.4}$$

Finally, given relations (8e.1)–(8e.4), we obtain

$$\mathcal{W}_{jz}/\mathcal{W}_j = \partial \log \mathcal{W}_j/\partial z_j = 1/z_j = \Lambda_{jz} > 0, \tag{8e.5}$$

$$\Lambda_{jg}(g_j, g_{-j}, \alpha) = \frac{1 - \sigma}{\rho + (\sigma - 1)g} - \frac{\alpha\sigma}{\rho + \sigma g}$$

$$+ \frac{[\sigma + 2(1/\beta - 1)A(0)/A_j(0)]\alpha}{\rho + \sigma g + 2(1/\beta - 1)g_j A(0)/A_j(0)}$$

$$+ \frac{(\alpha - 1)A(0)/A_j(0)}{1 - (\rho + \sigma g)^{-1}g_j A(0)/A_j(0)} \frac{\rho + \sigma g_{-j}}{(\rho + \sigma g)^2},$$

$$\frac{\partial^2 \Lambda_j}{\partial g_j \partial \alpha} = \frac{\sigma + 2(1/\beta - 1)A(0)/A_j(0)}{\rho + \sigma g + 2(1/\beta - 1)g_j A(0)/A_j(0)} - \frac{\sigma}{\rho + \sigma g}$$

$$+ \frac{A(0)/A_j(0)}{1 - (\rho + \sigma g)^{-1}g_j A(0)/A_j(0)} \frac{\rho + \sigma g_{-j}}{(\rho + \sigma g)^2}$$

$$= \frac{2(1/\beta - 1)(\rho + \sigma g_{-j})A(0)/A_j(0)}{(\rho + \sigma g)[\rho + \sigma g + 2(1/\beta - 1)g_j A(0)/A_j(0)]}$$

$$+ \frac{A(0)/A_j(0)}{1 - (\rho + \sigma g)^{-1}g_j A(0)/A_j(0)} \frac{\rho + \sigma g_{-j}}{(\rho + \sigma g)^2}$$

$$> 0, \tag{8e.6}$$

$$\mathcal{W}_{jg}/\mathcal{W}_j = \partial \log \mathcal{W}_j/\partial g_j$$

$$= \frac{\sigma + 2(1/\beta - 1)A(0)/A_j(0)}{\rho + \sigma g + 2(1/\beta - 1)g_j A(0)/A_j(0)} - \frac{\sigma}{\rho + \sigma g}$$

$$+ \frac{1 - \sigma}{\rho + (\sigma - 1)g}$$

$$= \frac{2(1/\beta - 1)(1 - \alpha)[\rho + (\sigma - 1)g]A(0)/A_j(0)}{(\rho + \sigma g)[\rho + \sigma g + 2(1/\beta - 1)g_j A(0)/A_j(0)]}$$

$$+ \Lambda_{jg} > \Lambda_{jg}. \tag{8e.7}$$

For each j, function (8e.3) is maximized subject to the employment constraints (8.2) and the union's incentive constraint (8.33), by the choice of inputs (z_j, g_j), holding input to research in the rest of the economy, g_{-j}, constant. The Lagrangean of this problem is given by

$$\mathcal{L}_j = \Lambda_j(z_j, g_j, g_{-j}, \alpha) + \xi_1[L_j(z_j, g_j, g_{-j}) - l_j(z_j, g_j, g_{-j})]$$
$$+ \xi_2[N_j(z_j, g_j, g_{-j}) - n_j(z_j, g_j, g_{-j})]$$
$$+ \xi_3[W_j(z_j, g_j, g_{-j}) - W_j(\bar{z}_j, \bar{g}_j, g_{-j})] + \xi_4 g_j, \qquad (8e.8)$$

where ξ_i are the multipliers satisfying the Kuhn–Tucker conditions

$$\xi_1[L_j(z_j, g_j, g_{-j}) - l_j(z_j, g_j, g_{-j})] = 0, \quad \xi_1 \geq 0,$$
$$\xi_2[N_j(z_j, g_j, g_{-j}) - n_j(z_j, g_j, g_{-j})] = 0, \quad \xi_2 \geq 0,$$
$$\xi_3[W_j(z_j, g_j, g_{-j}) - W_j(\bar{z}_j, \bar{g}_j, g_{-j})] = 0, \quad \xi_3 \geq 0,$$
$$\xi_4 g_j = 0, \quad \xi_4 \geq 0. \qquad (8e.9)$$

Noting (8e.5) and (8e.8), we obtain the first-order conditions

$$\partial \mathcal{L}_j / \partial z_j = [1 + \xi_3 W_j]/z_j + \xi_1[L_{jz} - l_{jz}] + \xi_2[N_{jz} - n_{jz}] = 0,$$
$$\partial \mathcal{L}_j / \partial g_j = \Lambda_{jg} + \xi_1[L_{jg} - l_{jg}] + \xi_2[N_{jg} - n_{jg}] + \xi_3 W_{jg} + \xi_4 = 0.$$
$$(8e.10)$$

Now we show the results one by one but not necessarily in the same order as in proposition 8.1.

(i) At least one of the labour inputs is fully employed.

Assume on the contrary that there is unemployment for both labour inputs, $n_j < N_j$ and $l_j < L_j$. Then given (8e.9) and (8e.10), we obtain

$$\xi_1 = \xi_2 = 0, \quad \partial \mathcal{L}_j / \partial z_j = [1 + \xi_3 W_j]/z_j > 0,$$

which is in contradiction with $\partial \mathcal{L}_j / \partial z_j = 0$. So the assumption cannot hold and either $n_j = N_j$ or $l_j = L_j$ must be true.

(ii) Composite input z_j can be expressed as a function of research inputs (g_j, g_{-j}) so that $\partial z_j / \partial g_j < 0$ for $g_j \geq \bar{g}_j$.

Consider first the economy in the vicinity of full employment (8.27). Now because $L_{jg} - l_{jg} < 0$ and $N_{jg} - n_{jg} > 0$ by (8e.4), and because cases $L_j < l_j$

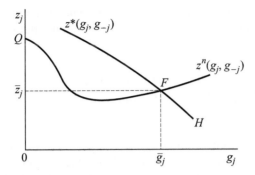

Figure 8e.1 The functions (8e.11).

and $N_j < n_j$ are impossible, a decrease in g_j below $\bar{g}_j$ (holding z_j and g_{-j} constant) implies $L_j > l_j$, and an increase in g_j above $\bar{g}_j$ implies $N_j > n_j$. Given (8e.4), (8e.9) and (8e.10), we obtain two relations:

$$\xi_2 = 0, \quad \xi_1[l_{jz} - L_{jz}] = [1 + \xi_3 W_j]/z_j > 0 \text{ and } l_{jz} > L_{jz}$$
for $n_j < N_j$ and $l_j = L_j$;
$$\xi_1 = 0, \quad \xi_2[n_{jz} - N_{jz}] = [1 + \xi_3 W_j]/z_j > 0 \text{ and } n_{jz} > N_{jz}$$
for $l_j < L_j$ and $n_j = N_j$.

Now given these relations, results (8.25), the full-employment conditions (8.27) and the relations (8e.4), we can define composite input z_j as a function of research input g_j:

$$z_j = \begin{cases} z^n(g_j, g_{-j}), \quad \partial z^n/\partial g_j = (N_{jg} - n_{jg})/(n_{jz} - N_{jz}) \\ \qquad\qquad \text{and } n_j = N_j \text{ for } g_j \leq \bar{g}_j, \\ z^*(g_j, g_{-j}), \quad \partial z^*/\partial g_j = (L_{jg} - l_{jg})/(l_{jz} - L_{jz}) < 0 \\ \qquad\qquad \text{and } l_j = L_j \text{ for } g_j \geq \bar{g}_j, \quad (8e.11) \end{cases}$$

$$z^n(\bar{g}_j, g_{-j}) = z^*(\bar{g}_j, g_{-j}) = \bar{z}_j,$$
$$\partial z^*(g_j, g_{-j})/\partial g_{-j} = [\partial L_j/\partial g_{-j} - \partial l_j/\partial g_{-j}]/(l_{jz} - L_{jz}) < 0,$$
$$\partial z^n(\bar{g}_j, g_{-j})/\partial g_j = [\partial z^n/\partial g_j]_{l_j = L_j} > 0.$$

In the (g_j, z_j) plane, this dependence can be illustrated as in figure 8e.1. The function z^* is decreasing, while the function z^n is increasing where it crosses z^*, but otherwise the slope of z^n is ambiguous. Since we assumed that the equilibrium with full employment, $(\bar{g}_j, \bar{z}_j)$, is unique, the crossing point F is unique. Now given result (i) above, curve QFH defines composite input z_j as a function of research input g_j.

(iii) The greater is the relative bargaining power α of union j, the more likely oligopolist j has some research of its own, $g_j > 0$.

Assume that oligopolist j has no research at all, $g_j = 0$. Now since $\bar{g}_j > g_j = 0$ by (8e.4), given the function (8e.11), there must be full employment for unskilled labour, $n_j = N_j$, but unemployment for skilled labour, $l_j < L_j$, so that $z_j = z''(0, g_{-j})$ holds. From this, relations (8e.4), (8e.9) and (8e.11), and the upper equation in (8e.10) it follows that

$$\xi_1 = 0, \quad \xi_2 = [1 + \xi_3 W_j]/[(n_{jz} - N_{jz})z_j] > 0, \quad n_{jz} > N_{jz},$$

$$\partial z''(0, g_{-j})/\partial g_j = (N_{jg} - n_{jg})/(n_{jz} - N_{jz}) > 0.$$

Given these equations and the lower equation in (8e.10), we obtain

$$0 > -\xi_4$$

$$= \left\{ \Lambda_{jg} + \xi_3 W_{jg} + [1 + \xi_3 W_j]\frac{1}{z_j}[(N_{jg} - n_{jg})/(n_{jz} - N_{jz})] \right\}_{g_j=0}$$

$$= \Lambda_{jg}(0, g_{-j}, \alpha) + \xi_3 W_{jg}(z''(0, g_{-j}), 0, g_{-j})$$

$$+ [1 + \xi_3 W_j][1/z''(0, g_{-j})]\partial z''(0, g_{-1})/\partial g_j. \tag{8e.12}$$

According to (8e.6), the increase in α increases Λ_{jg} and the right-hand side of inequality (8e.12). When α increases to a sufficiently high level, then inequality (8e.12) cannot hold, assumption $g_j = 0$ cannot hold and it must be the case that $g_j > 0$. Since, however, α cannot exceed one, we write this result in a milder form: the increase in α reduces the likelihood that there is no research by oligopolist j, $g_j = 0$.

(iv) If oligopolist j has some research, it employs all available skilled labour, $l_j = L_j$. Composite labour input z_j is a decreasing function of research input g_j, and the research input corresponding to full employment, $\bar{g}_j$, is the lower limit for g_j.

Assume on the contrary that oligopolist j does not employ all available skilled labour, $l_j < L_j$, and that it has some research, $g_j > 0$. Then, given relations (8e.4), (8e.9) and (8e.11) as well as the upper equation in (8e.10), we obtain

$$\xi_1 = \xi_4 = 0, \quad \xi_2 = [1 + \xi_3 W_j]/[(n_{jz} - N_{jz})z_j] > 0, \quad n_j = N_j,$$

$$n_{jz} > N_{jz},$$

$$g_j < \bar{g}_j, \quad \partial z^n/\partial g_j = (N_{jg} - n_{jg})/(n_{jz} - N_{jz}) > 0. \tag{8e.13}$$

From relations (8e.13), equality (8e.5), inequality (8e.7) and the lower equation in (8e.10) it follows that

$$\begin{aligned}
0 &= \Lambda_{jg} + \xi_2[N_{jg} - n_{jg}] + \xi_3 W_{jg} \\
&< W_{jg}/W_j + \xi_2[N_{jg} - n_{jg}] + \xi_3 W_{jg} \\
&= W_{jg}/W_j + (1 + \xi_3 W_j)(1/z_j)(N_{jg} - n_{jg})/(n_{jz} - N_{jz}) + \xi_3 W_{jg} \\
&= W_{jg}/W_j + (1 + \xi_3 W_j)(W_{jz}/W_j)\partial z^n(g_j, g_{-j})/\partial g_j + \xi_3 W_{jg} \\
&= (1/W_j + \xi_3)[W_{jg} + W_{jz}\, \partial z^n(g_j, g_{-j})/\partial g_j] \\
&= (1/W_j + \xi_3)dW_j(z^n(g_j, g_{-j}), g_j, g_{-j})/dg_j.
\end{aligned}$$

This and $\xi_3 \geq 0$ from (8e.9) implies

$$dW_j/dg_j|_{n_j=N_j} = dW_j(z^n(g_j, g_{-j}), g_j, g_{-j})/dg_j > 0. \tag{8e.14}$$

Noting $g_j < \bar{g}_j$ in (8e.13), result (8e.14) yields

$$W_j(z^n(g_j, g_{-j}), g_j, g_{-j}) < W_j(\bar{z}_j, \bar{g}_j, g_{-j}) \text{ for } g_j < \bar{g}_j,$$

which is in contradiction to (8.33). So the assumption cannot be true and inequalities $l_j < L_j$ and $g_j > 0$ cannot hold simultaneously. We conclude that if oligopolist j has some research, $g_j > 0$, then skilled labour is fully employed, $l_j = L_j$. Given this result and the function (8e.11), the following must hold:

$$z_j = z^*(g_j, g_{-j}), \quad \partial z^*/\partial g_j < 0 \text{ and } g_j \geq \bar{g}_j \text{ for } g_j > 0.$$

(v) In the Cobb–Douglas limiting case $\theta \to 1$, oligopolist j does research only if it employs all available skilled and unskilled labour, $n_j = N_j$ and $l_j = L_j$.

From (8.26), (8e.4), (8e.9) and (8e.10) it follows that

$$l_{jz} = L_{jz} = N_{jz} = 0, \quad \xi_2 = (1/n_{jz})[1 + \xi_3 W_j]/z_j > 0$$

and $n_j = N_j$. Given result (iv) above, we obtain the result that if oligopolist j has some research, then it must be the case that $l_j = L_j$ as well.

(vi) If there is unemployment for the members of union j, then the increase in the relative bargaining power of union j, α, increases the research input g_j of oligopolist j.

Assume that some members of union j are unemployed, and that oligopolist j has some research, $g_j > 0$. Then, given result (iv), only unskilled labour is unemployed, $n_j < N_j$, and given (8e.11) and (8e.9), it must be the case that

$$g_j > \bar{g}_j > 0, \quad \xi_2 = \xi_4 = 0. \tag{8e.15}$$

In such a case, the first-order conditions (8e.10) take the form

$$\begin{aligned}
\partial \mathcal{L}_j/\partial z_j &= [1 + \xi_3 W_j]/z_j + \xi_1[L_{jz} - l_{jz}] = 0, \\
\partial \mathcal{L}_j/\partial g_j &= \Lambda_{jg} + \xi_1[L_{jg} - l_{jg}] + \xi_3 W_{jg} = 0.
\end{aligned} \tag{8e.16}$$

On the other hand, from (8e.9), (8e.11) and the upper equation in (8e.16), it follows that

$$\begin{aligned}
\xi_1 &= [1 + \xi_3 W_j]/[(l_{jz} - L_{jz})z_j] > 0, \\
\partial z^*(g_j, g_{-j})/\partial g_j &= (L_{jg} - l_{jg})/(l_{jz} - L_{jz}) < 0.
\end{aligned}$$

Given these relations, inequality (8e.7) and the lower equation in (8e.16), we obtain

$$\begin{aligned}
0 &= \Lambda_{jg} + (L_{jg} - l_{jg})\xi_1 + \xi_3 W_{jg} \\
&< W_{jg}/W_j + (L_{jg} - l_{jg})\xi_1 + \xi_3 W_{jg} \\
&= W_{jg}/W_j + (1 + \xi_3 W_j)(1/z_j)(L_{jg} - l_{jg})/(l_{jz} - L_{jz}) + \xi_3 W_{jg} \\
&= W_{jg}/W_j + (1 + \xi_3 W_j)(W_{jz}/W_j)\partial z^*(g_j, g_{-j})/\partial g_j + \xi_3 W_{jg} \\
&= (1/W_j + \xi_3)[W_{jg} + W_{jz}\,\partial z^*(g_j, g_{-j})/\partial g_j] \\
&= (1/W_j + \xi_3)dW(z^*(g_j, g_{-j}), g_j, g_{-j})/dg_j.
\end{aligned}$$

This implies

$$dW_j/dg_j|_{l_j = L_j} = dW(z^*(g_j, g_{-j}), g_j, g_{-j})/dg_j > 0. \tag{8e.17}$$

Given $g_j > \bar{g}_j$ in (8e.15), result (8e.17) leads to inequality

$$W(z^*(g_j, g_{-j}), g_j, g_{-j}) > W(z^*(\bar{g}_j, g_{-j}), \bar{g}_j, g_{-j}).$$

This and (8e.9) yields $\xi_3 = 0$.

Given relations $\xi_3 = 0$ and (8e.15), the first-order conditions for the maximization of $\mathcal{L}_j$, (8e.9) and (8e.16), take the form

$$L_j(z_j, g_j, g_{-j}) - l_j(z_j, g_j, g_{-j}) = 0,$$

$$\partial \mathcal{L}_j / \partial z_j = 1/z_j + \xi_1[L_{jz}(z_j, g_j, g_{-j}) - l_{jz}(z_j, g_j, g_{-j})] = 0,$$

$$\partial \mathcal{L}_j / \partial g_j = \Lambda_{jg}(z_j, g_j, g_{-j}, \alpha) + \xi_1[L_{jg}(z_j, g_j, g_{-j}) - l_{jg}(z_j, g_j, g_{-j})]$$

$$= 0, \tag{8e.18}$$

where z_j, g_j and ξ_1 are endogenous and α and g_{-j} are exogenous variables. So when there is unemployment, $n_j < N_j$ and $g_j > \bar{g}_j$, the dependence of g_j on α, $\partial g_j / \partial \alpha$, can be obtained from (8e.18). Given (8e.6) and (8e.8), it must be the case that

$$\frac{\partial^2 \mathcal{L}_j}{\partial g_j \partial \alpha} = \frac{\partial^2 \Lambda_j}{\partial g_j \partial \alpha} > 0.$$

By the second-order conditions for the maximization of $\mathcal{L}_j$, the Jacobian of the system (8e.18), $\mathcal{J}$, must be strictly positive, so that by the comparative statics of the system, we obtain

$$g_j = G(\alpha, g_{-j}) \text{ with } \frac{\partial G}{\partial \alpha} = (1/\mathcal{J})[L_{jz} - l_{jz}]^2 \frac{\partial^2 \mathcal{L}_j}{\partial g_j \partial \alpha} > 0 \text{ for } g_j > \bar{g}_j.$$

This result can also be written in the form

$$g_j = \max[G(\alpha, g_{-j}), \bar{g}_j], \quad G_1 \doteq \partial G/\partial \alpha > 0, \quad G_2 \doteq \partial G/\partial g_{-j}. \tag{8e.19}$$

This completes the proof of result (vi).

Conclusions

In the case of fully centralized bargaining, for which $m = 1$, $g_j = g$, $z_j = z$ and $g_{-j} = 0$ hold, results (i)–(v) form proposition 8.1 as they stand. In the case of decentralized bargaining, for which $m > 1$ and $g_{-j} = \sum_{h \neq j} g_h$ hold, we deduce the proposition by the use of symmetry and the stability of oligopolistic equilibrium.

In the model, there is perfect symmetry over $j = 1, \ldots, m$. This has four immediate consequences. First, given (i) and (iv), skilled labour is fully employed, $l_j = L_j$, for all j. Second, given (iii), the greater the relative bargaining power α of all unions, the more likelihood there is of some growth, $g = \sum_h g_h > 0$. Third, denoting the balanced growth rate corresponding to full employment by $\bar{g}$, the full-employment level of research input is $\bar{g}_j = \bar{g}/m$ for every j. If there is some growth in the economy, then given (iv), it must be the case that $g = \sum_h g_h \geq \bar{g}$. Given this and the function (8e.11), we obtain

$$z_j = z = z^*(g/m, (1 - 1/m)g) \text{ with}$$

$$dz/dg = (1/m)[\partial z^*/\partial g_j] + (1 - 1/m)[\partial z^*/\partial g_{-j}] < 0.$$

Finally in the Cobb–Douglas limiting case $\theta \to 1$, given (v), there cannot simultaneously be growth and unemployment.

It remains to prove result (e) in proposition 8.1 for the case of decentralized bargaining. If there is unemployment, $n_j < N_j$ for all j, the function (8e.19) yields a system of m equations

$$Q_j = g_j - G(\alpha, g_{-j}) = 0, \quad j = 1, \dots, m,$$

with endogenous variables $g_1, \dots, g_m$. Differentiating this system, we obtain the coefficient matrix

$$[\partial Q_j/\partial g_h]_{m \times m}. \tag{8e.20}$$

Union j and oligopolist j act as if they were a single agent that behaves in a Cournot manner with respect to the other unions and oligopolists $h \neq j$: they choose input g_j taking g_h for $h \neq j$ as fixed. The reaction function of union and oligopolist j is given by (8e.19). Since there is perfect symmetry over $j = 1, \dots, m$, one of the sufficient conditions for the stability of the Cournot equilibrium requires that the coefficient matrix (8e.20) is subject to diagonal dominance:[11]

$$1 \pm (m-1)G_2 = \frac{\partial Q_j}{\partial g_j} \pm (m-1)\frac{\partial Q_j}{\partial g_h} > 0 \text{ for } h \neq j, \tag{8e.21}$$

where G_2 is defined by (8e.19). The interpretation of this stability condition (8e.21) is straightforward. Assume that the effect of the other quantities g_h ($h \neq j$) on the right-hand side of (8e.19) is negative and exceeds unity. Now let all quantities g_j be just above the level corresponding to the symmetric equilibrium $g_j = g/m$ for all j. Then $Q_j < 0$ for all j and all j will increase their quantities g_j. Since these increases in quantities g_j will in turn decrease Q_j for all j, there cannot be a stable outcome.

In symmetry $g_j = g/m$ and relation (8e.19) takes the form

$$g = mG(\alpha, (1 - 1/m)g).$$

Differentiating this and noting the stability condition (8e.21), we obtain

$$dg/d\alpha = mG_1/[1 - (m-1)G_2] > 0 \text{ for } g > \bar{g}.$$

---

[11] See, for example, Dixit (1986), p. 117. Here, the diagonal term 1 is positive so that the inequality must be greater than zero.

Noting the full-employment constraint $g \geq \bar{g}$, this result can also be written as follows:

$$g = \max[g^u(\alpha), \bar{g}], \quad dg^u/d\alpha > 0.$$

Appendix 8f. *The proof of proposition* 8.2

The optimization is carried out in the same way as in appendix 8e but, because the equalities $L_j \geq l_j$ are now replaced by equalities $L_j = l_j$, the task is here much simpler. Given (8.34), functions (8e.1) and (8e.3) take the form

$$\log \mathcal{W}_j = \log z_j - \log(\rho + \sigma g) - \log[\rho + (\sigma - 1)g]$$
$$+ \log[\rho + \sigma g + (1/\beta - 1)(2g_j - L_j)A(0)/A_j(0)]$$
$$+ \log A_j(0) + \text{constants}, \tag{8f.1}$$

$$\Lambda_j(z_j, g_j, g_{-j}, \alpha) \doteq \log \Omega_j = \alpha \log \mathcal{W}_j + (1 - \alpha) \log \mathcal{P}_j$$
$$= \log z_j - \alpha \log(\rho + \sigma g) - \log[\rho + (\sigma - 1)g]$$
$$+ \alpha \log[\rho + \sigma g + (1/\beta - 1)$$
$$\times (2g_j - L_j)A(0)/A_j(0)]$$
$$+ (1 - \alpha) \log[1 - (\rho + \sigma g)^{-1} g_j A(0)/A_j(0)]$$
$$+ \log A_j(0) + \text{constants}. \tag{8f.2}$$

Because $\mathcal{W}_j > 0$ in (8.34), it must be the case that

$$\rho + \sigma g + (1/\beta - 1)(2g_j - L_j)A(0)/A_j(0) > 0.$$

Now given this, (8e.2) and (8e.4), we see that the functions (8f.1) and (8f.2) yield the properties (8e.5)–(8e.7). This means that the results in appendix 8e hold as they stand.

Appendix 8g. *The proof of proposition* 8.3

Given (8.36), the maximization of the product (8.38) is equivalent to the maximization of the function

$$\Lambda_j^*(z_j, g_j, g_{-j}, s_j, \alpha) \doteq \log \Omega_j^*$$

$$= \alpha \log \mathcal{W}_j^*(z_j, g_j, g_{-j}, s_j) + (1-\alpha)\mathcal{P}_j^*(z_j, g_j, g_{-j}, s_j)$$

$$= \alpha \log[\mathcal{W}_j(z_j, g_j, g_{-j}) + s_j\mathcal{P}_j(z_j, g_j, g_{-j})]$$

$$+ (1-\alpha)[\log \mathcal{P}_j(z_j, g_j, g_{-j}) + \log(1-s_j)]. \tag{8g.1}$$

This is maximized subject to the limits of profit-sharing (8.35), the union's incentive constraint (8.37) and the employment conditions (8.2) – where the demand and supply functions are given by (8.25) – by the choice of (z_j, g_j, s_j). The Lagrangean of this problem is given by

$$\mathcal{L}_j^* = \Lambda_j^*(z_j, g_j, g_{-j}, s_j, \alpha) + \xi_1[L_j(z_j, g_j, g_{-j}) - l_j(z_j, g_j, g_{-j})]$$

$$+ \xi_2[N_j(z_j, g_j, g_{-j}) - n_j(z_j, g_j, g_{-j})]$$

$$+ \xi_3[\mathcal{W}_j^*(z_j, g_j, g_{-j}, s_j) - \mathcal{W}_j(\bar{z}_j, \bar{g}_j, g_{-j})]$$

$$+ \xi_4 g_j + \xi_5 s_j + \xi_6[1 - s_j], \tag{8g.2}$$

where ξ_i are the multipliers satisfying the Kuhn–Tucker conditions

$$\xi_1[L_j(z_j, g_j, g_{-j}) - l_j(z_j, g_j, g_{-j})] = 0, \quad \xi_1 \geq 0,$$

$$\xi_2[N_j(z_j, g_j, g_{-j}) - n_j(z_j, g_j, g_{-j})] = 0, \quad \xi_2 \geq 0,$$

$$\xi_3[\mathcal{W}_j^*(z_j, g_j, g_{-j}, s_j) - \mathcal{W}_j(\bar{z}_j, \bar{g}_j, g_{-j})] = 0, \quad \xi_3 \geq 0,$$

$$\xi_4 g_j = 0, \quad \xi_4 \geq 0, \quad \xi_5 s_j = 0, \quad \xi_5 \geq 0, \quad \xi_6[1 - s_j] = 0, \quad \xi_6 \geq 0. \tag{8g.3}$$

One easily observes from (8.36) that

$$\mathcal{W}_j^*(z_j, g_j, g_{-j}, 0) \equiv \mathcal{W}_j(z_j, g_j, g_{-j}),$$

$$\mathcal{P}_j^*(z_j, g_j, g_{-j}, 0) \equiv \mathcal{P}_j(z_j, g_j, g_{-j}),$$

$$\Lambda_j^*(z_j, g_j, g_{-j}, 0, \alpha) \equiv \Lambda_j(z_j, g_j, g_{-j}, \alpha),$$

$$\mathcal{L}_j^*(z_j, g_j, g_{-j}, 0, \alpha) \equiv \mathcal{L}_j(z_j, g_j, g_{-j}, \alpha),$$

where Λ_j and $\mathcal{L}_j$ are defined by (8e.3) and (8e.8). This connection with appendix 8e turns out to be very useful. From the functions (8g.1) and (8g.2) it follows that the first-order condition for the sharing ratio s_j is given by

$$\partial\mathcal{L}_j^*/\partial s_j = \partial\Lambda_j^*/\partial s_j + \xi_5 - \xi_6$$

$$= \frac{\alpha\mathcal{P}_j}{\mathcal{W}_j + s_j\mathcal{P}_j} - \frac{1-\alpha}{1-s_j} + \xi_5 - \xi_6 = 0. \tag{8g.4}$$

Now using (8g.3) and (8g.4), we obtain the following two cases.

Case I: either $\alpha = 1$ or $(1 - \alpha)/\alpha = [(1 - s_j)\mathcal{P}_j]/[\mathcal{W}_j + s_j\mathcal{P}_j]$ holds.

If $\alpha = 1$, then given (8g.3) and (8g.4), we obtain

$$\xi_6 = \xi_5 + \alpha\mathcal{P}_j/[\mathcal{W}_j + s_j\mathcal{P}_j] > \xi_5 \geq 0, \quad s_j = 1.$$

In this case, the union deprives the oligopolist of all profit, the workers earn all income and the function (8g.1) takes the form

$$\Lambda_j^* = \log[\mathcal{W}_j(z_j, g_j, g_{-j}) + \mathcal{P}_j(z_j, g_j, g_{-j})].$$

Next, assume $\alpha < 1$ and $(1 - \alpha)/\alpha = [(1 - s_j)\mathcal{P}_j]/[\mathcal{W}_j + s_j\mathcal{P}_j]$, which is equivalent to

$$s_j = 1 - (1 - \alpha)\mathcal{W}_j/\mathcal{P}_j < 1. \tag{8g.5}$$

Then conditions (8g.3), (8g.4) and (8g.5) imply $\xi_5 = \xi_6 = 0$. Given (8g.5), we obtain

$$\mathcal{W}_j + s_j\mathcal{P}_j = (1 - \alpha)(\mathcal{W}_j + \mathcal{P}_j), \quad (1 - s_j)\mathcal{P}_j = \alpha(\mathcal{W}_j + \mathcal{P}_j).$$

Substituting these into the function (8g.1) yields

$$\Lambda_j^* = \log[\mathcal{W}_j(z_j, g_j, g_{-j}) + \mathcal{P}_j(z_j, g_j, g_{-j})] + \text{constants}.$$

We conclude that, in this case, the maximization of (8g.1) is equivalent to the maximization of the discounted value of total income, $\mathcal{W}_j + \mathcal{P}_j$. For convenience, we define

$$\bar{\alpha} = \inf\{\alpha|(8g.3), \partial\mathcal{L}_j^*/\partial z_j = \partial\mathcal{L}_j^*/\partial g_j = 0 \text{ and}$$
$$(1 - \alpha)/\alpha = [(1 - s_j)\mathcal{P}_j]/[\mathcal{W}_j + s_j\mathcal{P}_j] \text{ hold}\}.$$

If $\alpha \to 0$, then, given (8g.3) and (8g.4), we obtain $\xi_5 = \xi_6 + 1/(1 - s_j) > 0$ and $s_j = 0$. This shows that $\bar{\alpha} > 0$. Because condition

$$(1 - \alpha)/\alpha = [(1 - s_j)\mathcal{P}_j]/[\mathcal{W}_j + s_j\mathcal{P}_j]$$

cannot hold for $\alpha = 1$ and $s_j < 1$, it must be the case that $\bar{\alpha} < 1$. Now $\mathcal{W}_j + \mathcal{P}_j$ is maximized for $\bar{\alpha} \leq \alpha \leq 1$. Replacing Λ_j^* by $\mathcal{W}_j + \mathcal{P}_j$ in (8g.2), one observes immediately that the Lagrangean (8g.2) becomes totally independent of α. This means that for $\bar{\alpha} \leq \alpha \leq 1$, the unions' relative bargaining power α has no effect on research inputs g_j and, consequently, on the balanced growth rate of the economy, $g = \sum_j g_h$.

Case II: both $\alpha < 1$ *and* $(1 - \alpha)/\alpha \neq [(1 - s_j)\mathcal{P}_j]/[\mathcal{W}_j + s_j\mathcal{P}_j]$ *hold.*

In this remaining case, it must be the case that $0 < \alpha < \bar{\alpha} < 1$. Because $(1 - \alpha)/\alpha \neq 0$ cannot be true for $s_j = 1$ by (8g.4), it must be the case that $s_j < 1$. Then conditions (8g.3) and (8g.4) and the assumption yield $\xi_6 = 0$ and

$$\xi_5 = \frac{1 - \alpha}{1 - s_j} - \frac{\alpha\mathcal{P}_j}{\mathcal{W}_j + s_j\mathcal{P}_j} > 0, \quad s_j = 0.$$

So the economy ends up with the ordinary wage system where only the basic wages are determined in collective bargaining, $s_j = 0$. This case is the same as the one that was analysed in appendix 8e. Consequently, proposition 8.1 holds as it stands for $0 < \alpha < \bar{\alpha}$.

Appendix 8h. *The proof of proposition* 8.4

The maximization of the utility (8.1) subject to the differential equations $\dot{A} = gA$ and (8.42) and the inequality $g \geq \bar{g}$ leads to the Hamiltonian

$$\mathcal{H} = U(C) + \lambda[y - C] + \mu Ag, \tag{8h.1}$$

where $U(C)$ is given by (8.1) and y by (8.41). The shadow prices for assets A and K evolve according to[12]

$$\dot{\lambda} = \rho\lambda - \partial\mathcal{H}/\partial K = [\rho - \partial y/\partial K]\lambda = [\rho - (1 - \beta)y/K]\lambda,$$

$$\dot{\mu} = \rho\mu - \partial\mathcal{H}/\partial A = (\rho - g)\mu - \lambda\partial y/\partial A = (\rho - g)\mu - \beta y\lambda/A,$$

$$\lim_{t \to \infty} \lambda Ke^{-\rho t} = 0, \quad \lim_{t \to \infty} \mu Ae^{-\rho t} = 0. \tag{8h.2}$$

The Hamiltonian (8h.1) should be maximized by the choice of consumption C and the growth rate g, given $g \geq \bar{g}$.

The first-order conditions for this problem are given by

$$\lambda = C^{-\sigma} > 0, \quad \frac{\partial\mathcal{H}}{\partial g} = \mu A + \beta\lambda\frac{y}{z}\frac{dz}{dg} \begin{cases} < 0 & \text{for } g = \bar{g}, \\ = 0 & \text{for } g > \bar{g}. \end{cases} \tag{8h.3}$$

For a balanced growth equilibrium, it must be the case that

$$\dot{\mu}/\mu = \dot{\lambda}/\lambda, \quad \dot{K}/K = \dot{C}/C = \dot{A}/A = g.$$

Combining this and $C^{-\sigma} = \lambda$ from (8h.3) yields

---

[12] The constraint $g \geq \bar{g}$ is independent of the variables K and A.

$$\dot{\mu}/\mu = \dot{\lambda}/\lambda = -\sigma\dot{C}/C = -\sigma g.$$

From this, (8h.2) and (8h.3), we obtain

$$\beta y\lambda/(A\mu) = \rho + (\sigma - 1)g \ \text{ for } g > \bar{g}$$

and

$$[\rho + (\sigma - 1)g](1/z)dz/dg = [(\beta y\lambda/(zA\mu)]dz/dg = -1 \ \text{ for } g > \bar{g}.$$

Substituting $\partial z/\partial g$ from (8.43) into this yields

$$1 = [\rho + (\sigma - 1)g]\varphi(g)/(\beta g) \ \text{ for } g > \bar{g}.$$

Rearranging this, we obtain (8.44):

$$\beta g/\varphi(g) = \rho + (\sigma - 1)g \ \text{ and } \ g[\beta/\varphi(g) + 1 - \sigma] = \rho \ \text{ for } g > \bar{g}.$$

9 Unions and international specialization

9.1 Introduction

The preceding chapter examined the relationship of growth and collective bargaining in a closed and fully unionized economy. Now we extend this analysis to a world of two economies: one unionized economy where labour contracts are determined by collective bargaining; and another non-unionized economy where, for some unspecified reason, the wages adjust to maintain full employment. Equivalently, one could consider a closed economy with a unionized and a non-unionized sector. It is instructive to see how unionization in one country (or in one sector) changes the patterns of growth and specialization.

The following features of the model are the same as in the preceding chapter. There are two labour inputs termed 'skilled' and 'unskilled' labour. Households can change their supply of these two labour inputs at some cost but they must do it before entering the labour market. Technological knowledge arises from intentional investment decisions made by profit-maximizing agents. Technology is a non-rival input and – since this leads to increasing returns to scale – the equilibrium is supported by monopolistic competition. Collective bargaining is due to the existence of monopoly profits, and it can be carried out at any level of centralization. Finally, because neither the government nor the unions can completely distinguish between inputs being used in research and elsewhere, there is no wage discrimination between research and ordinary production and the government cannot attain full efficiency through direct subsidies to research.

200

In models of international trade, two extreme specifications for the spillover of technology are commonly used.[1] One is that scientific and engineering information can be used only in the country where it has been developed, so that the nationwide stock of technological knowledge becomes an input to the production of new designs. In such a case, a 'big' country possesses a 'big' stock of knowledge and specializes wholly in the production of refined goods, while a 'small country' possesses only a 'small' stock of knowledge and specializes wholly in the production of primary products. The other is that scientific and engineering information is freely available to all researchers in the world when they are pursuing their innovation efforts, so that the worldwide stock of technological knowledge becomes an input to the production of new designs. Because we are interested in the case where both economies produce both refined and primary goods, we take this latter specification as a starting point.

So far, Kemp, van Long and Shimomura (1991) have made the most extensive attempt to integrate labour unions into the theories of growth and international trade. Their monograph consists of a number of essays which introduce unions either into a static Heckscher–Ohlin trade model or into a Solow-type growth model in which technological change is wholly exogenous. The common feature of their findings is that from the welfare point of view, union power is either harmful or insignificant. This chapter shows that after endogenous growth is properly incorporated into the model, the exercise of union power can be welfare-enhancing. We show that the unions lower the relative wage of the labour input that is more intensively used in research. Consequently, the existence of unions decreases the relative price for the construction of new designs and thereby boosts growth in that economy.

International specialization is commonly explained by Heckscher–Ohlin theory which claims that countries with an abundance of some resource will specialize in products that are intensive in this resource. This chapter gives another explanation for specialization, which is as follows. Since the unions lower the relative wage of the labour input being more intensively used in research, the relative price of new designs for refined goods is lower in the unionized than in the non-unionized economy. Consequently, the unionized economy constructs a greater number of new designs and specializes in refined products while the non-unionized economy specializes in primary goods.

---

[1] See, for example, Grossman and Helpman (1991), chs. 7 and 8. Attempts to construct 'intermediate' cases where the spillover of technology is internationally partial lead to very complicated models.

The plan of the study is the following. Sections 9.2 and 9.3 indicate briefly the institutional background, microfoundations and overall structure of the model. Section 9.4 specifies the fine details of the individual agents' behaviour and section 9.5 establishes the balanced growth equilibrium for the whole world. On the basis of this, section 9.6 constructs collective bargaining. The results are generalized for the case of non-unionized workers in section 9.7 and for the case of profit-sharing in section 9.8. Finally, section 9.9 considers the problem of when, from the welfare point of view, union power and involuntary unemployment are desirable.

9.2 The setting

9.2.1 The economies

The world under consideration consists of two economies, one unionized and the other non-unionized, which have the same technology and preferences. The unionized economy contains a fixed number m of similar sectors, each of which is controlled by a single labour union. In the non-unionized economy, there is a fixed number a of sectors which are otherwise similar to those in the unionized economy but in which the wages adjust to maintain full employment. Given this specification, both economies possess all primary resources in the same proportion m/a, and in the unionized economy, collective bargaining can be organized at any level of centralization: bargaining is centralized for $m = 1$ and decentralized for large m.

In both economies, each sector produces one primary product and a variety of refined goods so that the index of the level of technology in this sector determines the amount of this variety. It is assumed, for tractability, that refined goods are made from these primary goods according to CES technology. Furthermore, each sector contains one oligopolist that employs skilled and unskilled labour, produces the primary good and constructs new designs for refined goods by research, and a number of monopolists that assemble refined goods from primary products. After the oligopolist has constructed a design for a product, it sells that design to a monopolist that will complete the product and sell it back to the oligopolist. All firms, oligopolists and monopolists alike, behave in a Bertrand manner: when making production decisions, each firm assumes that the others hold their prices fixed. This specification has two advantages. The first one is that since the monopolists do not employ labour, each union will have the oligopolist as the only opponent in bargaining. Second, the free entry of monopolists will support the equilibrium with technology as a non-rival input.

Since the model lacks a monetary instrument, nothing pins down the price level at any time. This means that we are free to set the time path for one nominal variable and to measure prices at every moment of time against the chosen numeraire. We normalize prices so that nominal consumption expenditure in the whole world is equal to unity.

9.2.2 Input markets

Aggregate knowledge is an input to research and it can be proxied by the variety of refined products in the whole world. To obtain persistent growth, we assume that the productivity of research is in fixed proportion to aggregate knowledge. It is plausible to think that research uses one primary input (e.g. skilled labour) more intensively than the rest of the economy. However, for tractability, we transform this property into the extreme specification that research uses only skilled labour.

Because the model will in other respects be very complex, we assume that the primary good is composed from skilled and unskilled labour using Cobb–Douglas technology. In the preceding chapter, it was shown that if the elasticity of substitution between skilled and unskilled labour is one, then on the balanced growth path there will be full employment. In this chapter, however, the existence of a competitive economy ensures that growth and unemployment can coexist even when the elasticity of substitution is unity.

In each sector of the unionized economy, a union and an oligopolist bargain over the pay parameters for the union members given the latter's optimal demand for skilled and unskilled labour. We assume, for the moment, that labour contracts consider only the wages. Later, in section 9.8, we consider the case where the parties bargain simultaneously over the wages and the workers' profit share. Because there are several union–oligopolist pairs bargaining simultaneously, we specify that each pair behaves in a Bertrand manner, assuming that the wages being set by the other pairs are held fixed (in terms of the numeraire).

9.2.3 The households

All households in the world have the same preferences and they can earn both wages and profits. To make the parties to collective bargaining independent, we assume that a household does not own any part of its employer. The households can also purchase bonds being issued in both economies so that by arbitrage, the world interest rate is uniform. The unemployment risk is assumed to be the same for all workers in the same country and occupation. Then, these workers have the same expected labour income and they support themselves in periods of unemployment by evening out their consumption over the periods of employment and unemployment. We assume that a single worker's labour time is fixed and that spare time yields no utility. Otherwise, the substitution of consumption and spare time would excessively complicate the analysis.

It is assumed that only refined goods are consumed while primary products are used only as inputs. It would be possible to extend the model so that the consumers could spend a fixed share of their expenditure on the refined goods and the rest on the primary good. In such a case, the model would be similar to that of Grossman and Helpman (1991), where there is one low-tech good and a group of high-tech goods to be consumed. However, this extension would cause technical complications and add very little to the understanding of the basic problem of the study.

The households supply skilled and unskilled labour and they can change the relative supply of these two inputs at some cost. As in chapter 8, we assume that there is a convex transformation function so that when the supply of skilled labour increases, more unskilled labour must be transformed to get one more unit of skilled labour (and vice versa). Because a household must determine which labour it is going to supply *before* entering the labour market, it must make this decision according to the expected income (=the wage times the expected rate of employment).

9.2.4 Steady-state analysis

As in chapter 8, we focus entirely on the steady state of the model. Then one can use the generalized Nash product to explain the outcome of bargaining and use the weight on the union's objective function as a measure of the union's relative bargaining power. On a balanced growth path, the agents of the model – the households, oligopolists, monopolists, unions and the government of the unionized economy (or nature) – act as players in an extensive game. The strategic order of their decisions is as follows:

Stage 1 The government of the unionized economy (or nature) sets the environment for the labour market. This determines the relative power of a union and an oligopolist in collective bargaining.

Stage 2 In the unionized economy, the union–oligopolist pairs set the wages (and possibly the workers' profit share) in an alternating-offers game.

Stage 3 The oligopolists and monopolists decide on production.

Stage 4 The households choose their consumption as well as their supplies of skilled and unskilled labour.

The alternating-offers game between a union and an oligopolist forms a single stage for the extensive game. This extensive game can result in involuntary unemployment such that a single household wants to work more at given wages. It is assumed that the firms decide on production after the union–oligopolist pairs have reached their agreements. Stages 1–4 describe a strategic order: a player acting in a specific stage takes the instruments of those acting at earlier stages as given and the optimal responses of those acting at the later stages as constraints.

9.3 The overall structure of the model

9.3.1 Primary resources

The unionized economy contains a fixed number m of sectors and we label these as $j = 1, \ldots, m$. In the non-unionized economy, there is a fixed number a of sectors. All sectors in both economies have equal amounts of primary resources. To simplify the notation, we label the non-unionized economy as the sector $j = 0$ of the unionized economy. Then in each sector $j = 0, 1, \ldots, m$, oligopolist j makes a primary product from skilled and unskilled labour and monopolists assemble a variety D_j of refined products from the composite primary good.

Let L_j (N_j) be the supply of skilled (unskilled) labour and l_j (n_j) the demand for skilled (unskilled) labour in sector j. The households in sectors $j \neq 0$ are unionized, so that there can be unemployment for both labour inputs. In sector 0, i.e. in the non-unionized economy, the wages adjust to maintain full employment for both labour inputs. This leads to the employment constraints

$$L_0 = l_0, \quad N_0 = n_0, \quad L_j \geq l_j \text{ and } N_j \geq n_j \text{ for } j = 1, \ldots, m. \quad (9.1)$$

The households can change their supply of labour through the convex transformation function R as follows:[2]

$$N_0 = aR(L_0/a), \quad N_j = R(L_j) \text{ for } j = 1, \ldots, m, \quad R' < 0, \quad R'' < 0. \quad (9.2)$$

Because the marginal rate of transformation, $-R'$, increases with the supply L_j of skilled labour, more and more unskilled labour N_j must be

---

[2] Because sector 0 consists of a units that are similar to the other sectors $j \neq 0$, the transformation function R must be defined between N_0/a and L_0/a for $j = 0$ and between N_j and L_j for $j \neq 0$.

changed in order to create one more unit of skilled labour. This implies that there exists an equilibrium composition of the labour supply for the representative household.

9.3.2 Consumption

In line with Grossman and Helpman (1991), we assume that the representative household in the world is subject to the following preferences:

$$u = \int_0^\infty [\log C] e^{-\rho t} dt, \quad C = \left[\int_{D_0 \cup D_1 \cup \ldots \cup D_m} y(i)^{1/\theta} di \right]^\theta,$$

$$\rho > 0, \quad \theta > 1, \tag{9.3}$$

where t is time, ρ the subjective discount rate, θ the mark-up factor in pricing the refined goods, $y(i)$ the world consumption of refined variety i, and C an index of world consumption. At any moment of time, there is a finite number A_j of designs $i \in D_j$. This implies

$$\int_{D_j} di = A_j \text{ for } j = 0, 1, \ldots, m. \tag{9.4}$$

Let p_c be the world price for consumption C and $p(i)$ that for refined variety $i \in (0, \infty)$. The prices are normalized so that nominal consumption expenditure in the world, $p_c C$, is equal to unity. Given (9.3), this implies

$$\int_{D_0 \cup D_1 \cup \cdots \cup D_m} p(i) y(i) di = p_c C = 1. \tag{9.5}$$

Since each monopolist produces a different good, consumption magnitude $y(i)$ is also the production of good j in the world. If no firm produces good i, $y(i) = 0$, then we define $p(i) = \infty$. Now from (9.3) it follows that

$$p(i)/p_c = \partial C / [\partial y(i)] = [C/y(i)]^{1-1/\theta}, \quad y(i) = C[p_c/p(i)]^{\theta/(\theta-1)} \tag{9.6}$$

9.3.3 Primary and refined goods

Let w_j be the wage for skilled labour and W_j that for unskilled labour in sector j. Then the unit labour cost in sector j is given by

$$\phi_j = w_j^\gamma W_j^{1-\gamma}, \quad 0 < \gamma < 1, \tag{9.7}$$

where γ is the expenditure share of skilled labour. The composite primary good is made from primary products $i = 0, 1, \ldots, m$ according to CES technology. Since the purchasers of the primary goods (i.e. the monopolists producing refined goods) take the prices of these as fixed, then, by a proper choice of units, we obtain the unit cost function

$$p_l = [ap_{l0}^{1-\varepsilon} + p_{l1}^{1-\varepsilon} + \cdots + p_{lm}^{1-\varepsilon}]^{1/(1-\varepsilon)}, \quad \varepsilon > 1, \tag{9.8}$$

where p_l is the price for the composite good, p_{lj} that for primary product j and a is the relative weight of the primary product that is made in the non-unionized economy.[3] The condition $\varepsilon > 1$ means that primary products are close substitutes.

For each oligopolist j, there is symmetry over products $i \in D_j$. This means that the output of all varieties being produced is equal to some equilibrium value:

$$y(i) = Y_j \text{ for } j \in D_j, \quad y(i) = 0 \text{ for } j \notin D_0 \cup D_1 \cup \cdots \cup D_m. \tag{9.9}$$

Once refined good i has been invented, the fixed amount η of the primary good can be converted into one unit of good i. Given this, (9.4) and (9.9), the demand for the primary input by the monopolists of the whole world is determined as follows:

$$y_l = \eta \int_{D_0 \cup D_1 \cup \cdots \cup D_m} y(i) di = \eta \sum_{j=0}^m A_j Y_j. \tag{9.10}$$

From duality and the unit cost function (9.8) it follows that the demands for primary products are given by

$$\begin{aligned} y_{l0} &= y_l[\partial p_l/\partial p_{l0}] = ay_l[p_l/p_{l0}]^\varepsilon, \\ y_{lj} &= y_l[\partial p_l/\partial p_{lj}] = y_l[p_l/p_{lj}]^\varepsilon \text{ for } j = 1, \ldots, m. \end{aligned} \tag{9.11}$$

9.3.4 Research and development

Let y_{dj} be the output of new designs by oligopolist j. In research, the productivity of skilled labour, y_{dj}/g_j is in fixed proportion δ to the world stock of the designs for refined products, $A \doteq \sum_{h=0}^m A_h$. We choose, for convenience, the unit of designs so that $\delta = 1$. Because the production

---

[3] In the non-unionized economy (i.e. in sector 0), there are a times more producers as in any other sector of the unionized economy.

of new designs by oligopolist j increases the stock of designs for that oligopolist, $\dot{A}_j \doteq dA_j/dt = y_{dj}$, we obtain

$$\dot{A}_j = y_{dj} = g_j A, A \doteq \sum_{h=0}^{m} A_h \tag{9.12}$$

9.4 The behaviour of the individual agents

9.4.1 The households

Let, in sector j, w_j (W_j) be the wage and E_j ($\mathcal{E}_j$) be the expected wage income for skilled (unskilled) labour. A household must decide on which combination of labour inputs it will supply before entering the labour market. This decision must be based on the transformation function (9.2) and expected wage income for the two inputs. The representative household maximizes expected income

$$E_j L_j + \mathcal{E}_j N_j = E_j L_j + \mathcal{E}_j R(L_j)$$

by the choice of L_j. In equilibrium, the relative expected wage income must be equal to the relative marginal rate of transformation for the labour inputs:[4]

$$w_j \frac{l_j}{L_j} \bigg/ \left(W_j \frac{n_j}{N_j} \right) = E_j/\mathcal{E}_j = -R'(L_j). \tag{9.13}$$

Since r is the interest rate and p_c the price for consumption in terms of the numeraire, then $\dot{p}_c/p_c$ is the inflation rate and $r - \dot{p}_c/p_c$ the real interest rate for the consumer. The representative household in the world maximizes its welfare (9.3) by the choice of its real consumption C subject to the accumulation of wealth, taking the flow of income as given. On the balanced growth path the real interest rate $r - \dot{p}_c/p_c$ is held constant, so that the optimization by the household (see appendix 8a) and the normalization of prices, $p_c C \equiv 1$, yield

$$\dot{C}/C = r - \dot{p}_c/p_c - \rho, \quad \dot{C}/C = -\dot{p}_c/p_c. \tag{9.14}$$

From these relations it follows that on the balanced growth path, the interest rate is equal to the subjective discount rate:

$$r \equiv \rho. \tag{9.15}$$

---

[4] Since the unemployed do not earn any labour income, the expected wage income for skilled (unskilled) labour, E_j ($\mathcal{E}_j$), is equal to the wage w_j (W_j) times the probability of being employed, l_j/L_j (n_j/N_j).

9.4.2 The oligopolists

The profit of oligopolist j is given by $\Pi_j = p_{lj}y_{lj} - \phi_j y_{lj}$, where y_{lj} is output, p_{lj} the output price and ϕ_j unit cost. The oligopolist maximizes its profit Π_j given the demand for its output (9.11), taking aggregate demand y_l and the price index p_l as fixed. This leads to mark-up pricing

$$p_{lj} = (\varepsilon - 1)^{-1}\varepsilon\phi_j \text{ for } j = 0, 1 \ldots, m,$$

where $\varepsilon = -\partial(\log y_{lj})/\partial(\log p_{lj})$ is the price elasticity of demand. Substituting this into the unit cost function (9.8), the demand functions (9.11) and the definition of profit Π_j in (9.16) yields

$$p_{l0} = (\varepsilon - 1)^{-1}\varepsilon\phi, \quad y_{l0} = ay_l[\phi/\phi_0]^\varepsilon,$$

$$\Pi_0 = (p_0 - \phi_{l0})y_{l0} = \phi_0 y_{l0}/(\varepsilon - 1) = a\phi^\varepsilon\phi_0^{1-\varepsilon}y_l/(\varepsilon - 1),$$

$$y_{lj} = y_l[\phi/\phi_j]^\varepsilon \text{ and } \Pi_j = \phi_j y_{lj}/(\varepsilon - 1) = \phi^\varepsilon\phi_j^{1-\varepsilon}y_l/(\varepsilon - 1)$$
$$= \text{for } j \neq 0,$$
$$\text{where } \phi \doteq [a\phi_0^{1-\varepsilon} + \phi_1^{1-\varepsilon} + \cdots + \phi_m^{1-\varepsilon}]^{1/(1-\varepsilon)}. \tag{9.16}$$

Now by duality and by the functions (9.7) and (9.16), we obtain the labour demand functions

$$l_j - g_j = [\partial\phi_j/\partial w_j]y_{lj} = \gamma\phi_j y_{lj}/w_j = (\varepsilon - 1)\gamma\Pi_j/w_j \text{ and}$$
$$n_j = [\partial\phi_j/\partial W_j]y_{lj} = (1 - \gamma)\phi_j y_{lj}/W_j = (\varepsilon - 1)(1 - \gamma)\Pi_j/W_j$$
$$\text{for } j = 0, 1, \ldots, m, \tag{9.17}$$

where $l_j - g_j(n_j)$ is the employment of skilled (unskilled) labour in ordinary production and g_j skilled labour devoted to research by oligopolist j.

9.4.3 The monopolists

After monopolist i has produced refined good i, it sells this for a price $p(i)$. It takes its unit cost p_l, the consumer price p_c as well as aggregate consumption C as given, and it chooses its output price $p(j)$ on the demand curve (9.6) to maximize revenue $p(j)y(j)$ minus total cost $p_l y(j)$. Given (9.9), this leads to mark-up pricing:

$$p(j) = \theta p_l \text{ and } y(i) = Y_j = Y \text{ if } j \text{ is produced.} \tag{9.18}$$

Following the mark-up rule (9.18), a monopolist receives the profit

$$\pi_h(j) = [p(j) - p_l]Y = (\theta - 1)Yp_l \text{ if } i \text{ is produced.} \tag{9.19}$$

A monopolist decides to produce a new variety by a comparison of the discounted value of profit π_h and the cost p_d of the initial investment in design. Since the market for designs is competitive, in the steady state, the price for designs p_d must equal the present value of profit, π_h/r, where r is the interest rate. So given (9.19) and (9.15), we obtain

$$p_d = \pi_h/r = (\theta - 1)Yp_l/r = (\theta - 1)Yp_l/\rho. \tag{9.20}$$

9.4.4 Profits

Relations (9.4), (9.5), (9.9), (9.12) and (9.18) imply

$$1 = \int_{D_0 \cup D_1 \cup \cdots \cup D_m} p(i)y(i)di = \theta p_l Y \int_{D_0 \cup D_1 \cup \cdots \cup D_m} di$$

$$= \theta p_l Y[A_0 + A_1 + \cdots + A_m] = \theta p_l YA.$$

From this and (9.20) it follows that

$$AYp_l = 1/\theta, \quad p_d = (1 - 1/\theta)/(A\rho). \tag{9.21}$$

Given (9.10), (9.12), (9.16) and (9.21), we obtain primary output y_e and the oligopolists' profits π_j as follows:

$$y_l = \eta \sum_{j=0}^{m} A_j Y_j = \eta YA = \eta/(\theta p_l) = (\varepsilon - 1)\eta/(\varepsilon\theta\phi),$$

$$\Pi_0 = (\varepsilon\theta)^{-1}a\eta[\phi/\phi_0]^{\varepsilon-1}, \quad \Pi_j = (\varepsilon\theta)^{-1}\eta[\phi/\phi_j]^{\varepsilon-1} \text{ for } j = 1, \ldots, m. \tag{9.22}$$

9.4.5 Wages

The marginal revenue of skilled labour in research, μ, is equal to the productivity of skilled labour in research, A, times the price for designs, p_d. Given (9.21), we obtain that this marginal revenue

$$\mu \doteq Ap_d = (1 - 1/\theta)/\rho,$$

is constant and uniform in both countries. In sector 0 (i.e. in the non-unionized economy), marginal cost (=the wage for skilled labour) w_0 is always equal to marginal revenue μ. If sector $j \neq 0$, the wage for skilled labour w_j is set higher than unit revenue μ, then oligopolist j does not produce new designs, $y_{dj} = g_j = 0$. Otherwise, oligopolist j will produce new designs as long as there is a labour force available. This means that when $w_j \leq \mu$ for $j \neq 0$, labour input g_j takes the highest possible value within the employment constraints (9.1). This proves the conditions

$$g_j = \begin{cases} \max\{g_j | l_j = L_j\} > 0 & \text{for } w_j \leq \mu, \\ 0 & \text{for } w_j > \mu, \end{cases} \quad w_0 = \mu. \qquad (9.23)$$

9.5 Balanced growth

9.5.1 General equilibrium

It can be shown that, given (9.1), (9.2), (9.7), (9.17), (9.22), (9.13), (9.18), (9.21) and (9.23), the price for the primary good, the profits, the demand for and the supply of unskilled labour as well as research input are determined by unit costs as follows (see appendix 9a):

$$p_l(\phi_j, \phi_{-j}), \quad \Pi_j(\phi_j, \phi_{-j}), \quad n_j(w_j, \phi_j, \phi_{-j}), \quad N_j(w_j, \phi_j, \phi_{-j}),$$

$$g_0(\phi_j, \phi_{-j}), \quad g_j = \begin{cases} G_j(w_j, \phi_j, \phi_{-j}) & \text{for } w_j \leq \mu, \\ 0 & \text{for } w_j > \mu, \end{cases} \qquad (9.24)$$

and $N_j \geq n_j$ for $j = 1, \ldots, m$,

where ϕ_{-j} is some index of unit labour cost over the other sectors $h \neq j$. Finally, it can be shown that (see appendix 9a)

$$\partial \Pi_j / \partial \phi_j < 0, \quad \partial n_j / \partial w_j > 0, \quad \partial n_j / \partial \phi_j < 0,$$

$$dn_j(w_j, \phi, \phi)/d\phi < 0, \quad \partial G_j / \partial w_j > 0, \quad \partial G_j / \partial \phi_j > 0,$$

$$dG_j(w_j, \phi, \phi)/d\phi > 0, \quad \partial g_0 / \partial \phi_j < 0, \quad dg_0(\phi, \phi)/d\phi < 0,$$

$$[\partial N_j / \partial \phi_j]_{l_j = L_j} < 0, \quad [dN_j(w_j, \phi, \phi)/d\phi]_{l_j = L_j} < 0 \qquad (9.25)$$

and $[\partial N_j / \partial w_j]_{l_j = L_j} < 0$ for $j = 1, \ldots, m$,

$$d[\Pi_1(\phi, \phi) + \cdots + \Pi_m(\phi, \phi)]/d\phi < 0.$$

The results $\partial \Pi_j / \partial \phi_j < 0$, $\partial G_j / \partial w_j > 0$ and $\partial G_j / \partial \phi_j > 0$ can be explained as follows. Assume first $\partial \Pi_j / \partial \phi_j \geq 0$. Then given the wage w_j for skilled workers, the oligopolist could increase its profit by offering a higher wage W_j for unskilled workers. Since in such a case the wage W_j would increase indefinitely, there can be equilibrium only with $\partial \Pi_j / \partial \phi_j < 0$. If unit labour cost in ordinary production, ϕ_j, is held constant and the wage for skilled labour, w_j, is increased, then the households supply more, and ordinary production employs less, skilled labour. On the other hand, if the wage for skilled labour, w_j, is held constant but unit labour cost ϕ_j is increased, then ordinary production falls and employs less skilled labour. In both of these latter cases, there is more skilled labour to be used in research and G_j increases.

9.5.2 Steady-state conditions

If the economy is stable, it converges to some balanced growth path where the wages in terms of nominal consumption expenditure in the world, (w_j, W_j) for all j, are held constant. Now let us find out what such a path is. From (9.7) and (9.24) it follows that the unit costs, ϕ_j, the rates of profit, Π_j, and the world price for the primary good, p_l, are constants. Then the mark-up pricing (9.18) holds the prices $p(j)$ for refined goods constant for all j. Finally, given this, (9.6), (9.18) and (9.21), the terms $YA = 1/(\theta p_l)$ and

$$(C/Y)^{1-(1/\theta)} p_c = p(j)$$

must be constants, which implies

$$\dot{Y}/Y + \dot{A}/A = 0, \quad (1 - 1/\theta)[\dot{C}/C - \dot{Y}/Y] + \dot{p}_c/p_c = 0. \quad (9.26)$$

We define aggregate input to research in the whole world by

$$g \doteq g_0 + g_1 + \cdots + g_m. \tag{9.27}$$

This and results (9.12), (9.14) and (9.26) imply that the balanced growth rate of real consumption C must be in fixed proportion $\theta - 1 > 0$ to aggregate input to research g:

$$\dot{C}/C = -\dot{p}_c/p_c = (1 - \theta)\dot{Y}/Y = (\theta - 1)\dot{A}/A = (\theta - 1)g. \quad (9.28)$$

Given (9.12), (9.23), (9.28) and l'Hôpital's rule, we obtain the relative shares of designs for the case $w_j \leq \mu$ as follows:

$$A_j/A = A_j \bigg/ \sum_{h=0}^{m} A_h = \dot{A}_j \bigg/ \sum_{h=0}^{m} \dot{A}_h = g_j \bigg/ \sum_{h=0}^{m} g_h = g_j/g$$

for $w_j \leq \mu$. \hfill (9.29)

9.6 Unionized economy

9.6.1 Wage-setting

Consider the unionized economy for which $j > 0$. We make the plausible assumption that if the wage W_j for unskilled labour in sector j is increased and all the other wages are held constant, then net demand $n_j - N_j$ for unskilled labour in that sector j decreases. Given (9.17) and (9.24), labour income is equal to

$$B_j(w_j, \phi_j, \phi_{-j}) = w_j l_j + W_j n_j = w_j g_j + w_j(l_j - g_j) + W_j n_j$$

$$= w_j g_j(w_j, \phi_j, \phi_{-j}) + (\varepsilon - 1)\Pi_j(\phi_j, \phi_{-j}), \quad (9.30)$$

where g_j is defined by (9.24). Both parties in bargaining evaluate their income streams using the interest rate (9.15). Oligopolist j attempts to maximize the discounted value of profit, $\Pi_j/r = \pi_j/\rho$, while labour union j attempts to maximize the discounted value of labour income, $B_j/r = B_j/\rho$, within the limits of the full-employment constraint, $n_j \leq N_j$, by the choice of the wages (w_j, W_j). Let the relative bargaining power $0 < \alpha < 1$ be the same for all unions. Then, given (9.24), the outcome of collective bargaining is obtained as follows: maximize the generalized Nash product of the union's and oligopolist's objective functions,

$$Q_j(w_j, \phi_j, \phi_{-j}, \alpha) = (B_j/\rho)^\alpha (\Pi_j/\rho)^{1-\alpha}$$
$$= B_j(w_j, \phi_j, \phi_{-j})^\alpha \Pi_j(\phi_j, \phi_{-j})^{1-\alpha}/\rho, \qquad (9.31)$$

by the choice of the wages (w_j, W_j), given the full-employment constraint $n_j \leq N_j$ in (9.24). In appendix 9b, this optimization leads to the following outcome:

Proposition 9.1: Assume that there is unemployment in the unionized economy. Then the wage for skilled labour is uniform in the world, $w_j = \mu$ for $j = 0, 1, \ldots, m$, the production of primary goods is more expensive in the unionized than the non-unionized economy and the unit labour cost in ordinary production is an increasing function of the unions' relative bargaining power, $d\phi/d\alpha > 0$. The full-employment level of the unit cost ϕ is constant ϕ^f, and the full-employment constraint for the unionized economy is given by $\phi \geq \phi^f$.

This result can be explained as follows. If the parties to collective bargaining set the wage for skilled labour above the level that is paid abroad, then all new designs will be produced abroad. On the other hand, if the wage for skilled labour is below the level that is paid abroad, then, by increasing this wage but by holding unit labour cost in ordinary production constant, profits and labour income can be increased. This shows that in equilibrium, the wage for skilled labour must be uniform in the world. On the other hand, the production of primary goods uses unskilled labour more intensively. This means that if union power increases, then the unions claim higher wages for unskilled workers and primary goods become more expensive in the unionized economy.

9.6.2 International trade

In the model, consumption grows at the same balanced growth rate (9.28) all over the world but the effect of union power on this growth rate remains ambiguous. To show this, assume that the relative bargaining power of the unions, α, is increased. Then, according to proposition 9.1, unit labour cost $\phi_j = \phi_{-j} = \phi$ for primary products becomes higher in the unionized economy. This means that the production of primary goods decreases in the unionized but increases in the non-unionized economy. Consequently, skilled labour will be transferred from ordinary production to research in the unionized and vice versa in the non-unionized economy. Because of these two opposing effects, the worldwide construction of new designs as well as the balanced growth rate may increase or decrease.

Now consider the effect of unionization on world trade and specialization. The unionized economy purchases the amount

$$\eta \sum_{j=1}^{m} \int_{D_j} y(j)dj$$

of the composite primary good at price p_l and sells the amount y_{lj} of each primary good $j \neq 0$ at price p_{lj}. Thus in trading of primary goods, the unionized economy earns net surplus

$$M \doteq p_l \eta \sum_{j=1}^{m} \int_{D_j} y(j)dj - \sum_{j=1}^{m} p_{lj} y_{lj}. \tag{9.32}$$

If $M > 0$ ($M < 0$), the unionized economy imports (exports) primary goods and exports (imports) refined goods, and correspondingly the non-unionized economy exports (imports) the primary good and imports (exports) refined goods.

If there is full employment in the unionized economy, i.e. if $\phi = \phi^f$, then the wages are the same everywhere, the relative output of all goods is the same for both countries and, by symmetry, the net surplus (9.32) must be equal to zero. Given this, (9.9), (9.16), (9.17), (9.18), (9.21), (9.24), (9.25), (9.29) and (9.32), we obtain the following corollary to proposition 9.1 (see appendix 9c):

Proposition 9.2: If there is unemployment in the unionized economy, then the unionized economy exports refined goods and imports primary goods, $M > 0$ for $\phi > \phi^f$.

Since the unionized economy faces a relatively high unit cost in the production of the primary good and a relatively low unit cost in the production of new designs, it will produce relatively more refined goods and relatively less of the primary good than the rest of the world. With the consumers' preferences being similar all over the world, the unionized economy exports its surplus of refined products and imports its deficit of the primary good.

The patterns of specialization in production change the relative rates of growth for the trading economies. The aggregate rate of growth of manufactured output is a weighted average of the rates of productivity growth in the two manufacturing sectors, i.e. those producing primary and refined goods.[5] In forming this average, the shares of the respective sectors in the total value of the industrial output serve as weights. The production of refined goods grows at the same rate all over the world and comprises a larger share of the unionized economy. On the other hand, the production of the primary good does not grow at all and constitutes a larger share of the non-unionized economy. Consequently, manufactured output grows faster in the unionized than in the non-unionized economy.

9.7 Non-unionized workers

The results above show that the unions set the domestic wages for skilled labour at the level being paid abroad. As long as the workers are similar, having equal opportunities to change their occupation, all workers will benefit from the increase in the wage for unskilled labour due to unionization. Where the workers are not similar, skilled workers may have an incentive to leave the union. Therefore, this section considers the case where skilled workers are non-unionized.

To examine this problem, we modify the basic model as follows. First, assume that occupation cannot be changed, i.e. that $R' \to 0$ holds for the transformation function (9.2). This means that in each sector j, the supplies of both skilled labour, L_j, and unskilled labour, N_j, are fixed. Second, assume that each worker supplies either skilled or unskilled labour but not both. Third, since all skilled workers are non-unionized, we assume that the wages for skilled labour are at the level corresponding to full employment, $w_j = \mu$ for all j. Then the objective function for union j changes from (9.23) and (9.30) into the form

$$\tilde{B}_j = w_j l_j + W_j n_j - w_j L_j = B_j(w_j, \phi_j, \phi_{-j}) - \mu L_j.$$

Since μL_j is constant, the maximization of the union's objective function $\tilde{B}_j$ is equivalent to the maximization of the function B_j. This means that the analysis in section 9.6 also holds in this case. The result can be summarized as follows:

---

[5] See, for example, Grossman and Helpman (1991), p. 188.

Proposition 9.3: If there is no change of occupation, all workers supply only one labour input and skilled labour is non-unionized, then propositions 9.1 and 9.2 hold as they stand.

To keep the production of new designs within the country, the unions hold the wages for skilled labour at the level that is paid in the rest of the world. Given this, the unionization of skilled workers has no significance.

9.8 Profit-sharing

So far, it has been assumed that the labour market organizations bargain only over the basic wages w_j and W_j. Now we attempt to extend results to the case where union j and oligopolist j agree on both the wages (w_j, W_j) and the worker's profit share s_j. Since the profit share must be non-negative for both parties, it follows that

$$0 \leq s_j \leq 1. \tag{9.33}$$

Because only pure profits are to be shared, there will be no changes in the demand and supply functions. This means that only the objective functions of the oligopolist and the labour union must be revised. Since oligopolist j pays a fixed share s_j of its profit Π_j to the members of the union, the total labour income is equal to the sum of the wage income B_j and the profit share $s_j\Pi_j$ while the remaining profit for oligopolist j is equal to $(1 - s_j)\Pi_j$. Given this, the generalized Nash product (9.31) of the objective functions for union j and oligopolist j takes the form

$$Q_j^*(s_j, w_j, \phi_j, \phi_{-j}, \alpha) = [(B_j + s_j\Pi_j)/\rho]^\alpha [(1 - s_j)\Pi_j/\rho]^{1-\alpha}$$

$$= [B_j(w_j, \phi_j, \phi_{-j}) + s_j\Pi_j(\phi_j, \phi_{-j})]^\alpha \Pi_j(\phi_j, \phi_{-j})^{1-\alpha}$$

$$\times (1 - s_j)^{1-\alpha}/\rho, \tag{9.34}$$

where the constant α is the union's relative bargaining power. The product (9.34) must be maximized by the choice of (w_j, W_j), subject to the employment constraints $n_j \leq N_j$ and the limits of profit-sharing, (9.33). In appendix 9d, this maximization leads to the following result:

Proposition 9.4: There exists a critical level $\bar{\alpha} < 1$ such that when the relative bargaining power of the union is high enough, $\bar{\alpha} \leq \alpha \leq 1$, it has no effect on the unit cost ϕ and the allocation of resources. Otherwise, for $\alpha < \bar{\alpha}$, propositions 9.1 and 9.2 hold as they stand.

The explanation of proposition 9.4 is the following. If a union is strong enough, $\overline{\alpha} \leq \alpha \leq 1$, it can claim a share of profits on top of the basic wages. In such a case, the union and the oligopolist facing it share the profit in fixed proportion to their relative bargaining power but they both start maximizing national income by the choice of the wages. This means that the relative bargaining power of the union has no effect on the choice of the wages and, ultimately, on the allocation of resources in the economy. When a union is too weak to claim a share of profits, the choice of wages will depend on the strength of union power.

9.9 Welfare evaluation

To enable welfare comparisons, we assume that all households in the unionized economy are identical: they possess equal amounts of both skilled and unskilled labour, the risk of unemployment is the same for them, and all profits are evenly distributed among them. They can be thought to be, for instance, family households the members of which work in different occupations. We show that collective bargaining can improve efficiency even when the distributional aspects of bargaining are wholly ignored.

From proposition 9.1 it follows that $\phi_j = \phi_{-j} = \phi$ for $j \neq 0$ and $w_j = \mu$ for all j. Given (9.3), (9.4), (9.18), (9.21), (9.24) and (9.28), we obtain the steady-state consumption of the world as

$$
C = \left[\int_{D_0 \cup D_1 \cup \cdots \cup D_m} y(i)^{1/\theta} di \right]^\theta = Y \left[\int_{D_0 \cup D_1 \cup \cdots \cup D_m} dj \right]^\theta
$$

$$
= \frac{1}{\theta p_l A} \left[\sum_{j=0}^{m} \int_{D_j} dj \right]^\theta = (1/\theta) A^{\theta-1} / p_l(\phi, \phi), \tag{9.35}
$$

where C, $y(i)$, Y, A_j and A are functions of time t. From (9.16) we see that each oligopolist j earns income $w_j g_j + p_{lj} y_j = w_j g_j + \varepsilon \Pi$. Then, given (9.24), we can define the share of world income earned by the unionized economy as follows:

$$
\vartheta(\phi) \doteq \frac{\sum_{j=1}^{m} [w_j g_j + p_l y_j]}{\sum_{h=0}^{m} [w_h g_h + p_l y_h]}
$$

$$
= \left\{ \frac{\mu g_0(\phi, \phi) + \varepsilon \Pi_0(\phi, \phi)}{\sum_{j=1}^{m} [\mu G_j(\mu, \phi, \phi) + \varepsilon \Pi_j(\phi, \phi)]} + 1 \right\}^{-1}.
$$

Since all the households in the world are identical, then on the balanced-growth path the consumption/income ratio is equal for them and consumption in the unionized economy, C_D, must be equal to the unionized-economy share of world income times world consumption, $C_D = \vartheta(\phi)C$. Consequently, the welfare of the representative household in the unionized economy is given by

$$u_D(\phi) = \int_0^\infty \log C_D(t)e^{-\rho t}dt = (1/\rho)\log C_D(0)$$

$$= (1/\rho)[\log \vartheta(\phi) + (\theta - 1)\log A(0) - \log p_l(\phi, \phi)]$$

$$+ \text{ constants.}$$

Given proposition 9.1, there exists one-to-one correspondence from the parameter α to unit cost ϕ and the full-employment constraint $\phi \geq \phi^f$. Therefore, if the government of the unionized economy controls the relative bargaining power of the union α, the social optimum is obtained through the maximization of the utility function (9.3) by the choice of unit cost ϕ, given $\phi \geq \phi^f$. The maximization of the welfare of the unionized-economy household, u_D, yields the first-order condition

$$\rho[du_D/d\phi] = [d\vartheta/d\phi]/\vartheta - [dp_l/d\phi]/p_l \quad \begin{cases} = 0 & \text{for } \phi > \phi^f, \\ < 0 & \text{for } \phi = \phi^f. \end{cases}$$

Reorganizing this condition yields the following result:

Proposition 9.5: If the unit cost of producing the primary good in the unionized economy, ϕ^u, that is obtained by equalling the elasticities of the unionized-economy share of world income and the price of the primary good with respect to the unit cost,

$$\phi^u \vartheta'(\phi^u)/\vartheta(\phi^u) = [\phi^u/p_l(\phi^u, \phi^u)][dp_l(\phi^u, \phi^u)/d\phi],$$

is greater than the unit cost of producing the primary good in the unionized economy that corresponds to full employment, ϕ^f, then unemployment is socially optimal in the unionized economy. In such a case, the increase (decrease) of the relative bargaining power of the unions is welfare-enhancing as long as the unit cost of producing the primary good, ϕ, is below (above) ϕ^u.

For the following reason, from the welfare point of view, unemployment and the exercise of union power can be desirable. Assume that it is socially desirable to allocate a great amount of skilled labour to research. To take this amount of skilled labour from ordinary production, the unit cost for primary products must be set so high that the production of primary goods cannot employ all unskilled labour. Then, starting from the initial position of full employment, the increase in union power will promote both research and welfare in the unionized economy.

9.10 Conclusions

This chapter examined a world where growth is generated by research that produces new designs for refined goods, and where the existence of monopoly profits is the reason for collective bargaining. There are two labour inputs: unskilled labour which is used only in the production of goods, and skilled labour which can be used both in research and the production of goods. In the unionized economy, oligopolists, which maximize the discounted value of profits, and unions, which maximize the discounted value of labour income, bargain over the wages. This bargaining can be either at the level of the whole economy or it can be carried out simultaneously in different parts of the economy. The main outcome is that the economy with a unionized labour market exports refined and imports primary products, and the economy with a competitive labour market exports primary and imports refined products. This can be explained as follows.

Each union raises the wage for its unskilled members above the level that prevails abroad. This increases the unit cost for primary goods in the unionized economy. Consequently, in the unionized economy, the output of primary goods falls, employment and the wage for skilled labour falls and the unit cost for research decreases. Given this, the production of new designs and refined products will expand until the wage for skilled labour has increased back to the equilibrium level. The increased production of new designs leads to a higher stock of designs for the unionized economy relative to the rest of the world. Since the unionized economy now produces more of the refined products and less of the primary product, it will export the former and import the latter. The unions are interested in keeping the production of new designs in the economy. For this reason, they set the wages for skilled labour equal to the marginal product in research, and consequently these wages will be uniform all over the world.

Provided that the relative bargaining power of the unions is not very high, the results above also hold when profit-sharing is introduced into the economy. Only in the case where the unions are already very powerful in bargaining, does a marginal change in their power have no macroeconomic effects. Strong unions are interested in sharing the value-added directly rather than reducing profits by high basic wages. In such a case, it is in the interests of both parties to bargaining to maximize the 'total cake', so that the choice of wages, and consequently the allocation of resources, will be independent of the relative bargaining power of the parties.

The balanced growth rate of consumption is the same all over the world. Now assume that in the unionized economy, it is socially desirable to allocate a great amount of skilled labour to research. To take this amount of skilled labour from the production of primary goods, the unit cost for primary products must be set so high that not all unskilled labour will continue to be employed in the production of primary goods. In such a case, starting from the initial position of full employment, the increase in union power will promote both research and welfare in the unionized economy. Since, however, research in the rest of the world will contract, the change in the balanced growth rate of consumption remains ambiguous.

In chapters 8 and 9, the effect of unionization was examined by the use of two different growth models. Although a great deal of caution should be exercised when these highly stylized models are used to explain wage-setting, the following conclusions seem nevertheless to be justified. On the balanced growth path, skills that are more intensively used in research are fully employed. The unionization of workers promotes economic growth by making these skills relatively cheaper and the construction of new designs less expensive. If union power is very great, economic growth may even be excessive: the loss of current income due to high unemployment outweighs the benefits from faster economic growth and higher future income.

Appendix 9a. *The proof of relations* **(9.24)** *and* **(9.25)**

First, we define an index of labour cost over firms $j = 1, \ldots, m$ as

$$\phi_{-j} = \left[\frac{1}{m-1} \sum_{h>0, h\neq j} \phi_h^{1-\varepsilon} \right]^{1/(1-\varepsilon)}. \tag{9a.1}$$

Now from (9.16) it follows that

$$\phi = [a\phi_0^{1-\varepsilon} + \phi_j^{1-\varepsilon} + (m-1)\phi_{-j}^{1-\varepsilon}]^{1-\varepsilon},$$

$$p_l = \tilde{p}_l(\phi_0, \phi_j, \phi_{-j}) = (\varepsilon-1)^{-1}\varepsilon\phi \text{ with } \partial\tilde{p}_l/\partial\phi_j > 0 \text{ and} \tag{9a.2}$$

$$d\tilde{p}_l(\phi_0, \phi, \phi)/d\phi = m[\partial\tilde{p}_l/\partial\phi_j] > 0.$$

Given this, (9.22) and (9a.1), the foreign oligopoly profit becomes a function of unit costs ϕ_0, ϕ_j and ϕ_{-j}:

$$\Pi_0 = (\varepsilon\theta)^{-1} a\eta\phi^{\varepsilon-1}\phi_0^{1-\varepsilon}$$
$$= (\varepsilon\theta)^{-1} a\eta\{a + [\phi_j^{1-\varepsilon} + (m-1)\phi_{-j}^{1-\varepsilon}]\phi_0^{\varepsilon-1}\}^{-1}$$
$$\doteq \tilde{\Pi}_0(\phi_0, \phi_j, \phi_{-j}) \text{ with } \partial\tilde{\Pi}_0/\partial\phi_0 < 0, \ \partial\tilde{\Pi}_0/\partial\phi_j > 0 \text{ and}$$
$$d\tilde{\Pi}_0(\phi_0, \phi, \phi)/d\phi = m[\partial\tilde{\Pi}_0/\partial\phi_j] > 0. \tag{9a.3}$$

Given (9.1), (9.13) and (9.23), we obtain

$$\mu/W_0 = w_0/W_0 = -R'(L_0).$$

Differentiating this and noting (9.2) yields

$$L(W_0), \quad L_0' = \mu W_0^{-2}/R'' < 0, \quad N_0(W_0), N_0' = R'L_0' > 0. \tag{9a.4}$$

From this, (9.1), (9.7), (9.17), (9.23) and (9a.3) it follows that

$$\log N_0(W_0) = \log \Pi_0 - \log W_0 + \text{constants}$$
$$= \log \tilde{\Pi}_0(\phi_0, \phi_j, \phi_{-j}) - \log W_0 + \text{constants}$$
$$= \log \tilde{\Pi}_0(\mu^\gamma W_0^{1-\gamma}, \phi_j, \phi_{-j}) - \log W_0 + \text{constants}.$$

Differentiating this totally and noting (9a.3) and (9a.4), we obtain

$$W_0(\phi_j, \phi_{-j}) \text{ with } \partial W_0/\partial\phi_j > 0 \text{ and}$$
$$dW_0(\phi, \phi)/d\phi = [d\Pi_0(\phi_0, \phi, \phi)/d\phi]/H = m[\partial\tilde{\Pi}_0/\partial\phi_j]/H$$
$$= m[\partial W_0/\partial\phi_j] > 0, \tag{9a.5}$$

where

$$H \doteq (1/W_0 + N_0'/N_0)\Pi_0 - (\partial\tilde{\Pi}_0/\partial\phi_0)(1-\gamma)\mu^\gamma W_0^{-\gamma} > 0.$$

Substituting (9a.5) and $w_0 = \mu$ into (9.7) implies

$$\phi_0(\phi_j, \phi_{-j}) = \mu^\gamma W_0(\phi_j, \phi_{-j})^{1-\gamma} \text{ with } \partial\phi_0/\partial\phi_j > 0 \text{ and}$$
$$d\phi_0(\phi, \phi)/d\phi = m[\partial\phi_0/\partial\phi_j] > 0,$$

and substituting this into (9a.2) and (9a.3) yields

$$p_l(\phi_j, \phi_{-j}) = \tilde{p}_l(\phi_0(\phi_j, \phi_{-j}), \phi_j, \phi_{-j}) \text{ with } \partial p_l/\partial\phi_j > 0 \text{ and}$$
$$dp_l(\phi, \phi)/d\phi = m[\partial p_l/\partial\phi_j] > 0,$$
$$\Pi_0(\phi_j, \phi_{-j}) \doteq \tilde{\Pi}_0(\phi_0(\phi_j, \phi_{-j}), \phi_j, \phi_{-j}) \text{ with } \partial\Pi_0/\partial\phi_j > 0 \text{ and}$$
$$d\Pi_0(\phi, \phi)/d\phi = m[\partial\Pi_0/\partial\phi_j] > 0. \tag{9a.6}$$

Given this, (9.16) and (9.22), and noting the symmetry over $j = 1, \ldots, m$, we obtain

$$\sum_{j=0}^{m} \Pi_j(\phi_j, \phi_{-j}) = \frac{\phi^{\varepsilon} y_l}{\varepsilon - 1} [a\phi_0^{1-\varepsilon} + \sum_{j=1}^{m} \phi_j^{1-\varepsilon}] = \frac{\phi y_l}{\varepsilon - 1} = \frac{\eta}{\varepsilon \theta},$$

$$\frac{d}{d\phi} \sum_{j=1}^{m} \Pi_j(\phi, \phi) = -d\Pi_0(\phi, \phi)/d\phi < 0, \quad d\Pi_j(\phi, \phi)/d\phi < 0.$$

$$(9a.7)$$

Given (9.1), (9.17), (9.23), (9a.4), (9a.5) and (9a.6), we obtain

$$g_0(\phi_j, \phi_{-j}) = l_0 - (\varepsilon - 1)\gamma \Pi_0 / w_0$$
$$= L_0(W_0(\phi_j, \phi_{-j})) - (\varepsilon - 1)\gamma \Pi_0(\phi_j, \phi_{-j})/\mu,$$
$$\partial g_0 / \partial \phi_j = L_0'[\partial W_0 / \partial \phi_j] - [(\varepsilon - 1)\gamma / \mu]\partial \Pi_0 / \partial \phi_j < 0$$
and $dg_0(\phi, \phi)/d\phi = m[\partial g_0 / \partial \phi_j] < 0$ for $j = 1, \ldots, m$. $(9a.8)$

The function (9.7) can be transformed into

$$W_j = \phi_j^{1/(1-\gamma)} w_j^{\gamma/(\gamma-1)} \text{ for } j = 0, 1, \ldots, m. \qquad (9a.9)$$

Substituting (9a.7) and (9a.9) into (9.17) and noting the stability condition $\partial \Pi_j / \partial \phi_j < 0$ yields

$$l_j - g_j = (\varepsilon - 1)\gamma \Pi_j(\phi_j, \phi_{-j})/w_j \doteq \Omega_j(w_j, \phi_j, \phi_{-j}),$$
$$\partial \Omega_j / \partial w_j < 0, \quad \partial \Omega / \partial \phi_j < 0, \quad d\Omega_j(w_j, \phi, \phi)/d\phi < 0,$$
$$n_j(w_j, \phi_j, \phi_{-j}) \doteq (\varepsilon - 1)(1 - \gamma)\Pi_j / W_j$$
$$= (\varepsilon - 1)(1 - \gamma)\Pi_j(\phi_j, \phi_{-j})\phi_j^{1/(\gamma-1)} w_j^{\gamma/(1-\gamma)},$$
$$\partial n_j / \partial w_j > 0, \quad \partial n_j / \partial \phi_j < 0, \quad dn_j(w_j, \phi, \phi)/d\phi < 0,$$

$$(9a.10)$$

where $j = 1, \ldots, m$.

Finally, consider some $j \neq 0$ for which $l_j = L_j$ holds. Given $l_j = L_j$, (9.2), (9.17) and (9a.7), condition (9.13) takes the form

$$-R'(L_j)/R(L_j) = -R'(L_j)/N_j = w_j/(W_j n_j)$$
$$= (\varepsilon - 1)^{-1}(1 - \gamma)^{-1} w_j/\Pi_j(\phi_j, \phi_{-j}). \qquad (9a.11)$$

Given this and (9.2), we obtain that L_j and N_j are functions of the wage w_j and the unit costs ϕ_j and ϕ_{-j}:

$L_j(w_j, \phi_j, \phi_{-j})$ and $N_j(w_j, \phi_j, \phi_{-j})$ for $j = 1, \ldots, m.$ (9a.12)

The logarithmic transformation of equation (9a.11) is given by

$$\log[-R'(L_j)] - \log R(L_j) = \log w_j - \log \Pi_j(\phi_j, \phi_{-j}) + \text{constants}.$$

Differentiating this with respect to L_j, w_j and ϕ_j, we obtain

$$[R''/R' - R'/R]dL_j = dw_j/w_j - (1/\Pi_j)$$
$$\times [(\partial\Pi_j/\partial\phi_j)d\phi_j + (\partial\Pi_j/\partial\phi_{-j})d\phi_{-j}],$$

(9a.13)

where, noting the stability condition $\partial\Pi_j/\partial\phi_j < 0$, the multipliers of dL_j, dw_j and $d\phi_j$ are positive. Therefore, given (9.2), we can express the last equation in terms of partial derivatives as follows:

$$[\partial L_j/\partial w_j]_{l_j=L_j} > 0, \quad [\partial L_j/\partial \phi_j]_{l_j=L_j} > 0,$$

$$[\partial N_j/\partial w_j]_{l_j=L_j} = R'[\partial L_j/\partial w_j]_{l_j=L_j} < 0 \quad \text{and} \qquad (9a.14)$$

$$[\partial N_j/\partial \phi_j]_{l_j=L_j} = R'[\partial L_j/\partial \phi_j]_{l_j=L_j} < 0 \quad \text{for } j = 1, \ldots, m.$$

Furthermore, given (9a.13), we have

$$dL_j(w_j, \phi, \phi)/d\phi = -(1/\Pi_j)d\Pi_j(\phi, \phi)/d\phi > 0,$$
$$dN_j(w_j, \phi, \phi)/d\phi = R'[dL_j(w_j, \phi, \phi)/d\phi] < 0.$$

(9a.15)

If $g_j > 0$, then given (9.23), (9a.10), (9a.12), (9a.15) and (9a.14), we obtain $l_j = L_j$ and

$$g_j = G_j(w_j, \phi_j, \phi_{-j})$$
$$\doteq L_j(w_j, \phi_j, \phi_{-j})|_{l_j=L_j} - \Omega_j(w_j, \phi_j, \phi_{-j}),$$
$$\partial G_j/\partial w_j = [\partial L_j/\partial w_j]_{l_j=L_j} - \partial\Omega_j/\partial w_j > 0, \qquad (9a.16)$$
$$\partial G_j/\partial \phi_j = [\partial L_j/\partial \phi_j]_{l_j=L_j} - \partial\Omega_j/\partial \phi_j > 0,$$
$$dG_j(w_j, \phi, \phi)/d\phi > 0.$$

Results (9a.2)–(9a.16) are summarized in (9.24) and (9.25).

Appendix 9b. *The proof of proposition* 9.1

The maximization of the Nash product (9.31) by the choice of the wages (w_j, W_j) within the limits of the employment constraint $n_j \leq N_j$, holding the other wages (w_h, W_h) for $h \neq j$ constant, is equivalent to the maximization of the function

$$\Gamma_j(w_j, \phi_j, \phi_{-j}, \alpha) = [\log Q_j + \log \rho]/\alpha$$
$$= \log B_j(w_j, \phi_j, \phi_{-j}) + (1/\alpha - 1) \log \Pi_j(\phi_j, \phi_{-j})$$
$$= \log\{w_j g_j(w_j, \phi_j, \phi_{-j}) + (\varepsilon - 1)\Pi_j(\phi_j, \phi_{-j})\}$$
$$+ (1/\alpha - 1) \log \Pi_j(\phi_j, \phi_{-j}). \qquad (9b.1)$$

by the choice of (w_j, ϕ_j) within the limits of the employment constraint, holding (w_h, ϕ_h) for $h \neq j$ constant. The Lagrangean of this problem is given by

$$\mathcal{L}_j(\lambda, w_j, \phi_j, \phi_{-j}, \alpha) = \Gamma_j(w_j, \phi_j, \phi_{-j}, \alpha)$$
$$+ \lambda[N_j(w_j, \phi_j, \phi_{-j}) - n_j(w_j, \phi_j, \phi_{-j})], \quad (9b.2)$$

where the multiplier λ satisfies the Kuhn–Tucker conditions

$$\lambda[N_j(w_j, \phi_j, \phi_{-j}) - n_j(w_j, \phi_j, \phi_{-j})] = 0, \quad \lambda \geq 0. \qquad (9b.3)$$

We prove first that the wage for skilled labour, w_j, is always equal to constant μ for $j = 1, \ldots, m$. Assume first that there is full employment, $n_j = N_j$, so that in both economies the labour market is competitive. Now, since the technologies and preferences are the same for the two economies, given (9.23), the domestic wage w_j is equal to the foreign wage $w_0 = \mu$. Second, assume that there is unemployment, $\tilde{n}_j < N_j$. Now given (9.24), (9.25) and (9b.1)–(9b.3), we obtain $\lambda = 0$ and

$$\partial \mathcal{L}_j / \partial w_j = \partial \Gamma_j / \partial w_j \begin{cases} = 0 & \text{for } w_j > \mu, \\ > 0 & \text{for } w_j \leq \mu. \end{cases}$$

Since the purpose is to maximize $\mathcal{L}_j$ by the choice of w_j, this implies

$$w_j \geq \mu, \quad g_j \begin{cases} = 0 & \text{for } w_j > \mu, \\ > 0 & \text{for } w_j = \mu, \end{cases}$$

and

$$(w_j g_j)_{w_j = \mu} > 0 = (w_j g_j)_{w_j > \mu}.$$

From this and (9b.1) it follows that when the other instrument of optimization, ϕ_j, is held constant, it must be the case that

$$\Gamma_j(w_j, \phi_j, \phi_{-j}, \alpha)|_{w_j = \mu} > \Gamma_j(w_j, \phi_j, \phi_{-j}, \alpha)|_{w_j > \mu}.$$

To maximize Γ_j for given ϕ_j, the wage w_j is chosen equal to μ.

Given $w_j = \mu$, (9b.1) and (9b.2), the remaining first-order and second-order conditions for the maximization of $\mathcal{L}_j$ are (9b.3) and

$$\partial \mathcal{L}_j/\partial \phi_j = (1/B_j)(\partial B_j/\partial \phi_j) + [(1/\alpha - 1)/\Pi_j](\partial \Pi_j/\partial \phi_j)$$
$$+ \lambda[\partial N_j/\partial \phi_j - \partial n_j/\partial \phi_j] = 0, \tag{9b.4}$$

$$\partial^2 \mathcal{L}_j/\partial \phi_j^2 < 0.$$

Let ϕ_j^f be the unit cost corresponding to full employment, so that $\tilde{n}_j(\mu, \phi_j^f, \phi_{-j}) = N_j(\mu, \phi_j^f, \phi_{-j})$. We assumed that when the other wages are held constant, the increase in the wage W_j for unskilled labour in sector j decreases net demand $n_j - N_j$ for unskilled labour in that sector. Given $w_j = \mu$ and (9.7), this implies $\partial N_j/\partial \phi_j > \partial n_j/\partial \phi_j$ and

$$\phi_j > \phi_j^f \quad \text{for } n_j < N_j.$$

Consider now the case of unemployment, $\phi_j > \phi^f$ and $\lambda = 0$. Given (9.25) and (9b.4), we obtain

$$\partial^2 \mathcal{L}_j/(\partial \phi_j \partial \alpha) = -(\alpha^2 \Pi_j)^{-1} \partial \Pi_j/\partial \phi_j > 0.$$

This together with the second-order condition in (9b.4) yields

$$\phi_j = f(\alpha, \phi_{-j}) \quad \text{with}$$
$$f_1 \doteq \partial f/\partial \alpha = -[\partial^2 \mathcal{L}_j/\partial \phi_j \partial \alpha]/[\partial^2 \mathcal{L}_j/\partial \phi_j^2] > 0 \quad \text{and} \tag{9b.5}$$
$$f_2 \doteq \partial f/\partial \phi_{-j} \quad \text{for } j = 1, \ldots, m.$$

Since the technologies and preferences for the two economies are the same and there is perfect symmetry over $j = 1, \ldots, m$, the unit cost corresponding to full employment must be uniform in the world: $\phi_j^f \equiv \phi^f$ for $j = 0, 1, \ldots, m$. If there is unemployment, i.e. if $\phi_j > \phi^f$ for $j = 1, \ldots, m$, the functions (9b.5) yield a system of m equations

$$\Lambda_j = \phi_j - f(\alpha, \phi_{-j}) = 0 \quad \text{for } j = 1, \ldots, m \tag{9b.6}$$

with endogenous variables $\phi_1, \ldots, \phi_m$. Differentiating this system, we obtain the coefficient matrix

$$[\partial f_j/\partial \phi_h]_{m \times m}. \tag{9b.7}$$

Union j and oligopolist j act as if they were a single agent that behaves in Bertrand manner with respect to the other unions and firms $h \neq 0, j$: they choose unit cost ϕ_j taking ϕ_h for $h \neq 0, j$ as fixed. The reaction function of union j and oligopolist j is given by (9b.6). Since there is perfect symmetry over $j = 1, \ldots, m$, one of the sufficient conditions for the stability of the symmetric Bertrand equilibrium requires that the coefficient matrix (9b.7) is subject to diagonal dominance:[6]

$$1 \pm (m-1)f_2 = \frac{\partial \Lambda_j}{\partial \phi_j} \pm (m-1)\frac{\partial \Lambda_j}{\partial \phi_h} > 0 \text{ for } h \neq 0, j, \qquad (9b.8)$$

where f_2 is defined by (9b.5). The interpretation of this stability condition (9b.8) is straightforward. Assume that the effect of the other unit costs ϕ_h ($h \neq 0, j$) on the right-hand side f of (9b.5) is negative and exceeds unity. Now let all unit costs ϕ_j be just above the level corresponding to the symmetric equilibrium for all $j \neq 0$. Then $\Lambda_j < 0$ for all $j \neq 0$ and all j will increase their unit costs ϕ_j. Since these increases in ϕ_j will in turn decrease Λ_j for all j, there cannot be a stable outcome.

In symmetry $\phi_j = \phi$ for $j \neq 0$, relation (9b.6) takes the form $\phi = mf(\alpha, (m-1)\phi)$. Differentiating this and noting the stability condition (9b.8), we obtain

$$d\phi/d\alpha = mf_1/[1 - (m-1)f_2] > 0 \text{ for } \phi > \phi^f.$$

Noting the full-employment constraint $\phi_j \equiv \phi \geq \phi^f$, this result can also be written as follows:

$$\phi = \max[\phi^u(\alpha), \phi^f], \quad d\phi^u/d\alpha > 0.$$

So in the case of unemployment, the unit cost ϕ increases when the relative bargaining power of the union, α, increases.

Appendix 9c. *The proof of proposition* 9.2

From (9.4), (9.16), (9.18), (9.21), (9.29) and (9.32) it follows that

$$M \doteq p_l \eta \sum_{j=1}^{m} \int_{D_j} y(j)dj - \sum_{j=1}^{m} p_{lj}y_{lj} = p_l \eta \sum_{j=1}^{m} A_j Y_j - \sum_{j=1}^{m} p_{lj}y_{lj}$$

$$= \eta p_l Y \sum_{j=1}^{m} A_j - \varepsilon \sum_{j=1}^{m} \Pi_j = \frac{\eta}{\theta}\frac{1}{A}\sum_{j=1}^{m} A_j - \varepsilon \sum_{j=1}^{m} \Pi_j$$

$$= \frac{\eta}{\theta}\sum_{j=1}^{m} g_j \Big/ \sum_{h=0}^{m} g_h - \varepsilon \sum_{j=1}^{m} \Pi_j = \frac{\eta}{\theta}\left[1 + g_0 \Big/ \sum_{j=1}^{m} G_j\right]^{-1} - \varepsilon \sum_{j=1}^{m} \Pi_j.$$

---

[6] See, for example, Dixit (1986), p. 117. Here, the diagonal term 1 is positive so that the inequality must be greater than zero.

Thus, given (9.24), (9.25) and outcome $\phi_j = \phi$ for $j = 1, \ldots, m$ we can define the function

$$M(\phi) \doteq \frac{\eta}{\theta}\left[1 + g_0(\phi,\phi) \Big/ \sum_{j=1}^{m} G_j(\mu,\phi,\phi)\right]^{-1} - \varepsilon \sum_{j=1}^{m} \Pi_j(\phi,\phi),$$

for which

$$\frac{dM}{d\phi} = \frac{\eta}{\phi}\left[1 + g_0 \Big/ \sum_{j=1}^{m} G_j\right]^{-2}\left[\sum_{j=1}^{m} G_j\right]^{-2}$$

$$\times \left\{g_0 \sum_{j=1}^{m} \frac{dG_j}{d\phi} - \left[\sum_{j=1}^{m} G_j\right]\frac{dg_0}{d\phi}\right\} - \varepsilon \sum_{j=1}^{m} d\Pi_j(\phi,\phi)/d\phi$$

$$> \frac{\eta}{\phi}\left[1 + g_0 \Big/ \sum_{j=1}^{m} G_j\right]^{-2}\left[\sum_{j=1}^{m} G_j\right]^{-2} g_0 \sum_{j=1}^{m} \frac{dG_j}{d\phi} > 0.$$

This and outcome $M(\phi^f) = 0$ imply

$$M(\phi) > 0 \text{ for } \phi > \phi^f.$$

Appendix 9d. *The proof of proposition 9.4*

The maximization of the product (9.34) is equivalent to the maximization of the function

$$\Gamma_j^*(s_j, w_j, \phi_j, \phi_{-j}, \alpha) \doteq \log\left[\rho Q_j^*\right]$$

$$= \alpha \log[B_j(w_j, \phi_j, \phi_{-j}) + s_j \Pi_j(\phi_j, \phi_{-j})]$$

$$+ (1 - \alpha)[\log \Pi_D(\phi_j, \phi_{-j}) + \log(1 - s_j)]. \tag{9d.1}$$

This should be maximized by the choice of (s_j, w_j, ϕ_j), within the limits of the full-employment constraint $n_j \leq N_j$. The Lagrangean of this problem is given by

$$\mathcal{L}_j^* = \Gamma_j^*(s_j, w_j, \phi_j, \phi_{-j}, \alpha) + \lambda[N_j(w_j, \phi_j, \phi_{-j}) - n_j(w_j, \phi_j, \phi_{-j})]$$

$$+ \xi_1 s_j + \xi_2[1 - s_j], \tag{9d.2}$$

where λ, ξ_1 and ξ_2 are multipliers satisfying the conditions

$$\lambda[N_j(w_j, \phi_j, \phi_{-j}) - n_j(w_j, \phi_j, \phi_{-j})] = 0, \quad \lambda \geq 0,$$

$$\xi_1 s_j = 0, \quad \xi_1 \geq 0, \quad \xi_2[1 - s_j] = 0, \quad \xi_2 \geq 0. \tag{9d.3}$$

One observes easily from (9d.1) and (9d.2) that

$$\Gamma_j^*(0, w_j, \phi_j, \phi_{-j}, \alpha) = \Gamma_j(w_j, \phi_j, \phi_{-j}, \alpha), \quad \mathcal{L}_j^* = \mathcal{L}_j, \tag{9d.4}$$

where $\Gamma_j(w_j, \phi_j, \phi_{-j}, \alpha)$ and $\mathcal{L}_j$ are defined by (9b.1) and (9b.2). This connection with appendix 9b turns out to be very useful.

The first-order condition for the sharing ratio s_j is given by

$$\partial \mathcal{L}_j^*/\partial s_j = \partial \Gamma_j^*/\partial s_j + \xi_1 - \xi_2$$

$$= \alpha \Pi_j/(B_j + s_j \Pi_j) - (1 - \alpha)/(1 - s_j) + \xi_1 - \xi_2 = 0. \tag{9d.5}$$

Now, given (9d.5) and (9d.3), there are the following cases.

Case I: either $\alpha = 1$ or $(1 - \alpha)/\alpha = [(1 - s_j)\Pi_j]/[B_j + s_j \Pi_j]$ holds.

If $\alpha = 1$, then given (9d.1), the union deprives the oligopolist of all its profits so that the workers earn the whole national income:

$$\xi_2 = \xi_1 + \alpha \Pi_j/[B_j + s_j \Pi_j] > 0, \quad s_j = 1, \quad \Gamma_j^* = \log[B_j + \Pi_j].$$

Next, assume

$$\alpha < 1, \quad (1 - \alpha)/\alpha = [(1 - s_j)\Pi_j]/[B_j + s_j \Pi_j].$$

Then given (9d.3) and (9d.5), we obtain $\xi_1 = \xi_2 = 0$ and

$$s_j = 1 - (1 - \alpha)B_j/\Pi_j, \quad B_j + s_j \Pi_j = (1 - \alpha)(W_j + \Pi_j),$$

$$(1 - s_j)\Pi_j = \alpha(B_j + \Pi_j), \quad \Gamma_j^* = \log[B_j + \Pi_j] + \text{constants.}$$

We conclude that the maximization of (9d.1) is equivalent to the maximization of the discounted value of national income, $B_j + \Pi_j$. For convenience, let us define

$$\bar{\alpha} = \inf\{\alpha|(9d.3), w_j = \underset{w_j}{\operatorname{argmax}} \Gamma_j^*, \partial \mathcal{L}_j^*/\partial \phi_j = 0 \text{ and}$$

$$(1 - \alpha)/\alpha = [(1 - s_j)\Pi_j]/[B_j + s_j \Pi_j] \text{ hold}\}.$$

If $\alpha \to 0$, then, given (9d.5) and (9d.3), we obtain $\xi_1 = 1/(1 - s_j) + \xi_2 > 0$ and $s_j = 0$. This shows that $\bar{\alpha} > 0$. Since condition

$(1 - \alpha)/\alpha = [(1 - s_j)\Pi_j]/[B_j + \Pi_j]$ cannot hold for $\alpha = 1$ and $s_j < 1$, it must be the case that $\overline{\alpha} < 1$. Replacing Γ_j^* by $B_j + \Pi_j$ in (9d.2), one observes immediately that the Lagrangean (9d.2) becomes totally independent of α. This means that the relative bargaining power of the union, α, has no effect on the variables of optimization, (w_j, ϕ_j).

Case II: both $\alpha < 1$ and $(1 - \alpha)/\alpha \neq [(1 - s_j)\Pi_j]/[B_j + s_j\Pi_j]$ hold.

Here, it must be the case that $0 < \alpha < \overline{\alpha}$. Since $\alpha < 1$, it must be that $s_j < 1$, $\xi_2 = 0$ and

$$(1 - \alpha)/\alpha > [(1 - s_j)\Pi_j]/[B_j + s_j\Pi_j], \quad s_j = 0.$$

So the economy ends up with the ordinary wage system where only the basic wages are determined in collective bargaining. This case is the same as was analysed in appendix 9b. Consequently, propositions 9.1 and 9.2 hold as they stand for $\alpha < \overline{\alpha}$.

References

Atkinson, A.B. and J.E. Stiglitz (1980), *Lectures on Public Economics*. New York: McGraw-Hill.

Basar, T. and G.J. Olsder (1982), *Dynamic Non-cooperative Game Theory*. New York: Academic Press.

Bhagwati, J. and T.N. Srinivasan (1983), *Lectures on International Trade Theory*. Cambridge, Mass.: MIT Press.

Binmore, K., A. Rubinstein and A. Wolinsky (1986), The Nash bargaining solution in economic modelling, *Rand Journal of Economics* 17: 176–88.

Booth, A.L. (1995), *The Economics of the Trade Union*. Cambridge: Cambridge University Press.

Brecher, R.A. (1974), Optimal commercial policy for a minimum wage economy, *Journal of International Economics* 4: 139–49.

Calmfors, L. (1983), Centralization of wage bargaining and macro-economic performance – a survey, *OECD Economic Studies* 21.

(1985), Employment policies, wage formation and trade union behaviour in a small economy, *Scandinavian Journal of Economics* 84: 345–73.

Calmfors, L. and J. Driffill (1988), Bargaining structure, corporatism and macro-economic performance, *Economic Policy* 6: 12–61.

Calmfors, L. and H. Horn (1985), Classical unemployment, accommodation policies and the adjustment of real wages, *Scandinavian Journal of Economics* 87: 234–62.

(1986), Employment policies and centralized wage-setting, *Economica* 53: 281–302.

Calvo, G.A. (1978), Urban unemployment and wage determination in LCDs: trade unions in the Harris–Todaro model, *International Economic Review*, 19: 65–81.

Deaton, A. and J. Muellbauer (1980), *Economics and Consumer Behavior*. Cambridge: Cambridge University Press.

Diamond, P.A. and J.A. Mirrlees (1971), Optimal taxation and public production, I: Production efficiency, *American Economic Review* 61: 8–27.

Dixit, A. (1986), Comparative statics for oligopoly, *International Economic Review* 27: 107–22.

Dobson, P.W. (1997), Union–firm interaction and the right-to-manage, *Bulletin of Economic Research* 49: 213–29.

Driffill, J. (1985), Macroeconomic stabilization policy and trade union behaviour as a repeated game, *Scandinavian Journal of Economics* 87: 300–26.

Driffill, J. and F. van der Ploeg (1993), Monopoly unions and the liberalization of international trade, *Economic Journal* 103: 379–85.

Farber, H.S. (1986), The analysis of union behaviour, in *Handbook of Labor Economics*, vol. II, edited by O. Ashenfelter and R. Layard. Amsterdam: North Holland.

Fung, K.C. (1989), Unemployment, profit-sharing and Japan's economic success, *European Economic Review* 33: 783–96.

Grossman G. and E. Helpman (1991), *Innovation and Growth in the Global Economy*. Cambridge, Mass.: MIT Press.

Grout, P.A. (1984), Investment and wages in the absence of binding contracts: a Nash bargaining approach, *Econometrica* 52: 449–60.

Gylfason, T. and A. Lindbeck (1986), Endogenous unions and governments: a game-theoretic approach, *European Economic Review* 30: 5–26.

Hersoug, T. (1985), Workers versus government – who adjusts to whom? *Scandinavian Journal of Economics* 87: 270–92.

Hoel, M. (1991), Union wage policy: the importance of labour mobility and the degree of centralization, *Economica* 58: 139–53.

Hoel, M. and K.O. Moene (1988), Profit-sharing, unions and investments, *Scandinavian Journal of Economics* 90: 493–505.

Holmlund, B. (1997), Macroeconomic implications of cash limits in the public sector, *Economica* 64: 49–62.

Kamien, M.I. and N.L. Schwartz (1985), *Dynamic Optimization: the Calculus of Variations and Optimal Control Theory in Economics and Management*. Amsterdam: North Holland.

Kemp, M.C., V. van Long and K. Shimomura (1991), *Labour Unions and the Theory of International Trade*. Amsterdam: North Holland.

Layard, R., S. Nickell and R. Jackman (1991), *Unemployment*. Oxford: Oxford University Press.

Manning, A. (1987), An integration of the trade union models in a sequential bargaining framework, *Economic Journal* 97: 121–39.

McDonald, I. and R. Solow (1981), Wage bargaining and employment, *American Economic Review* 71: 896–908.

Myles, G.D. (1989), Ramsey tax rules for economies with imperfect competition, *Journal of Public Economics* 38: 95–115.

Nash, J.F. (1950), The bargaining problem, *Econometrica* 18: 155–62.

Nickell, S.J. (1978), *The Investment Decisions of Firms*. Cambridge: Cambridge University Press.

Osborne, M.J. and A. Rubinstein (1990), *Bargaining and Markets*. London: Academic Press.

(1994), *A Course in Game Theory*. London: MIT Press.

Osborne, M.J. and A. Rubinstein (1979), Wage determination in an economy with many trade unions, *Oxford Economic Papers* 31: 369–85.

(1982), The microeconomic theory of the trade union, *Economic Journal* 92: 576–96.

(1985), The economic theory of trade unions: an introductory survey, *Scandinavian Journal of Economics* 87: 160–93.

Palokangas, T. (1987), Optimal taxation and employment policy with a centralized wage setting, *Oxford Economic Papers* 39: 799–812.

(1989), Union power in the long run reconsidered, *Scandinavian Journal of Economics* 91: 625–35.

(1991a), Investment, profit-sharing and the degree of centralization, *Economic Letters* 35: 99–103.

(1991b), Tax incidence, partial policy improvements and centralized wage-setting, *Scandinavian Journal of Economics* 93: 439–46.

(1992), Binding contracts, profit-sharing and the degree of centralization, *Journal of Institutional and Theoretical Economics* 148: 260–73.

(1994), Taxation, cost-benefit analysis, and monopoly in an open economy, *European Journal of Political Economy* 10: 529–43.

(1996), Endogenous growth and collective bargaining, *Journal of Economic Dynamics and Control* 20: 925–44.

(1997), The centralization of wage bargaining, investment, and technological change, *Journal of Institutional and Theoretical Economics* 153: 657–73.

Pohjola, M. (1987), Profit-sharing, collective bargaining and employment, *Journal of Institutional and Theoretical Economics* 143: 334–42.

Rodseth, A. (1995), Are employment policies counterproductive when wage setting is centralized? *Scandinavian Journal of Economics* 97: 401–10.

Romer, P. (1990), Endogenous technological change, *Journal of Political Economy* 98: S71–S102.

Rubinstein, A. (1982), Perfect equilibrium in a bargaining model, *Econometrica* 50: 97–109.

Sampson, A. (1983), Employment policy in a model with a rational trade union, *Economic Journal* 93: 297–311.

Selten, R. (1975), Reexamination of the perfectness concept of the equilibrium points in extensive games, *International Journal of Game Theory* 4: 25–55.

Shapiro, C. and J.E. Stiglitz (1984), Equilibrium unemployment as a worker discipline device, *American Economic Review* 74: 433–44.

Sorensen, J.R. (1992), Profit-sharing in a unionized Cournot duopoly, *Journal of Economics* 55: 151–167.

Ståhl, I. (1972), *Bargaining Theory*. Stockholm: Stockholm School of Economics.

Steward, G. (1989), Profit-sharing in Cournot oligopoly, *Economics Letters* 31: 221–24.

Sutton, J. (1986), Non-cooperative bargaining theory: an introduction, *Review of Economic Studies* 53: 709–24.

van der Ploeg, F. (1987), Trade unions, investment and employment, *European Economic Review* 31: 1465–92.

von Neumann, J. and O. Morgenstern (1944), *Theory of Games and Economic Behaviour*. New York: Wiley.

Weitzman, M. (1984), *The Share Economy*. Cambridge, Mass.: Harvard University Press.

(1985), The simple macroeconomics of profit sharing, *American Economic Review* 75: 937–53.

(1987), Steady state unemployment under profit sharing, *Economic Journal* 97: 86–105.

Index

234